Content

Foreword   7

1. Knowledge Management as Practice   9
   Introduction   9
   The Notion of the Knowledge Society   10
   The Emergence of the Knowledge-Intensive Firm   13
   The Practices of Knowledge Management   16
   Strategic Management and the Practices of Knowledge Management   19
   Managing the Indeterminate   20
   Knowledge Management as Management Fad and Buzzword   23
   Outline of the Book   26
   Summary and Conclusion   27

2. The Strategic Management of Knowledge   28
   Introduction   28
   Content Perspectives   31
   Process Perspectives   48

3. Sharing Knowledge: Writing and Communication   56
   Introduction   56
   The Concept of Knowledge   57
   Organizations as Repositories of Knowledge   60
   Codified Knowledge: Practices of Writing   63
   Uncodified Knowledge: Practices of Communication   65
   Knowledge Sharing: Empirical Studies   71
   Summary and Conclusion   79

4. Knowledge Sharing at SCA Packaging   81
   Introduction   81
   The Eurobest Programme   85
   Eurobest and Performance   92
   Concluding Remarks   104

5. Knowledge Sharing at AstraZeneca   107
   With Jonas Roth, Knowledge Manager, Project Management
   Support Office, AstraZeneca
   Introduction   107
   Near and Far Transfer of Knowledge   108
   The Pharmaceutical Industry   109
   AstraZeneca   112
   The New Product Development Process   113
   Knowledge Sharing and Transfer in Clinical Study teams   116
   The Knowledge Facilitation Method   117
   Outcomes from the Knowledge Facilitation Method   120
   Knowledge Facilitation in Clinical Project Teams: Summary and Conclusion   122
   Project Management Support at AstraZeneca   123
   Working with Knowledge Transfer   125
   Knowledge Management as Practice at AstraZeneca   131
   Summary and Conclusion   132

6. Knowledge Sharing in Organizations   **134**
    Introduction   134
    Knowledge Sharing   135
    Knowledge Sharing in the Two Cases   137
    Revisiting the Literature on Knowledge Sharing   149
    A Framework for Knowledge Sharing in Organizations   158
    Summary and Conclusion   160

Appendix I: On Method   **162**
Collaborative Research   162

Appendix II: Research Methods   **165**
SCA   165
AstraZeneca   166

References   **168**

Tables and Figures

Table 3.1. Empirical research on knowledge transfer
Table 4.1. Simple correlations, absolute levels
Table 4.2. Selected simple correlations, relative levels
Table 5.1. International R&D intensities (1998).
Table 5.2. The basic elements of the knowledge facilitating method
    at AstraZeneca
Figure 4.1. The "Pickie-Stick": An explicit piece of production knowledge
Figure 4.2. Machine speed evolution
Figure 4.3. Productivity evolution
Figure 4.3. Machine speed evolution
Figure 5.1. The project organization of AstraZeneca
Figure 5.2. Overview of the drug research process

Foreword

Although the two of us were raised in the fair city of Gothenburg and spent four years at the Lund School of Economics and Management during the first half of the 1990s, we did not really cross one another's paths until we enrolled for the Ph.D. programme in Business Administration. During the next four years, Thomas became increasingly involved in strategic management theory in his thesis work while Alexander, who was paying some attention to strategic management theory without making it a key priority, delved into the TQM literature and books on Japanese management techniques and their transfer to the West. In late 1998, we finally decided to write a joint paper combining an analysis of the language used in resource-based literature with writing on deconstruction (represented by Jacques Derrida and others). The paper was eventually submitted to the Strategic Management Society's annual meeting in Berlin in 1999. Needless to say, the paper was a bit out of the ordinary in this stronghold of Compustat analyses and positivist research. But, to our great surprise, we nevertheless got a nice response from the audience at our session. For instance, the hard copies of the paper we brought to the session disappeared quickly and several participants claimed they were relieved to see some substantial criticism of the RBV literature. This mildly shocking experience — we thought after all that we would be treated as some kind of deviant case in the rather stodgy field of strategic management theory (this is Alexander's remark) — made us believe that there may be some inherent quality in mixing different worldviews and experiences.

Prevented from engaging in more collaborative work ever since the late 1990s due to various priorities, we finally decided to give it another go and make use of some of our post-doc studies in another co-authored text. For various reasons, we were both becoming acquainted with the emerging field of knowledge management, one of the conceptual innovations in the field of management during the 1990s, and decided that it was worth the effort to commit to this field. Hence, this book is the outcome of the merging of two individuals' different research interests. Therefore, it is not intended to capture the state-of-the art in one single field, but rather to pave the way for a more heterogeneous perspective on this thing called knowledge transfer and sharing. We have thus tried our best to view knowledge management as a multidisciplinary topic rather than an issue for, say, strategic management theorists or industry sociologists on their own. This book is thus a combination of worldviews rather than a pledging of allegiance to one single paradigmatic perspective.

We would sincerely like to thank Ola Håkansson at Liber whose support and willingness to discuss our ideas has been of great help during the project. We would also like to thank various representatives of SCA and AstraZeneca who have provided us with the insights and ideas that we have tried to make use of in this book.

Thomas Kalling acknowledges the efforts made by SCA Packaging in supporting and facilitating research projects over the years. To this particular study, the true renaissance man Frank Linnerz (Corporate Quality Manager) has contributed in many ways. An engineer by trade, Frank is currently finishing his MBA, and so was tremendously helpful as a keen and analytical critic of the concepts of strategy and knowledge management. I also wish to express my sincere gratitude to those numerous SCA Packaging representatives who over the years have supported the collaboration with the Institute of Economic Research at Lund University.

Alexander Styhre would like to thank his colleagues at the Department of Project Management at Chalmers University of Technology and the Fenix Research Program at Chalmers and the Stockholm School of Economics. I would also like to emphasize how rewarding my collaboration with Jonas Roth has been. Without Jonas' contribution I would have been completely lost amongst the multiplicity of acronyms used, organizational arrangements, and daily practices at AstraZeneca. But Jonas never lost his patience — as far as I was able to tell anyway — when faced with all my inquiries, sorting most of them out for me. In addition, I would like to thank Mats Sundgren, also at AstraZeneca, and Chalmers University of Technology, for their help and guidance when grappling with this thing called new drug development.

This book is dedicated to *Jakob* and *Simon*.

Thomas Kalling
Lund, June 2003

Alexander Styhre
Gothenburg, June 2003

Chapter 1

Knowledge Management as Practice

Introduction

This book aims to shed some light on how knowledge can be shared within and between organizations. Thus, it may be regarded as a contribution to the emerging field of knowledge management theory, one of the latest domains to be explored within management writing. Rather than providing solely theoretical examinations of major contributions to this debate or elaborating on its conceptual framework, we intend to present two cases of how knowledge may be shared at two different companies in two different industries. As in all management books, our presentation of the two cases will be examined on the basis of what is known as knowledge *management*, the management of knowledge. Even though this is a rather recent term in the field of management studies (Spender & Grant, 1996), we will argue that the knowledge management perspective draws on a number of different perennial perspectives and traditions from management studies. In brief, the management of organizations has been the management of knowledge from the outset. For instance, the so-called semi-skilled workforce that Frederick W. Taylor sought to make more "rational" use of at Bethlehem Steel in Pennsylvania in the beginning of the twentieth century was just as knowledge-intensive as the companies which today's knowledge management theorists examine, albeit with different forms of knowledge being employed. This does not, however, imply that knowledge management is merely a management fad or a buzzword signifying no particular qualities or processes. On the contrary, knowledge management theory has reinforced and articulated a number of theoretical perspectives that have previously been neglected, marginalized, or overlooked. Still, the knowledge management literature is highly normative and conceptual. It is more aimed at establishing knowledge management as a legitimate field within management studies than offering integrated and empirical studies of how knowledge management practices are implemented in contemporary organizations. This book is an attempt at making the somewhat elusive notion of knowledge more practical in terms of being a resource that the organization can actively deal with, and make use of, in its day-to-day activities.

In this opening chapter, we aim to establish the knowledge management discussion within a broader socio-economic and cultural framework. In our view, it is little wonder that intangible organizational resources such as knowledge have been in vogue for, say, the last ten years. Prior to the discussion on organizational knowledge, organizational culture was an area that attracted significant interest among academic researchers, consultants, and practitioners. In a society whose resources are increasingly being subjected to managerial practices and control, even the most intangible resources are treated as valuable, being regarded as what constitutes the difference between the "excellent" and the mediocre company or organization. Thus, we have seen a growth in interest in resources such as entrepreneurship, emotions, knowledge, creativity, etc. within recent time. Therefore, knowledge management is, we would say, a highly contingent phenomenon: What remains to be exploited in organizations is what remains tacit and intangible - what cannot be turned into manuals and artefacts — in brief what we call knowledge. In this chapter, we place the knowledge management debate within the discussions on dichotomies, e.g. modernity/postmodernity, fordism/postfordism, industrial/postindustrial societies, and concepts such as the consumer society and its accompanying concepts of the *McDonaldization* and *Las Vegasification* of society.

The Notion of the Knowledge Society

One of the most distinct characterizations of contemporary society, at least as debated among social scientists, is that our society is approaching a turning point or an end. Sociologists or philosophers talk about the end of modernity (e.g. Vattimo, 1992), an age characterized by an increasing emphasis and belief in technoscience (Lyotard, 1984), rational forms of social organization (Giddens, 1990), *entzauberung* (disenchantment) in Jakob Buckhardt's and Max Weber's sense, i.e. the loss of traditional beliefs and common sense explanations and the emergence of "rational forms" of social organization, and a steady growth in social welfare (Galbraith, 1958). The modern age has been a remarkably successful period in terms of technological innovations and social agreements, but it has also been a period of genocide (Bauman, 1991), ecological disaster (Serres, 1995), and the continuous inability to deal with poverty and social problems (see for instance Bourdieu, 1999; Hertz, 2000; Ehrenreich, 2001). In sociology and disciplines such as management, there is a discussion about the transition from the industrial to the post-industrial society (a thesis defended by Bell, 1973, and Touraine, 1971). In Touraine's (1971) analysis of what he calls the *programmed* or *technocratic* society, "[k]nowlege is a production factor" (Touraine, 1971: 12). Touraine employs Marxist terminology when sketching the qualities of this post-industrial society. In this society, "economic decisions and struggles" are no longer "of central importance" (Touraine, 1971: 3). Instead, the economy becomes dependent on knowledge and "creativity" (Touraine, 1971: 5) and new classes emerge on the basis of its control over knowledge: "[T]he new dominant class is defined by knowledge and a certain level of education" (Touraine, 1971: 51). In the post-industrial society, the notion of work — a concept of central interest to the Marxist perspective — is changed. Touraine (1971: 6) writes: "Work comes to be less and less defined as a personal contribution and more as a role within a system of communications and social relations". In consequence, it is "more useful to speak of alienation than of exploitation" (Touraine, 1971: 8). In addition, the university attains a new central role in society because virtually all sorts of knowledge may prove to serve as production factors. Touraine contends: "It is becoming increasingly more difficult to think of even highly formalized knowledge as being disinterested" (Touraine, 1971: 12. See also Lyotard, 1984).

The transition into the post-industrial society has been discussed from a number of theoretical perspectives. In operations management, industrial sociologists talk about the end of mass production (Kenney and Florida, 1993) and fordism (Hirst & Zeitlin, 1991) and the emergence of economic and managerial regimes such as mass customisation (Kotha, 1995), lean production (Womack, Jones & Roos, 1990), and postfordist modes of production such as flexible specialization (Piore & Sabel, 1984). Marxist writers such as Guy Debord (1977) talk about the *society of the spectacle* wherein the working class is no longer a subject of production and accumulation, instead becoming consumers, spectators, who are no longer needed in the production apparatus but who are still useful as consumers of the goods and services provided. In the same vein, Baudrillard (1998) talks about the *consumer society* wherein consumption is no longer simply an option but becomes an *institution*, an obligation. Writers who emphasize the importance of technological innovations adhere to a similar perspective. Best and Kellner (2001) use the concept of *technocapitalism* to denote the co-evolutionary nature of capitalism as an economic regime where new forms of technology (see also Featherstone & Burrows, 1995; Woolgar, 2002) support and interact with economic activities. Guattari (2000) has coined the concept of *Integrated World Capitalism* to capture the transnational and transregional nature of today's economic system (see also Castells, 1996). For Guattari (2000), there is no outside of the Integrated World Capitalism, only different modalities and contingent forms. Taken together, there are a great many perspectives, theories, models, and ideas on how contemporary society is on the verge of a new economic and technological regime that will, in many ways, differ from earlier regimes. It is, then, little wonder that the prefix "post" has been used in all sorts of discussions during the last ten years. For the anthropologist Clifford Geertz (2000), we are living in the "post-everything era". Therefore, it is only with great skepticism that old interpretative frameworks and taken-for-granted ideas are accepted. Writers too many and too diverse are too much in agreement that substantial social changes are, have been, or will be taking place. In consequence, there is a certain amount of anxiety among social writers that the future is unpredictable and that social changes may not be linear and easily controllable. The emergence of a complexity theory paradigm (Prigogone & Stengers, 1984; Prigogine, 1997; Cilliers, 1998; Holland, 1998) emphasizing points of bifurcations and non-linearity has also contributed to such anxiety. Although there are great institutional forces in society safeguarding the reproduction of certain conditions and relations (Bourdieu & Passeron, 1977), there are also writers who believe that society is more dynamic these days than it used to be.

It is within this general perspective of society being in a transitional phase between the industrial and post-industrial society that the knowledge management discussion should, in our view, be located. The knowledge management perspective, or the knowledge-based view of the firm (KBV), stresses organizations as being profoundly based upon the intellectual and emotional resources it controls and is able to make effective use of. In a world characterized by fluidity, ephemeral relations, uncertainty, and non-linearity, organizations may be regarded as repositories of knowledge rather than aggregates of humans and artefacts. Material resources may be considered temporal and easily controllable while knowledge resources are always virtual and fluid. The notion of knowledge is thus a very helpful analytical instrument in a society characterized by ambiguity and elusiveness because it is always very concrete and very abstract at the same time. On the one hand, one may say "I have the right knowledge of how to deal with this problem" in terms of making certain decisions and undertaking certain operations, but on the other hand, you can always talk about knowledge as a resource that captures all that we do not know or are able to explain ourselves. For instance, we may say that a medical doctor is very knowledgeable about a particular illness without knowing very much ourselves about that very illness. "Knowledge" is used here to denote all those abstract, tacit, embodied, and personal experiences and skills that the medical doctor makes use of when diagnosing or treating a patient. For the outsider, "knowledge" is certainly not something practical here, but is instead something very elusive and ambiguous. As a notion or concept, "knowledge" is, similar to concepts such as "power" or "society", both abstract and concrete at the same time, both practical and analytical, and gets its usefulness from this quality or from capturing double meanings. On the one hand, "knowledge" captures the most mundane and taken–for–granted of everyday practices (see for instance Garfinkel, 1967; de Certeau, Girard & Mayol, 1998), while on the other, it is used to denote the most complex forms of abstract thinking. In terms of knowledge management theory, the concept of knowledge is a useful construct because it provides opportunities for dealing with that which has previously been ignored or overlooked. The management of knowledge presupposes that knowledge may be dealt with just like any other organizational resource while everybody knows that this is impossible because knowledge can be anything, and just a subset of all the resources that can be regarded as knowledge are of interest from management's perspective to control and manage. Thus, knowledge management seeks to control what really cannot be fully controlled, but it is exactly in that ambition that the dynamics of the concept lie: To handle what cannot be fully captured.

In this book, we will try to show how knowledge can be used, shared within two companies. Although the knowledge management concept is characterized by tensions and contradictions, in practical terms, organizations can always aim to make use of their various resources. In order to exploit such intangible resources, firms and organizations need to develop practices wherein knowledge can be captured, understood, and shared by individuals, communities of practice or the organization *per se*. These practices may never be conclusive, but they contribute what Weick (2001) calls "small wins", i.e. individually insignificant contributions which, taken together, enable changes and improvements.

The Emergence of the Knowledge-Intensive Firm

The first and most important premise in the knowledge management literature is that access to, and superior use of, knowledge resources can provide a sustainable advantage. Davenport and Prusak (1998) write:

> Knowledge … can provide a sustainable advantage. Eventually, competitors can almost always match the quality and price of a market leader's current product or service. By the time that happens, though, the knowledge-rich, knowledge-managing company will have moved on to a new level of quality, creativity, or efficiency. The knowledge advantage is sustainable because it generates increasing returns and continuing advantage. Unlike material assets,

which decrease as they are used, knowledge assets increase with use: Ideas breed new ideas, and shared knowledge stays with the giver while it enriches the receiver. The potential for new ideas arising from the stock of knowledge in any firm is practically limitless — particularly if the people in the firm are given opportunities to think, to learn, and to talk with one another. (Davenport & Prusak, 1998: 17)

Davenport and Prusak depict knowledge as a dynamic organizational asset: It is used to create sustainable competitive advantage, it is subject to first-mover advantages, and grows when being used. Knowledge has the capability to continuously reproduce itself and gives rise to new ideas ("ideas breeds new ideas"). In a similar manner, Adler (2001: 216) says: "knowledge is a remarkable substance. Unlike other resources, most forms of knowledge grow rather than diminish with use". In Davenport and Prusak's account, knowledge offers great opportunities for organizations to outperform one another. Hence, the importance of "managing" knowledge. The emphasis on knowledge as a social and organizational resource of great importance is rarely questioned by critics of knowledge management, Instead, there is some controversy over the ontological, epistemological and political qualities of knowledge. For mainstream knowledge management writers such as Davenport and Prusak (1998), knowledge is treated very much as a functional resource that can more or less be managed in the same manner as any other tangible organizational resource. Against this backdrop, "locating" knowledge in certain departments, individuals, technological systems or social arrangements such as patents, a constructivist view of knowledge conceptualises knowledge more in terms of being, in Olkowski's (2002) words, a "social accomplishment". For instance, Alvesson (2001: 865) criticizes this functionalist view: "Knowledge — at least in the context of the business world and of management studies — is normally treated as a functional resource representing a 'truth' or at least something instrumentally useful on a subject matter and/or a set of principles or techniques for dealing with material or social phenomena" (Alvesson, 2001: 865). For Alvesson, much mainstream knowledge management theory seeks to reduce the most complex construct of knowledge to the level of clearly separated skills, operations, and "bits and pieces" of information and data. Knowledge is thus always defined on the basis of its instrumental and functional application. But knowledge is always more than its instrumental use. For Tsoukas (1996), knowledge is distributed throughout organizations rather than being located in certain places: "[f]irms are distributed knowledge systems in a strong sense: they are decentered systems. A firm's knowledge cannot be surveyed as a whole; it is not self-contained; it is inherently indeterminate and continually reconfiguring" (Tsoukas, 1996: 13). In consequence, firms and organizations always know more than they can make instrumental use of, which implies that there are always unexploited opportunities in organizations. For both Alvesson (2001) and Tsoukas (1996), mainstream knowledge management theorists tend to take the shortest route between "knowledge" and "management" and thus overlook some of the inherent problems in the construct of knowledge.

In addition to the ontological, epistemological and political debates, knowledge management theorists have to address what Kreiner (2002) calls a "double-sided concern", i.e. that of being able to manage existing resources and simultaneously develop new knowledge resources. Kreiner (2002) writes:

> Knowledge management needs to rest on a double-sided concern: to protect and utilize existing knowledge resources, on the one hand, and to facilitate the mobilization of new knowledge resources, on the other hand. It is my final contention that the knowledge management programme is in need of a better conceptualization of its own role and function — a conception that better reflects this double-sided concern. (Kreiner, 2002: 122)

Knowledge management practices are expected to handle the knowledge resources that exist, but they should also develop and gain access to knowledge that may provide sustainable competitive advantage in the future. These two objectives are not necessarily separated from one another. As was pointed out by Davenport and Prusak (1998) and Adler (2002), knowledge grows rather than diminishes with use. Thus, the management of existing knowledge resources may serve as a means of producing new knowledge in organizations. In consequence, there is no "management of knowledge" separated from the "generation of knowledge"; the two processes pre-require one another and are always entangled and implied in one another. From our point of view, this double-sided concern in knowledge management implies that it is not very useful, from a practical point of view, to separate abstract concepts of knowledge from their practical use, their practices. Knowledge is always articulated, expressed, and brought into being through various practices. Thus, we would like to align a practice-based view of organizations with a knowledge management view in order navigate between the normative knowledge management theorists' emphasis on managerial and normative aspects of knowledge and the critical theorists' discussions on the ontological and epistemological qualities of knowledge. Because knowledge is depicted as a dynamic resource that serves, when used effectively, to establish competitive advantage (or at least drive 'performance'), knowledge management is regarded here as a practice. Therefore, we will discuss theories of practice in association with a knowledge management perspective.

The Practices of Knowledge Management

The concept of practice is one of the most widely used concepts in social and organization theory. Sociologists such as Bourdieu (1977, 1990), de Certeau (1984), Garfinkel (1967), Bauman (1999) and social theorists such as Castoriadis (1987) have discussed the concept of practice as a key component of their theoretical frameworks. Schatzki, Knorr Cetina and Savigny (2001) even suggest a *practice turn* in social theory because practices operate on the intermediary level between the actor and the structure, the two elementary components of society whose relationship remains an *aporia* subject to continuous discussions among social theorists. The edited volume of Schatzki, Knorr Cetina and Savigny (2001) offer at least three different definitions of the notion of practice. The first is provided by Ann Swindler (2001):

> Practices can be routines of individual actors, inscribed in the ways they use their bodies, in their habits, in their taken-for-granted sense of space, dress, food, musical taste—in the social routines they know so well as to be able to improvise spontaneously without a second thought . . . Practices can also be trans-personal, embedded in the routines organizations use to process people and things, in the taken-for-granted criteria that separate one category of person or event from another. (Swindler, 2001: 75)

Stephen Turner (2001) associates practice with tacit components:

> 'Practice'... is defined as those nonlinguistic conditions for an activity that are learned. By 'a practice' I mean an activity that requires its genuine participants to have learned something of this tacit sort in order to perform. (Turner, 2001: 120)

Finally, Karin Knorr Cetina writes:

> Though much debate surrounds the exact specification of the relevant rules and habits ... most authors seem to agree that practices should be seen as recurrent processes governed by specifiable schemata of preferences and prescriptions. (Knorr Cetina, 2001: 175)

The notion of practice is thus a contested concept within social theory. For the sake of simplicity, we can characterize practice in the following terms: Practices are semi-structured operations and undertakings that draw on institutional behaviours and beliefs while giving the individual significant space for individual interpretations and idiosyncratic routines when performing a certain practice. For Bourdieu (1977, 1990), practices are internalized and embodied in terms of a *habitus*, i.e. the ability of the individual to operate smoothly within a particular field. De Certeau (1984) offers an analysis of the practices of everyday life wherein mundane activities such as walking, talking, cooking and eating are envisaged as social accomplishments embedded in shared agreements about what constitute proper and legitimate ways of walking, talking, cooking and eating. Garfinkel's (1967) ethnomethodological approach to practices aims to reveal such underlying agreements in order to show that social systems are always based on taken-for-granted beliefs and behaviours. For Bourdieu, De Certeau, and Garfinkel, practices represent a nexus between the actor and the structure; a practice is the act wherein the actor manifests and embodies social institutions and makes them produce practical effects. In organization theory, sociological theories regarding practice have been widely subscribed to. Various social constructivist, symbolic interactionist, feminist, and actor-network theory perspectives of organizations (to name a few) have emphasized practices. For instance, within the organization learning literature, the concept of *communities of practice* (see for instance Wenger, 2000; Wenger, McDermott & Snyder, 2002) has been suggested as one of the elementary entities for successfully learning and sharing knowledge in organizations.

Boden (1994) examines talk in organizations as practice. Drawing on the ethnomethodological work of Garfinkel (1967), Boden argues that most organizational activities are based on interaction through talk. Boden (1994) writes:

> The many coalitions of any organization or group of organizations . . . depend not so much on physical resources as on information. The information may be related to material resources but it is usually far more diffuse and multivalent. Much 'news' in organizations is soft — incomplete, fuzzy, and flexible — and it is the blur that needs to be classified, refocused, and occasionally completely realigned through talk. (Boden, 1994: 152)

For Boden, it is the practices of talking that make a fuzzy and incomplete reality coherent. Boden thus shares with Weick (1979) and Daft and Weick (1984) the view that organizations are always interpretative systems aiming to make sense of shared experiences. Weick (1979: 6) argues: "The basic raw material on which organizations operate are informational inputs that are ambiguous, uncertain, equivocal ... Organizing serves to narrow the range of possibilities, to reduce the numbers of 'might occurs'". What Weick (1979) calls *enactment* is what is taking place in symbolic interactions. Boden writes: "Through their timing, placing, pacing, and patterning of verbal interaction, organization members actually constitute the organization as a real and practical place" (Boden, 1994: 15). While Weick uses the notion of enactment,

Boden follows Garfinkel's notion (inherited from Husserl) of *bracketing*. Boden explains:

> To explore how everyday rationalities work, Garfinkel draws on the general phenomenological notion of 'bracketing'. According to this approach, social agents immersed in an intensive world of experience bracket out extraneous detail and selectively constitute a here-and-now mix of meaning and action . . . Everyday situations of action turn actors into 'practical theorists' who understand, to a profound degree, what Garfinkel came to call the 'etcetera principle', namely that in the real world no set of rules, no matter how general, clearly defined, or logically formulated, can ever be 'compete'. (Boden, 1994: 187)

Since there are no rules that can capture practices in their every detail, talk is what brings coherence to a scattered series of events. Boden (and Garfinkel) thus share with the proponents of a narrative view of organizations (see for instance Czaniawska, 1997; Boje, 2001; Gabriel, 2000) the emphasis on the importance of narrating practices and experiences. In a much-cited study of copy machine technicians, Orr (1996) studied how tacit knowledge and experiences were shared between technicians through anecdotes and storytelling. Here, the boundary between practice and narrative, referent and signifier became blurred. Lynch (1985) reports a study of the talk among scientists at a neuroscience laboratory, drawing on Garfinkel's (1967) ethnomethodology. Patriotta (2003) examined how shop floor work at carmaker FIAT relied on "detective story" narratives with a plot and a chronology that made sense of production breakdowns. Finally, Donnellon (1996) studied talk within project teams. For Boden (1994), and Orr (1996), Lynch (1985), Patriotta (2003), and Donnellon (1996), the concept of practice always includes the signifying framework, for instance talk, which denotes the practice.

In knowledge management theory, several writers have suggested that the concept of practice is an important analytical tool (for instance Gherardi, 2000; Hayes & Allinson, 1998). Tsoukas & Vladimirou (2001: 990) write that knowledge management is aimed at turning unreflected practices into reflected ones. Knowledge management activities should aim to make the processes of the organization more transparent to its members and to make sense out of complex activities. In a similar vein, Orlikowski (2002: 252-253) argues that knowledge is an "ongoing social accomplishment", constituted and reconstituted in everyday practice. Knowledge is what is embodied in practices rather than being some transcendental or extra-social process. Thus, organizational practices are of particular interest when examining knowledge-sharing in organizations.

The concept of practice enables the analysis of how knowledge is employed and developed in organizations without reducing it to the level of the individual co-workers, and without turning it into some structural quality of the firm. The concept of practice thus paves the way for a perspective on knowledge that captures the structural, community-based, and subject-centred qualities of knowledge. In Tsoukas' (1996) formulation, firms are fundamentally distributed knowledge systems and the notion of practice offers an analytical framework for capturing such a distributed organizational resource. In addition, the practice perspective does not imply a reductionist view of knowledge; while knowledge is distributed across the organization, it still serves as a strategic resource constituting competitive advantage for the organization.

Strategic Management and the Practices of Knowledge Management

Knowledge management is becoming a useful perspective on organizations for practitioners as soon as it provides practices, concepts, models and activities that help companies create competitive advantage. Thus, there is an explicit strategic management perspective in our view of knowledge management. Strategic management theory aims to understand how firms drive performance and create differences between themselves (Barney & Hesterly, 1999). Organizations control an idiosyncratic set of know-how, skills, experiences, and so forth, that they make use of when competing against other firms. Knowledge management, at least in its practical use, aims to exploit and make use of such intellectual capital and "knowledge-laden" resources. In this view of knowledge management as a practice-based, strategic matter, we draw on Penrose's (1957) classic *The Theory of the Growth of the Firm* (see also Kor and Mahoney, 2000) in order to underscore the fact that knowledge management practices may be fruitfully regarded as organizational capabilities. For Penrose, the "business firm" is "both an administrative organization and a collection of productive resources" (Penrose, 1959: 31). In addition, Penrose distinguishes between clear-cut administrative activities and the "productive resources" that serve as the basis for the competitive advantage of the firm. Penrose thus offers a most elegant and highly influential formulation of the firm, best captured in her own formulation: "A firm is basically a collection of resources" (Penrose, 1959: 77). Thus, Penrose's change in perspective from the dominant (at the time) structure-conduct-performance perspective in strategic management theory to a perspective emphasizing the interior of the firm enables a more affirmative attitude among strategic management theorists vis-à-vis the notion of heterogeneity. To quote Penrose; "it is the heterogeneity, and not the homogeneity, of productive services available that gives each firm its unique character" (Penrose, 1959: 75). Penrose's writing on organizational resources and firm heterogeneities has been greatly influential in the development of the resource-based view of the firm in strategic management theory. Although the RBV theory has spawned a significant debate on the nature of the firm and how competitive advantage is constituted and maintained (Priem & Butler, 2001; Barney, 2001b; Spanos & Lioukas, 2001; Eisenhardt & Martin, 2000), it represents a view of the firm that recognizes the notion of practices. Rather than being the outcome of a superior ability to position the firm in the marketplace vis-à-vis other competitors, sustainable competitive advantage is an effect of the use of heterogeneous organizational resources, RBV theorists contend. From a knowledge management perspective, the thinking of Penrose and her followers provides a useful theoretical framework for aligning the use of intangible intellectual resources and the firm's long-term competitiveness. The capabilities and competencies of the firm when making use of and sharing its various knowledge-based resources is what distinguishes the successful firm from the less successful one. In our view, such capabilities and competencies are always located in, and dependent upon, the practices of knowledge sharing. Therefore, the notion of practice is what serves to bridge abstract concepts such as competitive advantage and knowledge. Firms make use of their "productive resources" in practical activities and undertakings. Thus, the view of knowledge management in this book is directed towards active involvement with their intellectual resources. Knowledge management is not solely a matter of theoretical perspectives and sense-making mechanisms, such as metaphorical uses of the concept of knowledge, but is primarily a matter of sharing data, information, knowledge, and know-how. Thus, knowledge is not employed here as an abstract construct but as a resource that can be used in day-to-day practices.

Managing the Indeterminate

The management of intellectual resources such as knowledge implies that the concept of management is used to denote all sorts of planned activities aimed at organizing, categorizing, structuring and controlling practices in organizations. Thus, the knowledge management perspective shares a rather abstract notion of management with other managerial activities such as the management of emotions (Hochschild, 1983; Fineman, 1993), culture (Smircich, 1983; Deal & Kennedy, 1982, Hatch, 1986) or attitudes (Brief, 1998). Here, management is by no means used to control and make use of tangible resources, but seeks to handle all sorts of organizational resources, no matter how abstract and elusive these may be. Nevertheless, the management of intangible assets is always susceptible to processes that are indeterminate or not fully known. Speaking from the view of Reed and deFilippi (1990), there are always *causal ambiguities* inherent in such organizational resources that cannot be fully captured by managerial activities. In consequence, proponents of knowledge management and similar managerial projects tend to take on a rationalist, or even an instrumental or functionalist, view of managerial endeavours. Grint (1997) writes: "Management theory may not be composed entirely of 'pragmatic paradoxes' ... but, like many other forms of thought, it does tend to rationalize away the paradoxes, chance, luck, errors, subjectivities, accidents, and sheer indeterminacy of life through a prism of apparent control and rationality" (Grint, 1997: 9). Control and rationality are highly prized qualities (or conditions) in a managerialist ideology. Proponents of various forms of management tend to adhere to narratives emphasizing how such virtues are maintained. But the espoused theory of rationality and control (to use Argyris & Schön's [1978] formulation) may have a rather complicated relationship with the actual effects and outcomes of favoured managerial practices. In brief, what may appear to be a rational *modus operandi* may actually produce unintended or counterproductive effects. One particular example of the ambition to maintain a veneer of rationality and control in order to demonstrate an awareness of institutionalized values and objectives, is drug testing, a widely spread managerial practice in the U.S. setting (Cavanaugh & Prasad, 1994). For Cavanaugh and Prasad (1994), the effects of drug testing are insignificant or not very well known, while its costs are substantial. Thus, drug testing is undertaken in order to show how organizations conducting drug testing are committed to social control, responsibility, and other institutionalized values; in brief, to demonstrate a firm belief and an allegiance to control and rationality. Therefore, drug testing serves as a form of ritual testifying to certain social values and norms that are not, in themselves, necessarily aligned with other managerial objectives such as productivity and profits. Ehrenreich (2001), in her account of low-wage work in contemporary America, offers evidence that drug testing has, in Merton's (1957) formulation, latent and manifest consequences:

> There are many claims for workplace drug testing: supposedly, it results in reduced rates of accidents and absenteeism, fewer claims on health insurance plans, and increased productivity. However, none of these claims has been substantiated, according to a 1999 report from the American Civil Liberties Union, 'Drug testing: A bad investment'. Studies show that preemployment testing does not lower absenteeism, accidents, or turnover and (at least in the high-tech workplaces studied) actually lowered productivity — presumably due to its negative effect on workplace morale. Furthermore, the practice is

quite costly. In 1990, the federal government spent $11.7 million to test 29,000 federal employees. Since only 153 tested positive, the cost for detecting a single drug user was $77,000. Why do employers persist in the practice? Probably because of advertising by the roughly $2 billion drug-testing industry, but I suspect that the demeaning effect of testing may also hold some attraction to employers. (Ehrenreich, 2001: 128)

For Ehrenreich (2001), drug testing is a costly enterprise that aims to control and subsume low-paid workers further and serves to demonstrate a distrust for certain individual members of the workforce. Even though it is intended to have positive effects in its consequences — i.e. its latent consequences — it does not really contribute to a better working life or to better services. Notwithstanding the pros and cons of drug testing, it can be examined as a managerial practice that fiercely seeks to capture the inconsistencies and indeterminacy of everyday working life. In knowledge management theory, such inconsistencies and indeterminacy are only occasionally addressed and discussed. In most cases, these are examined on a rather superficial level. For instance, Pfeffer and Sutton (1999) speak about a "knowing-doing gap" wherein the firm's know-how is not fully exploited in its operations. But Pfeffer and Sutton (1999) do not aim to discuss the presence of such "gaps" from ontological or epistemological perspectives, rather they adhere to a managerialist view of organizations wherein knowledge and operations can be separated from one another and examined as such. Thus, the paradoxes of knowledge management are not very often examined and the management of organizational resources that are indeterminate or not fully known is not very often examined as something qualitatively different to the management of tangible resources. Therefore, the treatment of knowledge management as a set of interrelated practices aimed at turning unknown — or at least not *fully* known — processes into slightly better known processes recognizes Grint's (1997) idea that managerial practises tend to legitimise themselves thought their emphasis on control and rationality. One can say that the practice-based view of knowledge management follows Weick's (2001) insistence on emphasizing "small wins" in organizing. Weick writes:

A small win is a concrete, complete, implemented outcome of moderate importance. By itself, one small win may seem unimportant. A series of wins at small but significant tasks, however, reveals a pattern that may attract allies, deter opponents, and lower resistance to subsequent proposals. Small wins are controllable opportunities that produce visible results (Weick, 2001: 431)

It may be the case that the entire idea of managing such a thing as knowledge is wholly mistaken, but there may also be small wins that are gained from embarking on such a project. Knowledge may be distributed, scattered, elusive, uncoded, tacit, or whatever and there may only be limited possibilities of making it take full control of the organization, but the ethics of small wins will still enable some hope for more effective and "better" knowledge management practices. Knowledge management is always the management of what cannot be fully determined, but conceiving of knowledge management as a set of practices aimed at capturing at least parts of the firm's know-how and intellectual resources may have effects that will produce "visible results".

Knowledge Management as Management Fad and Buzzword

Even though the term "knowledge management" is a rather recent construct, the notion of knowledge has been examined in management writing for a long period. For instance, Etzioni (1964: 77) talked about the "organization of knowledge" and identifying one particular type of organization based on its access to specialized knowledge. Etzioni (1964) writes:

> Knowledge is produced, applied, preserved, or communicated in organizations especially established for these purposes. These are professional organizations, which are characterized not only by the goals they pursue but also by the high proportion of professionals on their staff (at least 50 per cent) and by the authority relations between professionals and non-professionals which are so structured that professionals have superior authority over the major goals of the organization. (Etzioni, 1964: 77-78)

Knowledge in organizations is not a new thing; knowledge management is. Therefore, one of the lingering concerns for the proponents of knowledge management theory is whether or not this particular perspective on organizations is to be regarded as a management fad or buzzword. Several writers point out that there has been a significant growth in the number of publications addressing the notion of knowledge management. Within organizational and management studies, an emerging field of research deals with what has been called "guru theory", and popular management books. At times, such a popular form of management theory has been debunked by academic researchers and dismissed in terms of being simplistic, managerialistic, or overtly functionalist. An alternative view is represented by, for instance, ten Bos (2000) who regards fashion in management thinking as serving a purpose in terms of making sense out of ambiguous realities for practicing managers. In a similar vein, Collins (2001: 32) writes: "[W]e might argue that in seeking 'to out' the myths of the guru industry, critical scholars have failed to engage with management practitioners, because the arguments advanced — *this is all just fads and rhetoric* — have failed to take managerial problems seriously, and so, have failed to recognize the capacity, which guru theory has to construct persuasive representations of reality, which resonate with the experiences and ambitions of managers". The social production of management concepts and models remains an intriguing matter for some management researchers. Collins (2000: 4), for instance, writes: "Management fads and buzzwords do not fall like rain. They do not occur naturally. They are *created* and disseminated by groups of people working within the apparatus, which has grown to become an industry in itself". Studies of management fads and buzzwords (see for instance Jackson, 2001; Collins, 2000; Huczynski, 1996) deal with this creation and dissemination of management ideas.

In order to discuss knowledge management theory in terms of management fads and buzzwords, a few definitions may be helpful. Collins (2000: 10) refers to *The Concise Oxford Dictionary* which tells us that a buzzword is "[a] slogan, or as a fashionable piece of jargon". A fad is defined as "a craze or a peculiar notion" (Collins, 2000: 14). Abrahamson (1996a: 257) defines management fads as "a relatively transitory collective belief, disseminated by management fashion setters". Gibson and Tesone (2001: 122-123) write: "We consider management fads to be widely accepted, innovative interventions into the organization's practices designed to improve some aspect of performance. Fads either evolve into new management practices or are abandoned as failures". Given these definitions, it is complicated to fully separate the "buzzword" from the "fad" or "management fashion". Collins (2000) writes:

> [W]hile 'culture' and 'empowerment' are buzzwords, Total Quality Management and Business Process Reengineering are not, properly, buzzwords. They may be 'buzz-phrases' but since 'buzz-phrases' is a rather clumsy conjunction and anyway, not listed in The Concise Oxford Dictionary, the terms 'fads' and 'buzzwords' have been selected in an attempt to capture the key terms applied in management. (Collins, 2000: 14)

Speaking of knowledge management, this may be regarded as a "buzz-phrase" rather than a single concept. As the literature suggests, fads and buzzwords are relatively transient linguistic or semiotic constructs, rapidly becoming part of everyday management vocabulary as soon as they are accepted as useful phrases or notions. As Gibson and Tesone (2001) note, management fads and buzzwords may both refer to highly useful management practices and models, but in most cases buzzwords or management fads are, by definition, management practices that fail to achieve the outcomes and effects their proponents have promised.

Studies of buzzwords and fads include the greening of industry discourse (Fineman, 2001), business process reengineering (Knights & Willmott, 2000; Benders & van Veen, 2001; Pruijt, 1998), new public management (Schofield, 2001), the practice of benchmarking (Walgenbach & Hegele, 2001), and the qualities of the "management guru literature" (Jackson, 2001; Huczynski, 1996). The concept of Total Quality Management (TQM) has been another area subject to both conceptual criticism (Xu, 1999; Zbaracki, 1998; Hackman & Wageman, 1995; Wilkinson & Willmott, 1995) and detailed empirical studies (Young, Charns & Shortell, 2001; Glover, 2000; Knights & McCabe, 1999; Edwards, Collinson & Rees, 1998; Wilkinson, Godrey & Marchington, 1997). Since knowledge management theory is a rather recent field of studies within organizational theory, one may argue that it is to be treated as a management fad and a buzzword. For instance, the grandiose declarations of the "knowledge society" or "post-industrial society" are susceptible to such a criticism. As Anthony Giddens points out: "Many authors speak of the emergence of an information society today, but in a broad sense, there has been an information society for centuries" (Giddens & Pierson, 1998: 99). In a similar manner, Thompson, Warhurst & Callaghan (2000: 137) call into question the embraced notion of the knowledge society on the basis of empirical evidence: "[T]he 'real' knowledge economy, such as the high-tech clusters in biotechnology or advanced electronics, is vital to the contemporary economy, but relatively small in scope and potential for employment growth". In addition, one critique of knowledge management is the strong emphasis on a de-contextualized and black-boxed notion of "knowledge" that is employed in a manner suggesting that the use of "knowledge" in organizations is of recent date, rather than being one of the integral components of the practices of organizing and organization. If one investigates the history of commercial enterprises (see for instance Braudel, 1992) one notices that all organizations throughout history have been dependent on certain skills, know-how and experience.

The objective of this discussion is not to say whether knowledge management "really is" or "is not" a management fad, but to point out that there is a discussion concerning the qualities, roles, and purpose of management fads and buzzwords. Nevertheless, one can argue, speaking from a symbolic management perspective as well as a sense-making perspective, that the construct of knowledge management appears to serve a purpose in terms of capturing some practical concerns and issues in the day-to-day work of organizations. Knowledge management may be fashionable and one may tick all the boxes when checking its management fad status, but it has still generated some interest among academic researchers, consultants, and practitioners.

Outline of the Book

In this chapter, it has been argued that the body of theory referred to as knowledge management theory is a contingent and socially-embedded concept whose "surface of emergence" (Foucault, 1972: 41) is the society wherein it is claimed by various groups that intangible resources make a difference in terms of organizational performance. In addition, it has been suggested that knowledge management is best examined on the level of practices, i.e. the immediate practical undertakings that firms and organizations become involved with under the banner of knowledge management. Thus, knowledge management practices are, in brief, the activities that firms and organizations refer to as knowledge management practices. Next, knowledge management practices were discussed in terms of being a strategic activity, and knowledge management practices will always seek to manage indeterminate and intangible resources. In consequence, knowledge management tends to overemphasize the rationalistic, functionalistic and instrumental aspects of it in order to demonstrate highly-prized and institutionalized values and norms in the business community. In practice, such a rationalistic approach to the management of knowledge is complicated to maintain because there will always be domains that cannot be fully captured by such managerial practice. Therefore, rather than depicting knowledge management as the next big thing in management (as most normative and popular management books in the area do), it is instead useful to speak in terms of small wins being an objective for knowledge management. Knowledge management should not overturn the entire organization, but it may influence some of its processes and practices in order to make more efficient use of the intellectual resources of the organization.

The outline of this book is as follows: in Chapter two, the strategic management theory is discussed in greater detail. In Chapter three, the debate on knowledge management theory and concepts such as the knowledge-based firm are examined. In Chapter four, the knowledge management practices of paper manufacturer SCA are examined. In Chapter five, a similar analysis is presented on the basis of pharmaceuticals manufacturer AstraZeneca. Finally, Chapter six provides an analysis of the two cases and their implications for knowledge management theory, and more specifically theories of knowledge sharing and learning.

Summary and Conclusion

Knowledge management theory represents a particular perspective on organizations, a perspective emphasizing intangible intellectual resources as the prime mover of organizational performance, competitive advantage, and managerial practices. This view of the firm is emerging from a broader discourse on the post-industrial consumer society. The notion of knowledge management is a concept developed and popularised during the 1990s, when interest in Total Quality Management, the most important managerial framework of the 1980s, seemed to have saturated and when new concepts such as Business Process Reengineering were both introduced and heavily criticized for not being capable of solving the managerial problems they promised to deal with (see for instance Knights & Willmott, 2000). In this perspective, knowledge management is just another fashionable label, denoting a set of managerial activities whose "time has come" (see Czarniawska & Jourges, 1996). TQM provided an integrated managerial framework explicitly addressing the notion of quality in various respects and BPR aimed at restructuring corporations in order to enhance productivity. In comparison with these two managerial frameworks, knowledge management theory does not focus on two distinctive organizational interests such as quality (TQM) or organization structure (BPR), rather it emphasizes the firm's internal resources and assets. More specifically, such resources and assets are often intangible and embodied. In consequence, knowledge management theory is departing from the more functionalist views of organization in terms of acknowledging resources that cannot fully be captured by managerial practices. Still, there are examples of good organizational practices actively engaging with the management of organizational knowledge. In this book, two cases of knowledge management practice will be examined. Knowledge management will be examined both as an organizational resource, from a strategic management perspective, and as a practice, i.e. a set of operations, undertakings and activities taking place within and between organizations.

Chapter 2

The Strategic Management of Knowledge

Introduction

In contemporary strategic management theory, knowledge takes a central position. But that has not always been the case. In its quest to explain drivers of performance, strategy theory has been concerned with a range of different matters over the last 40 to 50 years. Industry structure, asset endowments, organization, culture, and a number of other firm contents have been brought up at different points in time as being particularly central to firm success, i.e. strategy. However, over the last ten to fifteen years or so, the concept of knowledge has become increasingly important in strategic management. Concepts such as dominant logic and managerial cognition were introduced already in the 1980s, and core competencies, capabilities and skills were frequently addressed in strategy theory during the 1990s. They were addressed previously as well, but not as frequently as in the 1980s and the 1990s. Behind these concepts, the idea of knowledge is, of course, central. Today, knowledge management, or similar, makes up a significant proportion of the academic management field. Journals and research societies focusing on the role and management of knowledge in various forms are blossoming. The competence-based management perspective (Sanchez, 2001b) and the knowledge-based view (Conner & Prahalad, 1996; Grant, 1996) are examples of subfields conducting research into the strategic management of knowledge. In the strategy perspective, knowledge is seen as a potential resource, both independently and as a more fundamental factor behind other types of assets. Hence, knowledge can be a "direct" resource, e.g. knowledge of an oil well, or an "indirect" resource, e.g. knowledge of a way to manage brands. Not only is it seen as a potential resource, it is also seen as a potential driver of performance and competitive advantage. In addition, it is seen as something that needs to be managed, i.e. nurtured, evolved and fitted to the existing operations and organization – yet there is a debate about whether it can be managed or not (see for instance Grant, 1996; Sanchez, 1997; Boisot et al, 1997). Should firms attempt to manage knowledge, or should they just attempt to organize their businesses in a way that best deals with the cognitive abilities they have had the fortune, or misfortune, to be endowed with? The idea applied in this book is that while it may well be that certain pieces or aspects of knowledge cannot be "managed", it is obvious that organizations nonetheless try, with varying degrees of success. In this chapter, we will try to position knowledge management – and knowledge sharing – within the strategic management perspective. We will do so by describing the "general" strategy field and by focusing in more detail the contemporary turns into the resource-based and knowledge-centered perspectives.

Strategy is originally a Greek word referring to 'the art of warfare'. However, in contemporary lingo, used both by theorists and practitioners, the concept is diluted. Its meaning is subjective, and dependent on who is asked. Our view is that strategy refers to the factors that explain relative performance: a firm's performance in relation to some point in its past — last year, last quarter, during its previous executive management reign — or in relation to a comparable entity, such as competitors or stock brokers' expectations. Strategy has to do with factors that explain good or bad performance, typically *financial* performance. Strategic management, as a refinement, concerns the longitudinal processes along which strategies, or performance, evolve. These processes can be intentional and rational, based on managerial decisions and executive actions; but they can also be random and created through sheer luck and coincidence outside the control of decision-makers. The central theme of strategy is its normative orientation: it is ultimately concerned with the links between behaviour and success, including the obstacles to this connection, of course.

The management of knowledge is interesting to any theoretical field, but our primary focus is the organizational context. When knowledge is seen as a potential asset that can help organizations improve (their performance), and when strategy is defined in the way that we just have, strategy is the obvious umbrella under which to discuss knowledge management. In order to do so, we need to discuss strategy in the first place. Our primary focus in this chapter will be on theory that covers both strategy content and processes. The review is by no means exhaustive; our sole ambition is to discuss theory we believe to be of relevance when seeking to understand the economic, social, cognitive, normative mechanics behind the relationship between knowledge and strategy.

As indicated, there are many ways to view strategy. For example, it can be seen as a description of a firm's competitive position (Porter, 1980), as a long-term action plan (Ansoff, 1965), as a resource-base (Barney, 1991), as an ex post pattern of actions (Mintzberg, 1978), as a political process (cf. Bower, 1970), or as a sequential, industrial value chain configuration (cf. Porter, 1985). The execution of strategy can be seen as linearly rational (cf. Andrews, 1971) or as a less rational, random process involving evolutionary, Darwinist perspectives (Nelson & Winter, 1982). The focus of theories all concerns the relative well-being of firms and intra-industry dynamics. In order to separate perspectives, one simple way is to distinguish between strategy contents, or positions, on the one hand, and the longitudinal strategy process on the other (Chakravarthy & Doz, 1992; Foss, 1997).

In academic research, the former perspective is concerned with the relationship between certain features or characteristics and selected variables representing the concept of performance (typically relative profitability). This is evident, for instance, in the notion that a particular generic strategy is connected with a higher level of profitability (Porter, 1980); that a particular set of resource features is connected with sustained competitive advantage (Peteraf, 1993); that one particular organizational structure is more strongly associated with profit than another (Chandler, 1962; Rumelt, 1974), and so on. Research, both theoretical and empirical, is intent on studying and discovering correlations or connections between certain variables. What is particularly interesting, and a cause of debate, is identifying the independent variables behind the dependent performance variable: what sort of variables explain superior performance? As a direct extension, and a consequence of the maturity of the scientific field, the language of strategy has developed as well. When we speak about the variables that explain superior performance, we use concepts such as generic strategies, industry forces, firm resources, organization structure, factor market interactions and culture. Lately, we have also been referring to competence, skills, capabilities, assets, business models, business ideas, business equations, unique selling propositions – and knowledge. The consistency of these concepts is debatable, but in this chapter we shall try to propose ways of dealing with them. As will be discussed below, two perspectives dominate content-oriented strategy theory: industrial organization (Porter, 1980), which stipulates that success is determined by firm-external forces, and the resource-based view (Barney, 1991), which suggests that relative performance emanates from valuable and unique firm resources.

The latter perspective, what we refer to as the strategy process perspective, is concerned with the evolution of strategies over time. What is it that initially generates the variables that we correlate with performance? Of particular interest is the role of managers, notably senior managers, decision-makers. In a sense, one could say that the process perspective takes as its dependent variables the independent variables of strategy content research (Chakravarthy & Doz, 1992). As an example, a strategy process researcher will not primarily be occupied with whether or not a new competence will render a company greater profits (he or she will, but that is not the only concern), but rather what it was that created the new competence in the first place. The notion of bounded rationality (March & Simon, 1958) and the acceptance of the influence of potentially non-rational norms and values (Oliver, 1997) thus become important to the researcher. The random, unplanned events, which are so frequently taken for rational choice within content-oriented research, are important, consequently downgrading slightly our view of managers and decision-makers as strong, bold and clever leaders. A lot of strategy success has to be put down to luck and incidence.

In comparison to strategy theory, this book's position is resource-based and process-oriented. A topic such as knowledge sharing centres on the management of resources. The longitudinal and management-oriented character of the process view and the resource focus on the knowledge provided by the resource-based view suggest such a theoretical position. In what follows, we shall discuss the strategy content and process perspectives in more detail. We end the section with a brief connection with the role of knowledge in strategy and strategic management. The subsequent chapter specifically focuses on the management of knowledge.

Content Perspectives

One of the first management texts that referred to the concept of strategy was Chandler (1962), and his account of the history of four American companies. To him, strategy was defined as

> The determination of the basic long-term goals and objectives of an enterprise, and the adoption of courses of action and the allocation of resources necessary for carrying out these goals. (Chandler, 1962: 13).

In a way, Chandler's study can be seen as one of the early departures from straightforward organizational and management theories. As a result of the global economic progress following the Second World War, research into organizations became more focused on 'the big questions' that organizations and managers were facing. Up until then, organizational theory had primarily been biased towards matters which are seen today as fairly trivial and operational by strategists. Although revolutionary in extending our understanding of the management of organizations, scientific contributions by Taylor

(1911), Gilbreth (1911), Weber (1946), Fayol (1949), and Barnard (1938) typically did not concern problems associated with the "big issues", e.g. strategic, long-term decisions. They frequently focused on "smaller issues", including work organization, behaviour, decision procedures, rules, chains of command and so forth.

Institutions and Entrepreneurs

In his work on business administration, Newman (1951) used strategy to refer to the managerial work done outside of the daily routines required to administer an organization. Selznick (1957), who did not use the concept of strategy, took an institutional view of managerial work, and suggested that we separate organizations from institutions, where the former is seen as a skeletal system, a tool, a rational instrument that managers can change and alter as they desire, in order to improve efficiency, for instance. An institution, on the other hand, is a "natural product of social needs and pressures – a responsive, adaptive organism" (Selznick , 1957: 5). The institution refers to the position of the firm as an organism in a larger social context, in which the organization has to adapt to survive. In order to do so, the organization has to develop a distinct competence and a distinct set of interdependent norms and values. Managers of institutions work towards defining the long-term mission of the company and "infusing" the values required "beyond the technical requirements of the task at hand". The norms and values of the institution are in harmony with the environment.

Subsequently, Penrose (1959) studied the growth of businesses and was interested in the growth of both small and large companies. Entrepreneurship is manifest in the introduction of new ideas into the organization, which stimulates innovation, expansion and financial fund-raising. "Management" is subordinate to "entrepreneurship": management is supposed to execute entrepreneurial visions and operative issues. It reveals an intellectual relation to Selznick (1957) and his distinction between an organization and an institution. The view that the firm is "a collection of resources bound together in an administrative framework" is also evidence of links to Selznick. Despite having been slightly neglected, the work of Penrose has been a source of inspiration both for the resource-based view and for research into entrepreneurship.

So, at the end of the 1950's, research started to focus more on the context of firms, the increasing complexities that ensue, as well as the role of managers in this increasing complexity. Other sub-themes or concerns regarding the work of the manager, e.g. competition, global structure, and long term planning, were highlighted. Following the war, the economy had recovered and started to prosper. Firms grew fast, resulting in multinational and global companies, frequently in the shape of large, well-diversified conglomerates. This resulted in more intense competition between firms, increased uncertainty and a stronger focus on growth and relative performance. The openness of organizations was acknowledged and emphasized. The concept of 'strategy' was applied in order to define these 'big issues', and to distinguish them somewhat from the ordinary, day-to-day, internal organizational matters that managers had to deal with. As we approached the 1960s, the subject really took off.

Strategy and Tools for Strategic Analysis

The works of Chandler (1962), Ansoff (1965), Andrews (1971) are often seen as the roots of strategy theory (Porter, 1996). They provided theory and concepts that are still frequently used. What unites them is the analytical, linear approach, and the view that strategy has to do with the big things, and the big picture. An emphasis is evident on entities such as strategy and structure, strengths, weaknesses, opportunities and threats, and on the assumedly uncomplicated task of creating strategies. Strategy is very much a matter of analyzing and finally deciding on which actions to take – implementing these is not a big issue. Andrews has said, for instance, that strategy formulation is analytically objective, while implementation is primarily an administrative task.

Apart from the empirical data, Chandler's (1962) contribution to strategy is the discussion of strategy and structure and whichever comes first – in Chandler's view this is strategy. Management is not just confined to organizational issues, but also to the setting of long-term goals and objectives, and the planning and resource allocation necessary to achieve the goals. He explicitly addressed the need to structure the organization in order to make it support the strategy. So, somewhat paradoxically, Chandler's work came to centre upon structure and how to set a structure that fits the large, diversified firm emerging at that time. The most relevant structure appeared to be the M-form, or *multidivisional structure*, in which relatively distinct subunits were coordinated centrally but controlled themselves, independently of other subunits. This structure relieves top management from the daily, operative tasks, allowing it instead to focus on 'grand issues' like goals and plans. Like Penrose, Chandler was interested in scale and scope (size and diversification in Penrose's terminology). The companies that Chandler studied (Dupont, General Motors, Standard Oil and Sears, Roebuck & Co) had become successful because of their ability to fit structure to the complex growth strategy. The

M-Form structure allowed top management to concentrate on the big issues, while divisional managers could be made responsible for the implementation of different functions or business lines. Another field where Chandler was a pioneer was in the use of the case methodology in strategy research, which subsequently grew stronger at Harvard, whence Chandler had come, as well as at other universities where research into strategy was being conducted. This was an era when the positivist, mathematical ontologies and epistemologies of natural science and economics also reigned in social sciences such as management. Learning from the case, and using cases in teaching, has since become well established.

Chandler's ideas about strategy were subsequently supplemented with a bit more detail by Ansoff (1965), who integrated theories about strategy with decision-making and planning. According to Ansoff, the *corporate strategy* is the common thread that unifies choices regarding product-market scope, competitive advantage, synergy and make-or-buy decisions. Success is equal to economic return. Choices regarding the different strategy aspects had to be orchestrated and interrelated, and in terms of decision-making procedures, Ansoff was influenced by Simon's view of stages of problem solving (Simon, 1945). Although some of Ansoff's models, for instance his 'growth vector matrix', appear overly simplistic and linear in nature, some of the elements of the strategy choice are still valid.

Andrews (1971), another Harvard strategist, came to discuss two dichotomies that are still debated within strategy theory. An important idea in early strategy theory was the separation of *the environment* from *the firm*. Andrews emphasized this "dichotomy" and claimed that the industrial environment and its changes of it had to be matched by internal changes in the use of resources and competencies. To Andrews, strategy meant analyzing the external opportunities and threats and the internal strengths and weaknesses, and matching these factors so as to formulate a strategy. Thus, he gave rise to the widely applied SWOT (strengths, weaknesses, opportunities and threats) analysis, which is still a model used by practitioners in all sorts of fields. Andrews also emphasized another popular dichotomy at the time; between *analysis*, or formulation, and *implementation*. This perspective has not gone unanswered (cf. Mintzberg, 1978). The rationalistic assumption that it is possible to analyze, objectively, the strategic options and then administrate them is not applicable, since the perception of options and implementation is very difficult to envision *ex ante*, due to issues such as bounded rationality and norms and values, as well as organizational resistance to change. Strategic management is far more complex than Andrews implied.

The orientation towards analytical tools like the SWOT analysis was further emphasized during the 1970s, with the increasing influence of strategy consulting firms. Despite the increasing instrumentalism, practitioners still tended to find strategy theory a bit too conceptual (Rumelt et al., 1994). Instead, practitioners like the Boston Consulting Group (BCG), operationalized theory in order to be able to apply it to practical situations (McKinsey, a more established consulting firm, also developed their own models). Two models, in particular, emanating from BCG were important – and it is telling for the era that these were intended to improve the understanding of portfolio management and economies of scale, respectively. The *growth share matrix* (Henderson, 1973) was an analytical tool that helped managers to manage their portfolio of businesses. The central assumption of the model is that growth is good and important. Whether this is through industry growth, indicating demand growth, or growth by increased market share, does not matter. But why then, one might ask, are growth and size so important? This may be answered by the second influential analytical model provided by BCG, i.e. the *experience curve* (Yelle, 1979; Henderson, 1984; originally in 1968 by BCG), a model that actually addresses the role of knowledge in business. The assumption is that, with accumulated experience, organizations become increasingly efficient, albeit at a decreasing rate. This applies in particular to repetitive tasks such as production. The larger the factory – the higher the volume of production, and the greater the experience, but the lower the costs per product unit. Low costs were, as we know from Penrose for instance, central to the logic of growth. And relative market share was important not only in order to create low relative costs, but also to enable the erecting of so-called 'entry barriers' which complicated and possibly deterred potential competitors from entering the market. If firms could quickly take cost leadership positions, they could prosper for a long period of time. Economies of scale are assumed to be a constant issue for managers.

But cost is not the only means of competition, thus the validity of the experience curve is confined to areas related to productivity and efficiency. It says little about the quality of the product, and the ability to differentiate the product in relation to the competition. The experience curve implicitly assumes that size is the only means of competition and that all products are alike and experience the same level of demand. This is of course untrue. Even the most commoditized products (e.g. oil or power) are being differentiated from each other in terms of service, or other intangible properties like branding. A branded product is always unique in the eyes of the buyer. The influence of BCG and other consulting firms had a significant impact on practice in the 1970s. However, their models still had to cater for a broader range of strategy aspects.

Industrial Organization

In line with the interest in firm-internal and firm-external success factors, research into strategy has also been based on microeconomics. The notion of the industry, the clearly defined sector, has been important, because as long as we can define the industry we can define the market, and supply and demand. In order to discuss relative performance, competitive advantage, value chain configuration, differentiation and so on, the notion of industry must be accepted and the definition of the product has to be fixed. Doing this requires a clear orientation towards the product and the product market rather than, say, factor markets.

Drawing on the structure-conduct-performance (SCP) concept, and based on the reverse logic of industrial organization economics (I/O) (Bain, 1968), the Harvard strategist Michael Porter has created frameworks and explanatory models for strategy. Putting aside his Schumpeterian approach to the competitive advantage of nations (Porter, 1990), Porter's work includes three key models or sub-theories: the *five industry forces*, the *generic strategy* choice and the *value chain*. All three depend strongly on the notion of the industry and the dynamics and power of industry institutions. The two former Porterian models were introduced in 1980, and the value chain in 1985.

In practice, when business strategy theorists refer to I/O, they normally refer solely to Porter, 1980. The core idea of the 1980 book was that it is the industrial forces that determine the strategies of firms as well as the profitability, attractiveness, of the firms and the industry as such. In the first sentence of the book, Porter states;

> The essence of formulating competitive strategy is relating a company to its environment (Porter, 1980: 3).

Porter identified five structural determinants in the five forces model. *Threat of entry*: New entries put pressure on existing competitors and on profitability. Prices may go down, and in trying to hedge for price-competition competitors might be forced into investing in product quality enhancement or process improvements. Furthermore, fixed costs will be allocated on a smaller output. Margins are reduced. The threat of entry, however, depends on whether there are so-called *barriers to entry*. Porter claims that economies of scale, other cost disadvantages independent of scale, product differentiation, capital requirements, switching costs, access to distribution channels, and government policy all help to erect entry barriers.

Intensity of rivalry among existing competitors: According to Porter (1980: 17), "rivalry occurs because one or more competitors either feels the pressure or sees the opportunity to improve position". Tactics include price competition, advertising, product innovation, increased service and so forth. A number of factors drive intensity: numerous or equally balanced competitors, sluggish industry growth, high fixed costs, lack of differentiation or switching costs, and exit barriers.

Pressure from substitute products: A substitute product fulfils a function very similar to that of the original product, such as is the case with coffee and tea. Substitutes can limit the prices of the original product, since price increases that are too aggressive will trigger the search for functional fulfilment among other products. In severe cases, substitutes will wipe out an original product entirely – stencil copying is more or less dead these days, for instance. The substitutes that are most intensive are those subject to trends and those produced by industries earning high profits, according to Porter.

Bargaining power of buyers: Customers want to maximize quality in relation to price, or minimize price in relation to quality. Buyers tend to be powerful when purchasing a large proportion of the seller's total sales volume or the buyer's total purchase volume, when the product is standardized and the buyer knows about the cost structure, and when the sold product is unimportant in relation to the quality of the buyer's products. It is difficult but firms can deal with the behaviour and preferences of customers in different ways. Segmentation is one way, by means of which firms select customers that have the least power to influence the offering.

Bargaining power of suppliers: Suppliers can increase prices and possibly reduce the quality of their products and services, thus imposing a threat to the industry players. The factors that make suppliers powerful are almost the reverse of those imposed by customers.

Depending on the strength of the industrial pressure, firms that succeed and prosper either position themselves in a way that enables their capabilities of providing the best defence, or try to influence the forces by changing their strategy. One central type of defence is to diversify into more profitable industries and become less dependent upon the non-attractive industry. Porter's model has obvious practical advantages. But it also has severe limitations. For instance, the advice given to firms is relatively naïve and partly tautological. In addition, the model largely neglects the firm-internal factors that affect competitiveness. The implicit view that the firm is an incumbent organism, whose ultimate strategic alternative is to exit the industry and diversify into a more attractive industry where things are not so difficult, and firm profitability is completely in the hands of external factors, is indicative of a view that firms are incapable of changing the conditions or structure of an industry (e.g. Barney, 1991; making an exhaustive list of references to this criticism is pointless).

However, in 1980, Porter offered some further details of strategy choices when he introduced the concept of generic strategies which firms could apply

in their battle against industrial forces. According to Porter, there are principally two *generic strategies* for any given line of business (for select products
or markets). Achieving *cost leadership* is related to the experience curve concept discussed earlier. Primarily, it requires scale, but also the aggressive pursuit of cost savings, the constant rationalization of labour and capital,
process innovation, coordinated purchasing, and so forth. A low-cost strategy generates above-normal returns despite being under pressure: it can respond to all five forces. But a low-cost position can be risky, e.g. in relation to
product quality and service. The opposite of low-cost, one might say, is *dif-
ferentiating* the product in order that it appears unique in the industry. Successful differentiation results in a higher price: the customer is prepared to
pay more than he or she does for competing products, thus providing the dif-
ferentiating firm with above-normal profitability. Differentiation advantages
can be based on a particular design or brand loyalty. They can also be based
on technology, customer service or whatever makes it appear to have a
unique identity in the eyes of the market. One good example is so-called re-
newable energy, which has the same function as conventional energy, but is
produced in a more environment-friendly – and costly – way and commands
a higher price because consumers are prepared to pay for the environment.
Differentiation can be risky, in that it often means that firms have to trade
differentiation advantages for high costs.

It is important, Porter claims, that firms select *one* of the two strategies.
Logically, this means that attempts to achieve both cost leadership and differentiation for a given product are risky. This appears to contradict the intu-
itive logic that stipulates that companies should always seek to maximize
price and minimize cost. Porter's generic strategies are relevant precisely (and
only) from a generic perspective. For any firm with a profit and loss statement, two variables to look at are costs and sales turnover, which, divided by
product units sold, can offer the cost and calculation of a given product. But,
as is the case after having understood the logic of the external, industrial
forces, one issue remains: how do we achieve, i.e. formulate and implement, a
generic strategy? Many critics of Porter, such as advocates of the resource-
based view, claim that he did not produce this explanation. That is not entirely true. He gave some indications, as early as in 1980, during the discussion about actions that firms can take to combat industry forces, and an even
more firm-internal approach was offered with the value chain model.

Porter introduced the *value chain* in 1985 as the basic metaphor for firms
and the vehicle by which firms create low-cost or differentiation strategies.
The proposition was a complement to the five forces model and a response to
its critics. Porter stated that competitive advantage comes through cost or differentiation, which in turn are dependent upon the management of *activities*

in the flow of horizontal value addition, using the stream metaphor crossing vertically from industry to industry as raw materials are refined, sold, refined, sold and finally consumed. The value chain, however, could also be used for an individual business. Configuring the individual value chain is a matter of setting the boundaries of the firm and including activities that add value to the product, and grouping and gathering the internal drivers in a way that supports the improvement of costs and customer-perceived quality. Large-scale, for instance, is important for cost advantages and adds certain imperatives regarding internal organization. Product quality, another example, may require firms to integrate certain capabilities in order to enhance the quality of a certain product component. The concepts of value chains, activities and drivers constituted an explanation to the question of how firms and managers handle the issue of creating the generic strategies leading to competitive advantage. In describing what it is that actually makes an activity cost-effective or 'different', Porter identifies a number of 'cost drivers' and 'drivers of uniqueness'. *Cost drivers* are the structural factors that drive costs and have to be managed in a low-cost strategy. Economies of scale, learning and experience, capacity utilization, integration of activities, location and institutional factors (taxes, labour laws and so forth) are all examples. *Drivers of differentiation* are primarily based on policy choices and on linkages. Particularly important choices relate to product features and services, intensity of an activity (i.e. expenditure), technologies used, quality of inputs, procedures guiding certain activities, skills and experience, control of activities etc. Linkages to external and internal activities are sources of differentiation because they allow integration and cross-fertilization.

Porter's value chain model has been heavily criticized for a number of reasons, including its sequential orientation, its stream perspective, the obvious weaknesses in relation to service offerings, the neglecting of reciprocal interaction and learning, the rather superficial discussion about 'drivers', etc. But that has also resulted in widely ramified developments and extensions, including the 'value star' (Normann & Wikström, 1994), which opens up the sequential view of the value chain and looks at the entire network of stakeholders in value creation. Other buzzwords along the same lines include "value shops" (Stabell & Fjeldstad, 1995), "value nets" (Brandenburger & Nalebuff, 1996), "value innovation" (Kim & Mauborgne, 1997), "value webs" (Selz, 1999), and "value migration" (Slywotsky, 1995). As a final comment, the integration of Porter's models is not, perhaps, entirely simple. But Porter wrote one largely neglected paper in 1991 in which he discussed the cohesion and logic of his framework. The paper was partly a defence against the, by then, increasingly popular resource-based view.

The Resource-Based View

In direct contrast to I/O and the porterian framework, the so-called resource-based view (RBV) has emerged since the end of the 1980's (Wernerfelt, 1984; Barney, 1986, 1991). The core of the RBV, in relation to I/O, is the assumption that industries are heterogeneous and that the resources of firms are imperfectly mobile. These basic assumptions suggest that performance is ultimately driven by the resource base of firms – not external factors like industry forces. In consequence, rather than focusing solely on product market issues, firms should also pay attention to the factor market. Not only is it important to realize the value of skills and assets on the product market, it is also important to interact with factor markets in a way that allows firms to absorb, acquire and arrange resources in a cost-effective manner, in order that the resource-base can generate rents, preferably sustained (Conner, 1991; Peteraf, 1993). Factor market resources, like competence, might be scarce in supply, implying that the ability to interact and transact with the factor market is a key strategic issue and one that can sustain and enforce substantial resource differences. This is in contrast with the neo-classical view (Ricardo, 1817) that factor market supply is elastic (Barney, 2001a). In a sense, the RBV turns the porterian view upside down, and focuses on the performance of the resource-base: does it generate a payback? The factor market orientation of RBV does not hinder it from discussing product market issues, such as competitive advantage and relative performance. A competitive advantage, to the RBV (Barney, 1994b), is based on the individual resource. A resource which generates a rent and which competitors cannot imitate or substitute is a competitive advantage. This means that in the RBV framework, several companies in one industry can have a competitive advantage, albeit based on different resources. The concept of competitive advantage becomes entirely resource-centred: several firms can have competitive advantage, and one firm can have several competitive advantages (Barney, 1994b). In comparison with the I/O, in which competitive advantage is held by the company with the lowest cost or *the* company with the highest price in industry (and not necessarily the one with the highest profitability), RBV downplays the concept of competitive advantage. It is noteworthy that neither school equates competitive advantage with superior profits.

   Although I/O and RBV can be perceived as juxtapositions on the external-internal dimension, they share one feature, which is their orientation towards discussing contents, or positions, in strategy[1]. In I/O, this orientation is evi-

---

[1] They also share the view that demand curves slope to the South East, i.e. that marginal returns and utility decline with consumed volume. Uniqueness is important, be it on the product or the factor market, because exclusivity rather than 'inclusivity' generates payback. Network economies, where returns increase with consumption and value is generated through standardization and community, only serve to erode position (see Porter, 2001; but also Arthur, 1994).

dent in the focus on relations between genuine entities like value chains, generic strategies, industrial forces and so forth. It is also evident in the assumptions about the drivers of performance. A good example is the desire to estimate the relationship between generic strategies and performance. In RBV, the content orientation can be traced to the desire to set the characteristics and nature of resources, but also in the link between different types of resources and different types of resource attributes, e.g. whether a particular "organizational resource" is "valuable", "unique", and "costly to imitate". A relative lack of process orientation has been criticized all through the 1990s (Foss, 1997), and, as a result, there is a growing body of research trying to ask the (potentially time-consuming) question of where resources come from. This backtracking is logical to any strategy researcher, if we stipulate that firm performance is driven by resource-bases with certain characteristics and qualities. Thus, there are at least two 'content' sides to the RBV which are important. One refers to texts and research that discuss the *nature* of resources, while the other is connected with discussions about the *attributes*, or *qualities*, of resources necessary for generating competitive advantage. Below, we will first briefly discuss the qualities and attributes of resources, as well as views on the nature of resources. The process dimension of the RBV will be covered in the subsequent section.

Resource Attributes

RBV theorists have put a great deal of effort into trying to outline the resource characteristics needed for a resource to be strategic or a source of competitive advantage. Many writers focus on entire sets of attribute requirements (Dierickx & Cool, 1989; Amit & Schoemaker, 1993; Peteraf, 1993; Barney, 1994a; Collis, 1996), whereas others focus on single attributes (Reed & DeFillippi, 1990; Mahoney & Pandian, 1992; Liebeskind, 1996; Mosakowski & McKelvey, 1997). As a starting point, it might be useful to think of the attributes of strategic resources, i.e. sources of competitive advantage, as *value, uniqueness* and *costly imitation and substitution* (costly enough to deter attempts to imitate). A resource which is valuable and which nobody else holds is a source of competitive advantage. If it is costly to imitate and substitute, there will be prospects of sustaining the advantage.

A *valuable* resource lowers costs or raises the price of a product. It enables "a firm to conceive of or implement strategies that improve its efficiency and effectiveness" (Barney, 1991, p 106). Resources that exploit opportunities or neutralize threats "have the effect of lowering a firm's net costs and/or raising its net revenues more than would have been the case if they did not possess and use these skills" (Barney, 1994a, p 6). A link between the RBV and I/O is constituted by Collis's proposition (1996) that value is determined on the product market, when the firm "occupies a singular market position, so that the return to a factor of production it employs is greater than the return that factor can earn in any other use" (p 141). To obtain these market positions, firms exploit economies of scale, experience and skills to produce more effectively and to differentiate products – core features of I/O strategic management.

The fact that factor market prices strongly influence the value of a resource means that expectations regarding the future value of resources, i.e. what value a particular resource is expected to bring to individual firms and, consequently, what firms are willing to pay for a resource, are important (Barney, 1986; Peteraf, 1993). If all the competitors in an industry know which resource(s) will be important in the future and if the expected cash-flow is the same for all competitors, they will all acquire this resource, thereby creating nothing but parity for all competitors, because of the adjusted expectations and prices. According to Cool and Dierickx (1994), the effects on cash-flow created by a strategic investment may be divided into direct ones and indirect ones. If two firms acquire the same kind of resource for a price that is lower than the value of its use, the firm which has the ability to use the resource better will earn superior rents, even if both earn Schumpeterian rents. This also highlights the need for managers to combine the rational approach to future resources with a sense of idiosyncrasy. Finding *under-priced* resources, internally or externally, and seeing their potential and unique fit with existing stocks of resources, may create opportunities for competitive advantage. It is thus crucial that the identified resources are not common goods and that demand is a reflection of divergent expectations. If not, the resources will not be under-priced. It also shows that resources can be strategic, e.g. valuable, even if they are tradable, since price is an important determinant of the value of a resource. Yet many resources are not tradable or mobile, but products of firms' idiosyncrasies.

As a second precondition, resources must be *unique* and asymmetrically distributed across industry competitors. When a valuable resource is possessed by a large number of competitors, the strategy in question is easily duplicated, thereby eliminating the unique feature of the resource. Peteraf (1993) claims that the supply of superior resources cannot be expanded rapidly, meaning that there are windows for Schumpeterian rents. Consequently, inferior resources are brought to the market. Furthermore, although numerous actors may hold the same kind of resource, the uniqueness of the superiority of the resource is the crucial issue. "What is *key* is that the superior resources remain *limited* in supply" (Peteraf, 1993). Although two firms may hold valuable brands, one of the brands may be more valuable than the other.

Not only should the resource be unique, it must also be *costly to dupli-*

cate, in order to be a source of sustained competitive advantage. A valuable and rare resource acquired at an imperfect market price will only remain a source of advantage as long as competitors fail to realize the potential. A resource and its outcome can be duplicated either by building/acquiring the same resource (imitation) or by creating the same intermediate or final outcome using a different resource (substitution) (Dierickx & Cool, 1989; Barney, 1991, 1994a); Conner, 1991; Amit & Schoemaker, 1993; Peteraf, 1993). Eisenhardt and Martin (2000) elaborated upon this in the concept of "equifinality", referring to the tendency for the capabilities of competitors to converge over time, even if the paths leading to them may be idiosyncratic to the individual firm. According to Barney (1991, 1994b), the proper measurement of imitability is the costs required for a competitor to imitate. These costs depend upon three factors. *Unique historical conditions:* If the historical conditions under which one firm obtained its resources were particularly favourable, an imitating firm will have to pay more for the same kind of advantage, thus limiting the imitator's chance to gain competitive advantage. *Causal ambiguity:* Firms making numerous small resource decisions, rather than big public ones, may not attract much attention from their competitors. This, in turn, makes it difficult or costly for competitors to imitate the strategies, i.e. the resources. *Socially complex resources:* Resources that are tacit and dependent upon several intertwined "hubs", e.g. people or computer systems, may be impossible to imitate, because the imitator would have to deconstruct his own systems as well as create a new one.

Other writers have also addressed the factors behind costly imitation. Reed and DeFillippi (1990), focusing on the sources of causal ambiguity, claim that the tacitness, complexity and specificity of the resource are the prime determinants of ambiguity, and simultaneously, or consequently, of advantages. Mahoney and Pandian (1992) claim that the factors sustaining competitive advantage could be referred to as *isolating mechanisms*. Collis (1996) lists six different "constraints on imitability" and provides a framework for barriers to imitation that differentiates between stronger and weaker forms of imitability barriers. Two of them are more durable types of barriers: *Physical* constraints, such as natural resources and locations, and *legal* constraints, such as government regulations, patents etc. A third constraint is *time*, or rather time-compression diseconomy (Dierickx & Cool, 1989). It takes time to develop resources and often the same is true of duplication. In addition, *economic constraints, reputational threats* and *causal ambiguity* are proposed imitability constraints. The mechanisms and criteria discussed here are inter-related and, to some degree, sophistications of each other. The important conclusion is that in order to sustain the value and uniqueness of a resource, either it or its outcomes must be protected.

The Nature of Resources

There is a range of different texts within the RBV aiming to discuss resource typologies. In fact, this fascination occupies a lot of what is actually written on the subject of the RBV. Here, we shall briefly discuss some of them. Resources in general are not new phenomena in strategy theory (neither are they, of course, new empirical phenomena). Selznick (1957) and Penrose (1959) made early attempts to describe the 'core' of the firm. Subsequently, the SWOT analysis (Andrews, 1971) was introduced as a means of understanding strategy factors. With the RBV, the focus has been realigned to the internal factors, and although the names and the various characteristics proposed for the internal factors are different, they all can be referred to *strengths* as used in the SWOT analysis. This has not stopped the evolution of more or less sophisticated attempts to classify and label resources. During the 1990s, the RBV discourse was evolving along two basic tracks, partly because of ambitions to include the dynamics and evolution of resources and the impact of resources on activities and product offerings. One track focuses on the resources enabling certain firms to increase their performance relative to their competitors (Barney, 1991, 1994a; Conner, 1991; Grant, 1991; Hall, 1993, 1994, 1997; Peteraf, 1993; Hamel, 1994; Langlois, 1995; Wernerfelt, 1995; Winter, 1995; Conner & Prahalad, 1996; Rouse & Daellenbach, 1999; and others). The other track has come to highlight the so-called "capability" of firms to use and manage resources, competencies, assets, skills, knowledge and so forth (Grant 1991; Leonard-Barton, 1992; Stalk et al, 1992; Amit & Schoemaker 1993; Durand, 1997; Teece et al, 1997; Chatterjee, 1998; Kazanjian & Rao, 1999; Yeoh & Roth, 1999; Eisenhardt & Martin, 2000; Winter, 2000; and others).

Along the "resource track", a number of different definitions and phenomena have been presented, not without linguistic confusion (Chiesa & Manzini, 1997; Kalling & Styhre, 1999). In some cases, seemingly identical definitions describe different phenomena, whereas in other cases similar phenomena are given different definitions. Dierickx and Cool (1989) differentiate between *asset stocks* and *flows* of resources, where the former refers to the current set up of resources and the latter to the leakage and development of resources. Amit and Schoemaker (1993) talk about strategic assets, meaning either resources (possessed factors converted into products, for instance know-how) or capabilities (the capacity to deploy resources). Grant (1991) suggests that resources are financial, human, physical, technological, reputational or organizational. Another separation made is the one between intangible and tangible resources. Hall (1993, 1994, 1997) focuses on *intangible resources* and classifies these into four subgroups: *Regulatory* capabilities are intangible assets that are legally protectable, including trademarks, patents, copyrights, registered design, databases etc. *Positional* capabilities are intangible assets that are not legally protectable, including reputation, organizational and personal networks etc. *Functional* capabilities refer to the competence to do specific things, including employee, supplier, and distribution know-how etc. *Cultural* capabilities are competencies concerning attitudes, beliefs, values and norms. Miller and Shamsie (1996) made a similar distinction between property-based and knowledge-based resources. Ginsberg (1994) discusses two types of resources: physical (plants, equipment) and socio-cognitive resources (human and organizational capital). Black and Boal (1994) address the complex nature of resources and distinguish between *contained resources*, which are identified, simple bundles of resource factors that can be monetarily valued, and *system resources*, which are complex networks containing many direct and indirect linkages between a large number of factors made up of nested system resources, contained resources and other resource factors. Others, like Lado et al. (1992), Brumagim (1994), and Yeoh and Roth (1999), suggest that we regard resources in a hierarchical sense. Lado et al distinguish between, on the one hand, managerial competence and strategic focus, and on the other, resource-based, transformation-based and output-based competencies. The managerial competence and the strategic focus refer to the ability of top managers to acquire and mobilize the resources needed to match the environment of the firm, as perceived and envisioned by top management.

The discourse on resources has also drawn on the *competence* concept, which appears to equate the meanings of the concepts of resources, skills, assets and strengths with one another (Prahalad & Hamel, 1990; Bogaert et al, 1994; Hamel, 1994; Hamel & Prahalad, 1995; Sanchez et al, 1996; Chiesa & Manzini, 1997; Durand, 1997). Even though many would argue that competence means different things when compared to resource, it is used here as an equivalent, or as one specific type of resource. Based on Selznick (1957), Prahalad and Hamel (1990) introduced the concept of *core competence* as the foundation of firm strengths, and described it as technological: Core competencies are the broader technological abilities that apply to different products. The concepts of competence and competence-based management have become widely institutionalized. Some examples of literature on competence and its strategic impact are anthologies such as Moingeon and Edmondson (1996), Sanchez and Heene (1997) and Sanchez (2001b). As it appears, the somewhat colonialist expansion of RBV lingo might be confusing. Some have emphasized this, like Barney (1991), whose definition of a resource covers all areas of strengths:

> All assets, capabilities, organizational processes, firm attributes, information, knowledge etc. [...] that enable the firm to conceive of and implement strategies that improve its efficiency and effectiveness. (Barney, 1991: 101)

Barney has also argued that differences between resources and other concepts such as competencies and skills are not likely to stand up to application. Similarly, Mahoney and Pandian (1992) commented on various classifications of resources and stated that the "subdivision of resources may proceed as far as is useful for the problem at hand", but that a suitable primary classification may be land and equipment, labour and capital.

Along what can be referred to as the "capability track", there is partial confusion as well. Among those who do not equate capabilities directly with resources or the effects of resources (cf. Grant, 1991; Collis, 1994; Nanda, 1996), most writers refer to capability as the capacity to manage, develop, and use resources (Teece et al, 1997; Eisenhardt & Martin, 2000). The distinction between resources, on the one hand, and the capability to manage these resources, on the other, is probably important. Both Barney (1994a) and Prahalad and Hamel (1990) raise the question of the 'organization of resources'. These kinds of suggestions have been emphasized in a number of articles focusing on the *managerial* and *organizational capabilities* of managing resources. Included concepts are, according to Henderson and Cockburn (1994), "integrative capabilities" (Lawrence & Lorsch, 1967), "dynamic capabilities" (Teece et al, 1997), "organizational architecture" (Nelson, 1991), "combinative capabilities" (Kogut & Zander, 1992), "managerial systems", "values and norms" (Leonard-Barton, 1992) and "invisible assets" (Itami, 1987).

Teece et al (1997) discuss the *dynamic capabilities* of firms as regards integrating and reconfiguring internal and external resources and activities in order to match the environment. They suggest that strategy is about processes, paths and position, and that dynamic capabilities refer to management's ability to manage these issues. These capabilities allow the firm to create new products and processes and respond to changing markets. In a previous working paper (Teece et al, 1990), it was proposed that capabilities constitute the abilities of firms to create and utilize resources so as to improve their performance. Capabilities, in turn, are based on learning, accumulated experience, technological opportunities and the nature of the environment of the firm. Leonard-Barton (1992) also claims that *core capabilities* are something "larger" than resources, skills or competencies, and that they consist of particular skills, technical systems, managerial systems, all of which are grounded in the norms and values that the firm has built up during its existence. In their definition of dynamic capabilities, Eisenhardt and Martin

(2000) connect with Teece et al. (1997) claiming that dynamic capabilities consist of "specific strategic and organizational processes like product development, alliancing, and strategic decision making that create value for firms within dynamic markets by manipulating resources into new value-creating strategies". However, dynamic capabilities assume different forms depending on the nature of the market. When markets are stable, or 'moderately dynamic', dynamic capabilities assume the form of regular routines. They become complex, linear, analytic processes relying on existing knowledge bases. In more dynamic markets, so-called "high-velocity markets", dynamic capabilities are different in character. They then become simple, unstable processes relying on the swift development of new knowledge and iterative deployment to generate adaptive outcomes. In short, the more complex the environment - the simpler the nature of the capability. In both instances, dynamic capability refers to the ability to develop and use resources in a way that will improve the strategic position.

The distinction between resources and the ability to manage them seems fruitful. Capabilities are broader concepts and include managerial and organizational solutions to problems or challenges needing to be solved in order to utilize the full potential of a resource. However, viewing resource management as a capability – a "content", not a practice or act – initiates an infinite search for the origins of competitive strength (Collis, 1994; Spender, 1996). If resource management is seen as a cross-sectional entity that is either good or bad for the firm, the next step in the search for the origins of competitive strength is bound to be finding the "management of the resource management capability" in question; or the resource behind the resource behind the resource... and so forth. We will have to backtrack to the dawn of civilization. Being able to manage resources (a capability) is a resource in itself (Barney, 1991). Thus, one could argue that the growing interest in capabilities is a result of a desire to explain the roots of resources that in turn constitute the roots of competitiveness. However, it could be a problem, we maintain, if the managerial and organizational, evolutionary processes of building and using resources are converted into an entity *per se*.

The RBV has been criticized for many things, including neglecting the product market and demand side of resources (Priem & Butler, 2001), tautology ("successful firms have valuable and inimitable resources"), for not being applicable to empirical study (Williamson, 1999), for being static and unable to explain shifts in industry (D'Aveni, 1994, Eisenhardt & Martin, 2000) — and for neglecting the dynamics of resources and the processes by which they are managed (Collis, 1996; Foss, 1997).

Hence, we have connected to the discussion that started this chapter: strategy theory, or at least research within strategy theory, can be structured in terms of whether one has a content-oriented or process-oriented view of things. If we want to understand where resources and competitive advantages come from, there is a risk of constantly referring to a second-order resource entity. It is probably important to halt the content-biased process of inquiry in order to see and study the longitudinal, random or managed resource evolution: what role do managers and decision-makers have; how do we secure leverage of strategic resources; what are the impacts of bounded rationality, or norms and values, on the management of resources; what role does luck play; and so on. Below, we discuss the so-called strategy process perspective, which deals explicitly with the dynamics and evolution of strategic content like resources, capabilities, value-chains, cost leadership and so forth.

Process Perspectives

Whereas much strategy theory has been content-oriented, like I/O and straightforward economics-oriented RBV, for a long time there has been a parallel track of research focusing on the dynamics of strategy processes, the managerial challenges in decision making situations, the impact of bounded rationality and institutional forces such as norms and values, the politics of organizational change, the uncertainty, complexity and risk of strategic choice, the psychological factors in play in such situations, and other constraints on strategic management. Furthermore, in a process perspective, the longitudinal dimension is important: how do cross-sectional strategy contents evolve over time, what are the causalities and what is the role of incidence?

On Impetus and the Political Character of the Strategy Process

There are several important texts dealing with strategy process issues. Donaldson's (1969) work within the area of finance, an area typically occupied with developing analytical tools (such as, for instance, the capital asset pricing model, CAPM, or the Black & Scholes options evaluation model), was based on the overarching problem of acquiring financial resources. The firm and the financial director were treated as part of larger system, where decision processes, actions and management had to progress in the face of cognitive and political obstacles. One of the conclusions was that firms need financial mobility in order to survive in the long-term, and this requires the ability to act swiftly when problems arise, to be able to interpret the problems and motivate staff and managers.

Similarly, in his study of resource allocation processes in conjunction with capital investments, Bower (1970) found that such processes include different phases or sub-processes. The first phase is the *definition process*, in which a discrepancy between objectives and the available capacity is observed. The definition process often takes place on lower levels of the organizational hierarchy, closer to day-to-day operations. The next phase involves *impetus*, which is aimed at securing attention and commitment from those in charge of allocating resources to solve the discrepancy. The impetus phase is highly political because it forces debate between antagonists and decision-makers, and it forces people to clarify their views on suggested changes and the investments required. Both the definition process and the impetus process are bottom-up processes. People on lower levels define the need for change and try to persuade their superiors to pursue the question further up the hierarchy. A third process, however, has more of a top-down character: the *manipulation of the structural context*. This is essentially a task for the corporate level. Manipulating the structural context means designing a political and administrative structure that provides corporate management with influence over the proposals made by staff. By shaping the structure, top management indirectly shapes the strategy of the firm.

Burgelman (1983, 1988) continued the work of Bower and addressed the hierarchical dimension of the strategy process. He wanted to show that much of the decision-making process is actually a bottom-up process. He also stressed that strategy often follows structure in the sense that political and administrative mechanisms, embodied in rules and structures, shape the way problems are identified, presented and solved within organizations. Burgelman (1988) puts the emphasis on the interplay between cognition and action in strategy-making. Here, he claims that learning through action, such as through ordinary work or experimentation, influences cognitive development in a reciprocal fashion, eventually leading to the creation of knowledge and political consensus supporting new courses of action. When such a "cognition-action" spiral is successful, the project is institutionalized and constitutes a strategic change. Again, Burgelman stresses the bottom-up character of the process. The cognition-action spiral is initiated on lower hierarchical levels in operations, and as action and learning continue, the results become known to middle management and subsequently to corporate management. The influence that corporate management has on this process is based on the formal power to allocate commitment and funds once it has been informed about the ideas, but also on the cognition-action process as such, through the way top management structures and deals with entrepreneurial activities within the organization. But strategic management is not solely a cognitive issue. For top management, it also has a strong political component: It is important that local entrepreneurs stimulate innovation. In order to stimulate it in a particular direction, managers have to make sure that the organizational entrepreneurs favour certain directions of capability development (Burgelman, 1988).

Strategy Process Theories

Apart from the earlier works on strategy processes by Donaldson, Bower and Burgelman, Quinn (1978) and Mintzberg (1978; 1994) were among the first to make theoretical declarations about the need for a process orientation. Mintzberg (1978) claimed that the strategy definitions provided by Chandler and others during the 1960s over-simplify true strategy work, which is far more complex than writing down plans. Strategy is not a grand plan, nor is it an idea about what the company is. Strategy, according to Mintzberg, is what firms actually do. Strategy can be seen as a problem-solving process, by which firms deal with specific problems as they occur. The realized, emergent strategy is a mix of planned and unplanned actions. The main divergence here is between formulation and implementation (cf. Andrews, 1971).

Unlike the RBV or the I/O, there have not been any formal declarations, central articles or books starting off the field. Instead, what we refer to as the strategy process perspective includes a range of different texts focusing on the problems and complexities that strategists encounter. Chakravarthy and Doz (1992: 5) describe the process field thus:

> Strategy process research addresses a number of fundamental questions that are of interest to general managers. The subfield is at the heart of all research in strategic management. It focuses on how a general manager can continuously influence the quality of the firm's strategic position through the use of appropriate decision processes and administrative systems. By the term administrative systems we mean the organizational structure, planning, control, incentives, human resource management, and value systems of a firm. The strategy process research subfield is concerned with how effective strategies are shaped within the firm and then validated and implemented efficiently.

Chakravarthy and Doz (1992) claim that, although process and content strategy research are both concerned with performance, process research focuses on how firms reach the positions that they hold. Hence, process research is concerned with the factors and variables behind the positions, rather than how the positions affect performance. The independent variables of content research become the dependent variables of process research. The independent variables of process research are found in fields related to management and organization. Two assumptions make strategy process research unique, according to Chakravarthy and Doz, and these are the acceptance of 'bounded rationality' and the pluralist view of the organizational unit and its participants and interactions.

Process-oriented research has evolved with a sophisticated focus on the managerial and decision-making function. For instance, the process-based school has prospered from the research field of the cognitive and socio-cognitive processes of managers, including the work of Weick (1979), Prahalad and Bettis (1986, 1994), Johnson (1987), Huff et al, (1992) and Ginsberg (1994). The 'cognitive map' of a decision maker and the 'dominant logic' of a firm are claimed to have an impact on the way firms behave, or on how they can be predicted to behave. Also, maps and dominant logics are regarded as constraints on changes that are too revolutionary in organizations, thus limiting the strategic scope of firms unable to challenge them. In an extension of the cognition-based view of management processes, interest in complexity theory and chaos theory has increased among strategists, particularly during the 1990s. Stacey (1993), von Krogh and Roos (1995) and Brown and Eisenhardt (1998) are examples of such texts.

Strategy Process and the RBV

Although much of the early RBV can be treated as content-based research, a lot has happened during recent years, which has directed the RBV into a more process-based domain. We are not going to dive into it in great detail, because we are now approaching the core of the theoretical focus of this book: the management of knowledge. And this will be dealt with in the subsequent chapter. But a lot of the process-oriented RBV centres on the management of knowledge. A core assumption, as previously stated, is that knowledge is the "ultimate" strategic resource. This is a potentially tautological assumption, but this has not stopped RBV theorists from studying its dynamics and the processes by which firms manage knowledge in various forms in order to gain competitive advantage. That is what distinguishes the RBV of knowledge management from mainstream knowledge management or organizational learning. In fact, RBV researchers have even tried to stipulate knowledge-based theories of the firm.

Spender (1996) claims that a knowledge-based theory of the firm pictures the firm as a "dynamic, evolving, quasi-autonomous system of knowledge production and application" (p. 59). Spender goes on to claim that knowledge is not an 'asset' in the positivist sense, but "a qualitative aspect" of the activity system. Four heuristics help to define the firm as a knowledge-based activity system: interpretive flexibility is required in order to evolve and activate the system. Boundary management is necessary in order to be able to ex-

pand or contract the activity system as knowledge evolves. Institutional influences, such as those external to the organization, need to be understood in relation to knowledge management. The distinction between systemic and com-
ponential characteristics needs to be understood as well, including both the
meaning and the mechanisms of knowledge processes. When managing these
heuristics, managers have the platform for creative strategic leadership. In the
same (special) issue where Spender published his knowledge-based theory of
the firm, Grant (1996) characterizes the firm as an institution for integrating
knowledge. Grant claims, contrary to other theories of knowledge, that the
primary role of the organization is to apply rather than explore knowledge.
The main organizational issue, according to a knowledge-based view and
when given the role of knowledge, is to balance the trade off between specialized and generalized knowledge, and the role of common language. Firms
need to be endowed with broad ranges of heterogeneous yet specialized
knowledge. Creating such heterogeneity results in communication difficulties:
specialized knowledge requires specialized language, so managers have to
choose between excessive coordination costs (an effect of heterogeneous, specialized knowledge), and the costs of being inflexible – and less competent (an
effect of commonality). In Grant's view, the benefits are greater with heterogeneous, specialized knowledge. Others have also launched knowledge or
competence-based views, or theory declarations, of the firm. Sanchez and
Heene (1997) claim that competence management is a matter of both process
and content, and that the two are not readily separable. In managing competencies, firms build and leverage competencies – this is the main strategic issue, and it requires the subtle understanding of a number of different issues in
association with competencies.

> Competence building occurs when firms acquire and use new and qualitatively
> different assets, capabilities and modes of coordination. [...] [Leveraging com-
> petences means] coordinated deployment of resources in ways that do not re-
> quire qualitative changes in the assets, capabilities, or modes of coordination
> used by the firm. (Sanchez & Heene, 1997: 8)

In an attempt to outline the resource and its causal function and attributes,
Sanchez & Heene (1997) suggest an overall model of the firm as an open system, wherein strategic logics and management processes create intangible and
tangible assets, in turn creating operations/activities that build up product offerings potentially rendering the firm competitive advantage.

Apart from the more declarative knowledge-based approaches to strategy,
there is a range of work claiming to belong to either a resource- or a knowledge-based view that explicitly deals with the strategic role of knowledge

from a process perspective. Here, we are going to discuss a couple of the ones we find particularly important. Amit and Schoemaker's (1993, 1994) work on the decision-processes underlying the decision to invest in resources, and the mechanics by which firms can make resource decisions that are unique in comparison to their competitors, is one such important contribution. They claim that the complexity managers face as regards the causes shaping the environment forces them to simplify their decision process. Cognitive limitations and biases towards past experience and known solutions will create homogeneity across companies. However, this increases the opportunities for others to gain competitive advantage based on the complacency and convergence of less bold and radical competitors (Amit & Schoemaker, 1993). The strategic management challenge is then how to direct the decision making process and to obtain knowledge of the relationships between resources and success, without being hampered by false assumptions and obsolete or biased wisdom. According to Schoemaker and Amit (1994), the cognitive challenge for managers includes estimating the subset of resources that is most important in view of the competition, assessing how the existing resource stock can be changed over a given period of time, and communicating the desired changes to others within the organization. Cognitive limitations and biases distract the decisions "away" from rationality. Moreover, the decision context is often multivariate, something with which human cognition has a problem (Schoemaker & Amit, 1994). Non-linearity is hard for humans to detect. As an example, diminishing or increasing marginal returns may thus be hard to detect, creating over- or under-investment in resources. Another type of bias relates to *interaction effects*, suggesting that complementarities and synergies are often ignored by humans. For instance, the negative or positive effects of integrating resources may be overlooked. A third potential bias is that the attention paid to equally relevant variables may be asymmetric and subjectively weighted due to emphases on fewer variables. This narrowness creates simplification, and decision processes may exclude relevant resources. According to Schoemaker and Amit, there are two basic ways in which people assess causal relationships; *correlational reasoning* and *causal reasoning*. Correlational reasoning means relying on perceptions of co-variation or partial correlation between resources and future rents (or any other dependent variable, in strategy often being connected with performance). This kind of reasoning is inductive. Causal reasoning is based on theory and is fundamentally deductive. Data-driven correlational reasoning, however, may be difficult since humans tend to disregard smaller correlations if they have no guiding, pre-existing theory or well-designed statistical analysis at hand. This means that the effects of a resource may be largely underestimated. On the other hand, when an *a priori* theory about a relationship between resource and a future rent (i.e. causal reasoning) exists, people tend to overestimate the correlation. These *a priori* theories are strong in the sense that they are acted upon even if evidence to the contrary is presented. Schoemaker and Amit (1994) conclude that when managers tend to base their resource decisions on past data, they will have difficulties in identifying the weaker correlations between resource and rent, thus underevaluating a valuable resource. If they base their decision on business theory, for instance, they will probably overestimate the resource. So, the contribution of Amit and Schoemaker (1994) lies in the focus on the cognitive factors that drive or hamper decisions regarding resources that can turn out to be unique in competition. It is partly a process that relies on luck and informative feedback from the market, and it is partly a process that is dependent upon knowledge, existing knowledge as well the acquisition and creation of new, and courage: being courageous enough to experiment and tread paths that others will not is often a prerequisite for competitive advantage.

Along similar lines, Oliver (1997) stresses the fact that the RBV in general has paid little attention to the institutional context (rules, norms and beliefs surrounding economic activity that define and/or enforce socially acceptable economic behaviour) of decision-making. She also claims that the RBV has not addressed "the process of resource selection, that is, how firms actually make, and fail to make, rational resource choices in pursuit of economic rents" (p 698). In a suggestion to extend the RBV to include the social obstacles, she proposes the insights provided by neo-institutional theory (cf. Meyer & Rowan, 1977; DiMaggio & Powell, 1983; Scott, 1995). Firms function in a social context of norms, values and beliefs that constrains or biases decisions. The way firms comply with norms and values may serve as a barrier to economically rational behaviour. In fact, as some suggest, firms conforming to norms and values may be regarded as successful, even though the action does not increase the profitability, which is the economic view of successful behaviour. So, while institutional theory suggests that firms are successful when they conform to predominant norms and values, the RBV suggests that firms are successful when they *break with* common views and create heterogeneity and success in terms of idiosyncratic and valuable resources (Oliver, 1997). Decisions about resource selection will be influenced by the institutional context, on the individual, firm and industry levels. On the individual level, the RBV and institutional perspectives differ in terms of their view of the nature of the decision process, the decision constraints, the resource allocation process, the decision objective, the nature of sunk costs, the resource attributes and the decision outcomes. For instance, whereas the key attributes of resources in the RBV are efficiency and inimitability, in institutional theory they are longevity and legitimacy. Moreover, as Oliver (1997) points out, when the normative bias is too strong, decisions will be economically irrational. For firms managing the normative bias better, the opportunities will arise to make more economically efficient resource decisions. The institutional factors are also in play on the firm-level, in this respect as isolating mechanisms hindering the acquisition of resources that do not have the cultural or political support of the organization. In the institutional view, isolating mechanisms are "barriers to imitation which result from a firm's reluctance to imitate or acquire resources that are incompatible with the firm's cultural or political context" (Oliver, 1997: 704). On the third level, isomorphic pressures serve to sustain industry homogeneity. These pressures include regulatory pressure, by which governments restrict possible resource behaviour, thus making it difficult to create heterogeneity. In conclusion, Oliver suggests that we view sustainable competitive advantage as consisting of both resource capital and institutional capital. In using institutional capital, Oliver refers to "the firm's capability to support the value-enhancing assets and competences". Oliver thus focuses on the management of the institutional context of resource decisions. In that sense, Oliver extends the cognitive view of strategic resources that Amit and Schoemaker introduced, to also include the potentially non-rational influence of norms and values on the individual, firm and industry levels. It is not only cognitive obstacles which limit the decision processes which foster unique resources: being able to challenge conventional wisdom and attached norms and values is often necessary in order to create competitive advantage.

The above RBV references are examples of a process orientation, evident in their ambition to describe the hardships by which organizations attempt to move their knowledge-base further towards being a source of uniqueness and competitive advantage. They all imply the acceptance of limited rationality, the impact of norms and values, and politics. They are also evidence of the pluralistic nature of the subject, including theory on psychology, cognition, economics, sociology and even law. There are numerous other similar RBV attempts, including a range of anthologies (e.g. Edmondson & Moingeon, 1996; Sanchez & Heene, 1997; Sanchez, 2001b), wherein both empirical and conceptual texts aim to describe the processes firms go through when aiming to amass knowledge that is both valuable and unique.

We comply with the process-oriented, resource-based view of knowledge sharing, and see it as an organizational practice that can be a source of competitive advantage and performance improvements, thus positioning this book in that field. In the next chapter, we will specifically go into more detail about knowledge management and knowledge sharing, including that which does not directly represent a resource-based approach.

Chapter 3:

Sharing Knowledge: Writing and Communication

Introduction

In this chapter, the notion of knowledge management will be examined. Scarborough and Swan (2001) write: "Knowledge Management is not easy to define and many definitions supplied in the literature are highly ambiguous. The ambiguity of the concept, however, is itself a clue to the fashion-setting possibilities of this discourse; ambiguity makes KM amenable to multiple interpretations and remouldings which potentially extend its relevance across different communities of practice" (Scarborough & Swan, 2001: 3). Knowledge management is thus a broad and ambiguous concept and has emerged as a rather new perspective on organizations (Spender & Grant, 1996). Some strategic management theorists even talk about a knowledge-based view of the firm as a distinct theory of the firm similar to that of the resource-based view of the firm. While most other "theories of the firm" integrate various tangible and intangible resources, the knowledge-based view of the firm and knowledge management theories operate with a set of resources that are to be regarded as what Itami (1987) calls *invisible assets*, assets whose elementary forms are not materialized into documents and artefacts but primarily distributed in organizational routines, practices of communication, and individuals' skills and know-how. Such assets are more complicated to manage because they do not only escape any determinate system of reference, such as accounting practices, but are also complicated to pin down in clear categories. Invisible assets such as knowledge tend to transgress the boundary between what is a useful resource and what is not; for instance, knowledge of the organization not only includes useful and strategic information about markets, competitors and products, but equally includes old justified beliefs, outmoded ideas, and other forms of "knowledge" that are no longer regarded as useful. The entire pool of knowledge that an organization can make use of (we are talking in metaphorical terms here) thus consists of both highly valuable knowledge and non-valuable knowledge. Being able to manage what is known in organizations is thus a most challenging endeavour (Soo, Devinney, Midgley and Deering, 2002).

In this chapter, the concepts of knowledge and knowledge management will be examined and discussed in detail. The most important concept of this discussion is, however, the concept of *knowledge sharing*, i.e. the idea that knowledge, no matter how intangible or fuzzy, is capable of being disseminated, transferred, diffused, shared, and distributed within and between organizations, communities of practices and departments. Knowledge sharing is perhaps the single most important knowledge management practice because it embodies all the opportunities and challenges associated with managing intangible invisible assets. While it is possible to view organizations as repositories of knowledge from an analytical perspective, it is more complicated to take an active part in sharing knowledge within firms as an active managerial operation. As the cases presented in Chapters four and five of the book will show, it is possible for management to take such an active role in order to share knowledge and learning across organizations.

The Concept of Knowledge

Knowledge, Data, Information

To start off the discussion, we may, for the sake of simplicity, make use of a formal definition of knowledge offered in knowledge management and its related literature. Liebeskind (1996: 94) defines knowledge as "information whose validity has been established through test of proof" (Liebeskind, 1996: 94). Another much-cited definition of the concept of knowledge is provided by Daniel Bell (1973). For Bell, knowledge is "[a] set of organized statements of facts or ideas, presenting a reasoned judgement or an experimental result, which is transmitted to others through some communication medium in some systematic form" (Bell, 1973: 175, original in italics). Both Liebeskind's and Bells' definitions are complex; they invoke notions such as "information", validity", "tests", "proofs", "facts", "ideas", "judgement", "experimental results", "communication", and so forth. Rather than offering pure operational definitions; Liebeskind and Bell instead point to the various practices that are commonly associated with the notion of knowledge. Knowledge cannot be defined on the basis of ostensive definitions ("there is knowledge, look at it!") because it is not a "simply located" and clearly bounded entity. Instead, the notion of knowledge is employed to denote either the input or the output of complex intellectual, perceptual, emotional, and political practices. For instance, Liebeskind's definition suggests that knowledge is what integrates information, validation processes, and the notion of proof. Here, knowledge is what emerges when I have access to some information whose validity I test through an experimental activity. Thus, knowledge is, here, an emergent property that is an outcome of rather complicated processes. One of the elementary forms of knowledge is *information*. Information is in turn often suggested to be based on *data*. Sanchez (2001a) writes:

> Data are representations of the events that people notice and bring to the attention of other people in the organization. Data consists of qualitative and quantitative descriptions of events. As descriptions, data are always incomplete representations—some aspects of an event are noticed and recorded in some way, while other aspects either are not noticed or are not included in the representation of the event. How the event becomes represented in data depends on what aspects of an event an observer notices and thinks will have significance, personally or for the organization. Just as it has been noticed that 'all facts are theory laden', all data are selective representations of events, implicit in which are some presumptions about which events and which aspects of these events are likely to have significance in some context of interest. Thus the data entering an organization are greatly influenced by the interpretative frameworks ... that determine which events are noticed and how those events are represented by the organization. (Sanchez, 2001a: 5)

Even the most elementary form of knowledge, data, seems to be complicated to define in ostensive terms. If data is defined as what people tend to observe, then the concept of knowledge is founded on human ignorance of details. An alternative definition of data is offered by Hacking (1992). Hacking is speaking from the perspective of the laboratory sciences and does not rely on what people pay attention to, rather the uninterpreted material provided by laboratory experiments: "By data I mean uninterpreted inscriptions, graphs recording variation over time, photographs, tables, displays" (Hacking, 1992: 48). In this definition, data is what is yet to be examined (for Hacking, this comprises the three steps of *data assessment, data reduction*, and *data analysis*) rather than what is extracted from an external empirical reality, as in Sanchez's (2001a) view.

Data is generally regarded as the basis of information. Information is often treated as data accumulated and processed. Thus, the same kind of problem applies to information as to data and knowledge: It is always, to some extent, incomplete, situational, context-dependent, and emergent. Munro (2001: 202) writes: "The image of information is exactly one of neutrality:

impersonal, factual, technocratic, boring". Information is often regarded as provided from a God's-eye view, a view from nowhere that enables objective evaluation. But, as we have suggested, data, information, and knowledge are always concepts filled with absences and tension. There are simply no lexical definitions of data, information and knowledge that match the practical work being done on such concepts. Therefore, to claim to have data regarding an event, to be informed about a matter and to be knowledgeable about a certain topic, always implies that there is data missing, the lack of some information, and particular areas that are ignored, overlooked or simply not focused on. Boisot (1998) writes:

> Knowledge builds on information that is extracted from data. In practice the three terms are often confused. Data is discrimination between physical states—black, white, heavy, light, etc.—that may or may not convey information to an agent. Whether it does so or not depends on an agent's prior stock of knowledge ... whereas data can be characterized as a property of things, knowledge is a property of agents predisposing them to act in particular circumstances. Information is that subset of the data residing in things that activates an agent—it is filtered from the data by the agent's perceptual or conceptual apparatus... Information, in effect, establishes a relationship between things and agents. Knowledge can be conceptualized as a set of probability distributions held by an agent and orienting his or her actions. (Boisot, 1998: 12)

Operating on the basis of intangible intellectual resources, e.g. data, information and knowledge, is dealing with these inconsistencies and the fuzziness of such resources.

Knowledge is Situational

Another property of the concept of knowledge is its being what Donna Haraway (1991) calls *situational*, i.e. it is always qualified as knowledge from a particular point of view. Knowledge is situational because it is inherently social in nature; knowledge serves to establish relations in society and therefore it is never value-neutral, but always already emergent from specific social interests and concerns (see for instance Sole & Edmondson, 2002; Lam, 1997). The positivist doctrine regarding knowledge — and more specifically scientific knowledge — as produced *sine ira et studio* is forcefully rejected by analysts of technoscience such as Haraway (1991). Gherardi and Nicolini (2001) write:

> Every attempt to label something as 'knowledge' is made by a specific social community belonging to a network of power relations, and not by a world consisting purely of ideas. Hence, no knowledge is universal or supreme; instead, all knowledge is produced within social, historical, and linguistic relations grounded in specific forms of conflict and the division of labor. (Gherardi & Nicolini, 2001: 44)

As a consequence, there is no knowledge *per se*. There may be certain *facta bruta*, but most things constituting operational knowledge in organizations are more or less contested, more or less commonly agreed upon, more or less subject to negotiation. Since we here conceive of knowledge as firstly being based on inconsistent and fragmented data and information, and secondly as being inherently social in nature, knowledge management practices may take a most pragmatic approach to the use of knowledge in organizations. We can thus adhere to the *pragmatic instrumentalism* suggested by Dewey (1929) in terms of making use of knowledge without being too concerned about whether or not such knowledge is really, really true as long as its works in practice. Thus, it is important to distinguish the truth-claims of academic knowledge management theorists, aiming to establish the knowledge-based view of the firm as a legitimate analytical perspective within management studies, from the practicing knowledge manager who wants to make effective use of organizational resources. But, in order to become a good practicing knowledge manager, one needs to point to the fundament for a pragmatic in-strumentalism, i.e. the inconsistencies in the concept of knowledge. Thus, theory and practice are mutually dependent and inform one another, but since they seek different outcomes, they need to be separated, to some extent.

Organizations as Repositories of Knowledge

One of the axial principles of knowledge management theory is that organi-zations are social formations which control significant amounts of knowledge as well as possess the capability to develop, share, and transform that know-ledge into either competitive advantage or new forms of knowledge (Stewart, 1997). In brief, the organization is founded on knowledge, but also equally serves as an arena wherein knowledge is developed and used. Hedberg and Holmqvist (2001) write:

> All organizations are repositories of knowledge, but some organizations are more knowledge-intensive and knowledge-dependent than others. Knowledge is lodged in the brains of organization members as well as in explicit rules,

that is, artificial memories, which include files, records, and other documents ... Knowledge is also stored in organizational routines, that is, repetitive modes of acting, and standard operating procedures. (Hedberg & Holmqvist, 2001: 737)

In Hedberg and Holmqvist's account, knowledge pervades all spheres of the organization; it is located in the minds of the co-workers, embodied in organizational routines, stored in databases and other technical devices designed for codified knowledge. Hedberg and Holmqvist's (2001) image of the organization as a social formation saturated with knowledge captures the two dominant views of the knowledge-based view of the firm. On the one hand, knowledge is seen as socially embedded, expressed in practices of communication and through storytelling, in brief as highly dependent on what is commonly referred to as human capital, i.e. human beings. On the other hand, knowledge is regarded as an organizational resource that is primarily to be captured and distributed through various technological systems such as computer databases and intranets. One tradition is affirmative towards various social perspectives on knowledge, while the other emphasizes the technological applications within knowledge management. To say the least, the technological orientation of the field has dominated the normative literature. More social perspectives on knowledge management are, however, dominating the field of organizational studies. For instance, Tsoukas and Vladimirou (2001) write: "Knowledge management then is primarily the dynamic process of turning an unreflected practice into a reflective one by elucidating the rules guiding the activities of the practice, by helping give a particular shape to collective understandings, and by facilitating the emergence of heuristic knowledge" (Tsoukas & Vladimirou, 2001: 990). They continue: "Managing organizational knowledge does not narrowly imply efficiently managing hard bits of information but, more subtly, sustaining and strengthening social practices ... In knowledge management digitalisation cannot be substituted for socialization" (Tsoukas & Vladimirou, 2001: 991). In the same vein, Orlikowski argues: "[k]nowledge is an ongoing social accomplishment, constituted and reconstituted in everyday practice. As such, knowing cannot be understood as stable or enduring. Because it is enacted in the moment, its existence is virtual, its status provisional" (Orlikowski, 2002: 252–253). In both these quotes, knowledge is conceived of as a frail social convention, an outcome of subtle interactions wherein small nuances tend to make a difference. Knowledge is thus always contested and subject to discussions and controversy. For Leonard-Barton, one could also add that knowledge is a resource that evolves slowly:

> Knowledge accumulates slowly, over time, shaped and channeled into certain directions through nudging of hundreds of daily managerial decisions. Nor does knowledge occur only one time; it is constantly aborning... knowledge reservoirs in organizations are not static pools but well-springs, constantly re-plenished with streams of new ideas and constituting an ever-flowing source of corporate renewal (Leonard-Barton, 1995: 3)

Here, knowledge is an outcome of various managerial decisions and under-takings. Knowledge is again an emergent property that is produced through interactions in the face of new opportunities and challenges. But Leonard-Barton also suggests, which is contrary to the general attitude among the pro-tagonists of knowledge management who tend to affirm knowledge as a solely positive resource, that knowledge can always serve as a core rigidity within firms. For instance, an automotive company praising itself and taking great pride in its technical expertise may have a problem overcoming its core rigidities constituted by these experts, in time, where customers value and search for other qualities, e.g. design or safety. Leonard-Barton thus suggests that even though knowledge is an important significant resource in organiza-tions, it may also become an impediment to change. Haradon and Fanelli (2002) write: "Deviations from expected action represent threatening shifts in previously established scripts, goals, or identities that will elicit responses, likely negative, from other participants in the ongoing process. The result is the apparent constraint that latent knowledge has on the generation of novel action" (Haradon & Fanelli, 2002: 298). In practical work, knowledge is em-bodied in particular behaviours and "scripts, goals and identities". When such behaviours are poorly aligned with organizational objectives, i.e. the un-derlying knowledge is less valued in terms of achieving such objectives, cogni-tive dissonance may occur. That is, some individuals do not perceive the same things as their co-workers because they are biased by their identity and their previous experiences. For instance, in a company, certain groups of experts may not understand, nor are they willing to work in accordance with, new company strategies because their knowledge base is less valued in the new strategic regime.

Organizations may thus be regarded as repositories of knowledge but such statements should not be conceived of as solely one-dimensionally posi-tive statements. Knowledge may be both enabling and dysfunctional. The practices of knowledge management are aimed at dealing with such chal-lenges and opportunities.

Codified Knowledge: Practices of Writing

There are two dominant ways of conceiving of knowledge. On the one hand, it is regarded as accumulated data and information, which implies that knowledge is more or less the sum of the data and information embodied in the knowledge. In such cases, knowledge is often conceived of as an organizational resource that is possible to break down into its smallest components and to codify. Such operations on the organizational knowledge-base pave the way for various applications of technological systems. In this perspective, the notion of writing is of key interest. On the other hand, knowledge is conceived of as a social practice, arrangement or—in Orlikowski's (2002) formulation—an "accomplishment". Here, knowledge is what is produced through interactions in communities of practice and work teams, in communication and discussions, at social events such as seminars and courses. In this perspective, knowledge is an outcome of communicative practices rather than something based on codification and de-codification.

Knowledge as Writing

Perhaps the single most important human innovation is the practice of writing (Ong, 1982). Anthropologist Claude Lévi-Strauss (1992) would like to draw a line between writing and non-writing people as a decisive demarcation between civilization and its previous societies. Lévi-Strauss (1992) writes:

> There are people with, or without writing; the former able to store up their past achievements and to move with ever-increasing rapidity towards the goals they have set for themselves, whereas the latter, being capable of remembering the past beyond the narrow margin of individual memory, seem bound to remain imprisoned in a fluctuating history which will always lack both a beginning and any lasting awareness of an aim (Lévi-Strauss, 1992: 298)

Writing enables historical memory; the writing human being can easily transcend the individual or collective human mind. Even though it is frequently pointed out that non-writing people have advanced mnemotechniques (Grosz, 1995: 133) at their disposal, Lévi-Strauss still thinks that writing practices entail tremendous implications for a society. Marshall McLuhan (1962) especially emphasizes the printed word as an important social innovation because it enables the segmentation, codification, and transmission of messages across time and space:

At any rate, with the Gutenberg technology, we move into the age of the machine. The principle of segmentation of actions and functions and roles became systematically applicable wherever desired ... The Gutenberg technology extended this principle to writing and language and the codification and transmission of every kind of learning. (McLuhan, 1962: 155)

Taken together, the emergence of writing and the reproduction of written texts in particular constitute a significant event in history. Michel Callon (2002) has examined the practices of writing and codification in organizations as an approach to dealing with complexities. Callon (2002: 191) writes: "Without tools for collecting, constructing, processing, and calculating information, agents would be unable to plan, decide or control. In brief, organized action would be impossible". Writing practices have certain merits in terms of being capable of dealing with complexities without eliminating such complexities (Callon, 2002: 193). Callon concludes: "[W]riting devices lie at the heart of the organization in action and ... without them the organization would not exist, as it does, in a location between knowing and doing" (Callon, 2002: 212). On the one hand, organizations are capable — this anthropomorphism is applied here in a metaphorical sense — of knowing things; on the other hand, they do things. Knowing and doing need to be aligned in one way or another. Such mechanisms are standard organizational operating procedures (Cyert & March, 1963), routines (Nelson & Winter, 1982), and scripts and handbooks (for instance, McDonald's "Bible" prescribing in detail the preferred order of things). Although routines may appear to be a most bureaucratic concept suitable for environments characterized by stability, studies suggests that routines are, in fact, highly dynamic scripts that can be applied to various situations (Feldman & Amit, 2002; Feldman, 2000; Pentland & Rueter, 1994). Nevertheless, writing practices are, at least in Callon's (2002) account, even more capable of dealing with "complexities" than routines and standard operating procedures. Kallinikos (1996a) writes: "[B]ureaucracy is inextricably bound up with writing and the codifying forms and techniques whereby predictable and recurrent sequences of acts are conceived and instrumented" (Kallinikos, 1996a: 13). Here, we need to acknowledge Kallinikos' (1996b) distinction between what he calls *speech-forms of writing*, "writing that represents a written transformation of speech", and *alphanumerical techniques*, "i.e., words and numbers, for recording information and which do not necessarily exhibit serial and verbal character of language and speech" (Kallinikos, 1996b: 25. See also Yakhlef & Salzer-Mörling, 2000). In Callon's (2002) view, writing is primarily thought of as the former type of writing, wherein activities are broken down into instructions about how different practices should be dealt with.

One example of how writing practices based on codification are employed in a knowledge management perspective is the use of what Mouritsen, Larsen and Bukh (2001) call *intellectual capital statements* in annual reports for the formal representation of companies. Mouritsen, Larsen and Bukh (2001: 740) write: "Intellectual capital statements are not about knowledge per se. They are about the actions and activities that managers put in place in the name of knowledge. Such activities are complex sets of interventions that cannot be captured easily". Since the knowledge of the firm or organization is complicated to capture in standard accounting practices, intellectual capital statements point out how particular intellectual resources are used in organizations (see also Kreiner & Mouritsen, 2003; Mouritsen, 2000).

Organizing and management are generally regarded as based on the practice of writing the particular into the universal. Tsoukas and Chia (2002: 573) say: "[O]rganizing implies generalizing; it is the process of subsuming particulars under generic categories". Thus, all managerial practices have to deal with paradoxes and complexities (Clegg, et al, 2002). In terms of knowledge management, individual competencies and experiences that are to be codified will always have to fit into the "universal" categories that have been developed. Personal and idiosyncratic knowledge becomes codified into written facts and figures in a database, or on a web page on the intranet. Knowledge management operates through such practices of codification.

Uncodified Knowledge: Practices of Communication

The Dutch historian Johan Huizinga, speaking about the establishment and growth of the medieval university, writes; "All knowledge — and this naturally includes philosophy — is polemical in nature, and polemics cannot be divorced from agonistics" (Huizinga, 1949: 156). The mediaeval university was a highly scattered and fragmented unity; a multiplicity, composed of various faculties, fraternities, interest groups, communities, and schools. That kind of fragmented organization is still present in the university system. For Huzinga (1949), this arrangement is an outcome of the inability to find a shared ground for antagonists and opposing beliefs. This knowledge is a passionate concept: A good antagonist in knowledge–intensive fields may make up an entire intellectual career. Spinoza needed Descartes to develop his philosophy of immanence; quantum theory is opposed to Newtonian physics; modern aesthetics can be seen as a revolt against the tradition. Knowledge is the offspring of conflict and controversy.

Knowledge may be codified, i.e. written into documents using *speech-*

forms of writing or alphanumerical techniques as suggested by Kallinikos (1996b). In some cases, knowledge may not benefit from being transferred via codification. For instance, the notion of tacit knowledge is a very frequent topic of discussion in the knowledge management literature. In its classic formulation, provided by Michael Polanyi (1958), tacit knowledge is knowledge which we can make use of but which we cannot formulate and provide with proper expression. In Polanyi's account, tacit knowledge is an effect of what Chomsky (1968) calls *speech performance*, i.e. the ability to formulate experiences and ideas (Styhre, 2002). As one may easily realize, speech performance capabilities are unevenly distributed across a population. Some people may be able to give very detailed and adequate accounts of their experiences while others may be incapable of saying a lot about what they experience. Thus, tacit knowledge is a function of individual eloquence. For instance, a great poet may be able to express very elegant and emotional formulations on the experience of being in love, while the love-struck adolescent may struggle to find an adequate expression of this most multifaceted experience. In cases where the tacit component of knowledge is significant, it may be complicated to code and decode it. Instead, practices of communication may be an applicable method. While practices of codification are aimed at breaking down knowledge into categories, practices of communication are aimed at narrating knowledge, i.e. telling stories and free accounts of how tacit and explicit knowledge are used in practical work. The codification practices serve to break down knowledge into its elementary forms; the communication practices, on the contrary, aim to align particular forms of knowledge with resources that lie *outside* of the knowledge in order to make it appear intelligible to an outsider. For instance, a surgeon's work may be possible to break down into scripts and standard operation practices that can be printed in medicine textbooks used as educational material in undergraduate courses (Wenger, McDermott & Snyder, 2002). These scripts and texts capture some of the fundamental operations of the profession. But once the medical student starts getting acquainted with the "basics", issues that are harder to capture in scripts and texts may be raised (Becker, Geer, Highes & Strauss, 1961; Mol, 2002). Here, experienced surgeons may need to develop a metaphorical and colourful language that can share the intellectual, embodied and emotional experience of performing an operation. Practices may be described in poetic terms, or compared with everyday life practices. Since surgery is a very specialized expert-based practice that not only requires a long and detailed formal training, but should also be regarded as a life-long learning experience, it requires a shared analytical framework, a set of concepts, metaphors and illustrations, in brief a narrative structure to fully capture the complexity of the activity. For instance, Lynch (1985), in his ethnomethodological study of neuroscience laboratory work, points to the various tools and heuristics that scientists make use of in their day-to-day work: "[I]nteractions between scientists utilize such non-vocal materials and formulations as written equations, notes, illustrative or analytical diagrams, electron micrographs, oscillographic data inputs, and styrofoam models of lattice structure" (Lynch, 1985: 155). Uncodified knowledge is shared through various interactions wherein talking is perhaps the single most important, but not the only, medium for joint learning. Thus knowledge sharing in the laboratory sciences is dependent on the use of heterogeneous materials and conceptual developments. In Pickering's (1995) formulation: "[S]centific knowledge should be understood as sustained by, and as part of, interactive stabilizations situated in a multiple and heterogeneous space of machines, instruments, conceptual structures, disciplined practices, social actors and their relations, and so forth" (Pickering, 1995: 70).

Practices of communication are not, however, a trivial matter in which individuals sharing an expertise or a profession are brought together in order to discuss what they know in new terms. Communication includes the processing of data and information which organization members regard as important. Weick (1979: 6) writes: "The basic raw material on which organizations operate are informational inputs that are ambiguous, uncertain, equivocal... Organizing serves to narrow the range of possibilities, to reduce the numbers of 'might occurs'". Organizations are thus always interpretative systems: "To survive, organizations must have mechanisms to interpret ambiguities and to provide meaning and direction for participants" (Daft & Weick, 1984: 293). Moore (1996), discussing the notion of *virtual actions* in Bergson's philosophy, provides a nice passage capturing human beings' selective attention paid to their environment:

> Living organisms...are selectively sensitive to their environment. For the simplest organisms, only a very limited set of properties of surrounding objects will evoke response. Thus a body capable of action acts as a kind of 'filter' of the properties of these objects. It does not react to all properties; it need not represent any property, but it does tend to respond to the properties important to it. That is why representation is a bad picture of perception. Perceiving, in a living body, is not making a picture of an object, but selecting just some of its properties in the light of that body's needs and projects, of what Bergson calls its *virtual actions*. (Moore, 1996: 27)

Human beings collect a number of impressions based on their perceptual abilities. These impressions are interpreted in social settings; ambiguities are dealt with, actions are given meaning, events are located within a frame of reference. The French sociologist Gabriel Tarde, Emile Durkheim's contemporary and critic, argues that "social evolution" is driven by acts of *invention* and *imitation*, the "elementary social acts" (Tarde, 1969: 178). For Tarde, it is conversations—"nonessential discussions" [*entretien de luxe*] (Tarde, 1969: 308) — between individuals which enable inventions and imitations. Tarde writes:

> By conversation I mean not only dialogue without directs and immediate utility, in which one talks primarily to talk, for pleasure, as a game, out of politeness. This definition excludes juridical inquiries, diplomatic or commercial negotiations, and even scientific congresses, although the latter abound in superfluous chatter. (Tarde, 1969: 308)

Tarde continues: "It [conversation] is ... the strongest agent of invention, of the propagation of sentiments, ideas and modes of action". (Tarde, 1969: 308). In Tarde's sociology of invention and imitations, conversation plays a decisive role. Knowledge is thus distributed and shared through what may be regarded as everyday speech.

Thus, one mechanism serving to make sense out of a set of fragments from a complex and confusing reality is storytelling in organizations (Gabriel, 2000; Boje, 1991). For Boje (1991: 106), stories "make sense out of an equivocal situation". Stories have the quality of being shared by a number of individuals in organizations; they are always social in nature, distributed across the tiers of the organization. In addition, stories are always, for Boje (1991), continuously altered and improved upon. Things are added to the storyline, new "facts" are integrated, new consequences of an event are formulated. Boje (1991) writes: "Each performance is never a complete story; it is an unravelling process of confirming new data and new interpretations as these become part of an unfolding story line" (Boje, 1991: 106). But what does storytelling really tell? What are the limits of storytelling and of language? The writings of Niklas Luhmann offers some ideas.

Storytelling in organizations is one particular form of communication. For Niklas Luhmann, the notion of communication lies at the heart of social formations. In fact, in Luhmann's view, social systems are communicative systems by definition (Bakken & Hernes, 2002; Anoldi, 2001). Luhmann (1982) writes: "We can speak of a 'social system' whenever the actions of several persons are meaningfully interrelated and are thus, in their interconnectedness, marked off from an environment. As soon as any communication whatsoever takes place among individuals, social systems emerge" (Luhmann, 1982: 70). Luhmann's theory on communication draws on theories of self-organization. It radically calls into question many theories of communication in terms of not making any explicit claims of the outcome of communication. Thus, Luhmann is strongly opposed to the theories of communicative rationality advocated by Habermas:

> Often, it is more or less implicitly supposed that communication aims at consensus, that it seeks agreement. The theory of rationality of communicative action developed by Habermas is built upon these premises. One can also communicate in order to mark dissent, one can desire to argue; and there is no compelling reason to hold the search for consensus to be more rational than the search for dissent. That depends entirely on themes and partners. Communication is obviously impossible without any consensus, but is also impossible without any dissent. (Luhmann, 2002: 162. See also Leydesdorff, 2000)

For Luhmann, communication always brings together three different processes: "Communication brings about a unity (and with possible contradiction) by integrating a threefold selection. Information, utterance, and understanding (with or without acceptance) are practiced as a unity however different the conscious contents of the participants and their selective horizons might be and remain" (Luhmann, 1995: 364). Communication is what enables information, utterance and understanding to take place simultaneously. Thus, Luhmann criticizes the popular sender-receiver model of communication research because it puts forth too simplistic a view of communication assuming that some kind of transmission is taking place: "The metaphor of transmission is unusable because it implies too much ontology: It suggests that the sender gives up something that the receiver acquires ... The entire metaphor of processing, having, giving, and receiving, the entire 'thing metaphor' is unsuitable for understanding communication" (Luhmann,, 1995: 139). Instead, in Luhmann's account, communication is *autopoetic*; it is based on what it is capable of producing. For instance, an utterance aimed at communicating some information is misunderstood. This misunderstanding is responded to by another utterance that provokes further misunderstanding. The communication system is based on its own production of utterances, information and understandings. Thus, it is a self-organizing activity. As a consequence, Luhmann refuses to accept that communication *per se* is capable of solving any antagonistic relationships:

> In principle, reducing conflicts to a failure of communication misses the target (as if communication were something 'good' that could break down). Communication is the autopoetic process of social systems, which continues over and beyond cooperative or antagonistic episodes, so long as it carries on. Conflicts serve to continue communication by using one of the possibilities that communication holds open, by saying no. (Luhmann, 1995: 389)

In order to make sense out of a complex social reality, human beings, members of an organization, for instance, can make use of communication. Communication aims to create shared meaning. But communication is, Luhmann argues, a fickle instrument for meaning production (see also Lyotard, 1990, on the limits of communication). Yet, it is what social systems are founded upon. Therefore, communication is not a linear one-dimensional process wherein utterances, information and understanding are effectively disseminated. In organization theory, Gabriel (2000), examining storytelling in organizations, has suggested that storytelling not only makes sense, it may also actively destroy meaning: "[S]tories are not the only things that generate and sustain meaning, nor indeed do all stories generate and sustain meaning— some stories may actually undermine and destroy meaning". Such an account helps to make Luhmann's point. Since communication is autopoetic, there is always a possibility of refusing to understand, of saying no. Therefore, there is no such thing as an innate rationality in communication. Communication is autopoetic, not rational in the conventional sense. It operates in accordance with its own logic.

Returning to knowledge management, much of the resources that are labelled organization knowledge are in fact what emerges from within processes of communication. Martin Wood argues: "[K]nowledge is not a commodity 'out there', nor is its movement a question of the starting or finishing of use or production. Rather it is the elusive subject of what happens 'in-between' " (Wood, 2002: 153). Knowledge is what is produced when members of the organization either work together or communicate with one another. In all cases, communication is an important component of the production of knowledge in an organization. As will be suggested by the second case study, that of AstraZeneca in the pharmaceutical industry (Chapter Five), knowledge is shared through seminars and courses during which co-workers get together and share their experiences and learning. In our two generic practices for knowledge sharing — writing practices enabling databases and documentation and practices of communication — knowledge is what is defined in the realm between the observation of a fact, its formulation, and its documentation. Knowledge is not simply located at a singular point in the organization but distributed between various processes and activities. Thus, knowledge is what happens in-between the *seeing* and the *saying* (see Foucault, 1973; Deleuze, 1988). If knowledge includes a tacit component, it is most effectively communicated in an uncodified form; if it is possible to codifiy the knowledge, it may be captured by documents and stored in databases.

Knowledge Sharing: Empirical Studies

Regardless of whether we use the reservoir or network metaphors (cf. Boisot & Griffiths, 2001) to describe knowledge, regardless of whether we assume it to be a "truth" or an interpretation or a construct, regardless of whether we see it pragmatically or "scientifically", we can agree that, under certain circumstances, knowledge can be a source of organizational improvement, perhaps even financially. Organizations learn in different ways, but one viable and economical means of learning is to make use of knowledge that is already part of the organization, in practices or "restored" in documentation. Internal knowledge sharing is thus one learning strategy, comparable with other methods, including R&D, experimentation, external absorption, study, and so forth. The advantages of internal knowledge sharing are the lower costs of managing, the idiosyncratic fit and leverage.

The study of knowledge sharing in organizations has emerged as an individual field within the knowledge management literature (Boland, et al, 2001; Seely-Brown & Duguid, 2000). Empirical knowledge-sharing studies can be categorized on the basis of focus. One perspective focuses on analyzing what part(s) of the organization is involved in the knowledge sharing. Here, *communities of practice* (Wenger, McDermott & Snyder, 2002), *teams* (Postrel, 2002), *departments* (Dixon, 2000), *professional service firms* (Empson, 2001), or *networks* (Spencer, 2003; Brusoni & Prencipe, 2001; Augier & Thanning, 1999; Dyer & Nobeoka, 2000; Seufert, von Krogh & Bach, 1999) have been suggested as organizational entities wherein knowledge has been shared. In this perspective, knowledge sharing will be managed differently depending upon what level of organization is taking place. For instance, in communities of practice, a group of individuals who share an expertise or interest, knowledge is shared differently than in, say, a network of organizations. A more normative stream of research aims to identify tools and mechanisms for knowledge sharing (Pawlowsky, Forslin & Reinhardt, 2001). In this body of texts, strategic mapping (Ambrosini & Bowman, 2002), intranets (Newell, Scarborough, Swan & Hislop, 2000), specific physical places (Nonaka, Toyama & Konno, 2002), knowledge brokers (Hargadon, 1998), leadership practices (Hansen & Oetinger 2001), and organizational interventions (Dixon, 2000) have all been examined. In this perspective, knowledge sharing is a matter of establishing good managerial techniques and mechanisms in organizations, enabling individuals on various levels to participate in the joint production and sharing of knowledge. Yet a third perspective focuses on the different conceptual frameworks that enable or hinder knowledge sharing. Concepts such as *stickiness* (von Hippel, 1998; Szulanski, 1996), *resource absorption* (Cohen & Levinthal, 1990;

Van den Bosch, Volberda, & Boer, 1999), *structural ambiguities* (Ravasi & Verona, 2001), *translation* (Gherardi & Nicolini, 2000), *cultural barriers* (De Long & Fahey, 2000), *organizational structure* (Oliver & Montgomery, 2000), or *tacit knowledge* (Baumard, 1999, 2002; Kreiner, 2002; Lam, 2000) have been invoked as key components for understanding knowledge sharing. Furthermore, the role of *motivation* is occasionally addressed (Gupta & Govindarajan, 2000, Stein & Ridderstråle, 2001). In this perspective, knowledge sharing is examined from a more theoretical perspective, aiming to establish a more formal theory (see Glaser and Strauss, 1967) on knowledge sharing.

When it comes to discussing the managerial implications of knowledge sharing, all three of the perspectives above are interesting. However, from a strategy perspective, a key concern is, of course, the relationship between knowledge sharing and success in some form, as well as the mechanisms and obstacles by which knowledge sharing is managed and facilitated in order to become a source of competitive advantage, or simply a means of improving performance. What is perhaps a bit disturbing, even among the strategy-oriented knowledge-sharing studies, is a relatively narrow focus on knowledge and learning, meaning that the primary focus of much empirical research is outlining whether or not sharing has *occurred*, been *accomplished* (von Hippel, 1994; Darr et al, 1996; Szulanski, 1996). Few empirical studies address the wider implications of sharing — for instance whether or not sharing has resulted in performance improvements (exceptions include Tsai, 2000). This research strategy exhibits a rather non-contextual view of knowledge, and, to make matters worse, displays a view of knowledge as inherently "good", regardless of contextual setting. The dependent variable in much knowledge transfer and sharing theory is thus accomplished transfer *per se*, although it has occasionally been extended to performance proxies, e.g. rate of innovation, long term survival, product quality and project efficiency (e.g., Tsai, 1999; Levin, 2000; McEvily & Chakravarthy, 2002). Table 3.1 gives an overview of empirical work carried out on knowledge transfer and sharing.

Cognitive Factors

The independent, explanatory variables are subject to greater variation. The nature of the transferred knowledge is often addressed as an important factor, as is the absorptive capacity of knowledge "recipients". Information is "sticky" when it is costly to acquire, transfer and use in a new location. Under such conditions, problem-solving tends to be concentrated to one location (i.e. knowledge is not transferred), or solved interdependently by involved units (von Hippel, 1994).

TABLE 3.1. Empirical research on knowledge transfer

Reference	Independent variable/factors	Dependent variable	Comments
Epple et al. (1991)	Training, Geographical proximity	Transfer accomplished	Dependent variable operationalised as labour hours per unit of output
von Hippel (1994)	The nature of knowledge	Transfer accomplished	
Zander & Kogut (1995)	Structure, Shared coding schemes. Knowledge commonalty, the pace of recombinating skills	Transfer accomplished, Imitation	
Darr et al (1996)	Geographical proximity, Level of communication	Transfer accomplished	Dependent variable operationalised ascost per unit of output
Epple et al. (1996)	Managerial and engneering attention	Transfer accomplished	Dependent variable operationalised as labor hours per unis of output
Szulanski (1996)	Absorptive capacity, Casual ambiguity, Nature of relationships	Transfer accomplished	Studied several other factors, but found limited support
Ingram & Baum (1997)	Proximity	Long term survival	"Proximity" refers to being part of a chain of bsinesses
Hoopes & Postrel (1999)	Knowledge sharing, Cooperation, Coordination	Prevention from "glitches"	Glitches refer to project errors
Simonin (1999)	Ambiguity, in turn driven by Tacitness, Complexity, Experience, Cultural and Organisational Distance	Transfer accomplished	
Argote & Ingram (2000)	Social subnetworks	Transfer accomplished	Also discuss imitation
Gupta & Govindarajan (2000)	Value of knowledge stocks, Motivation, Richness of transmission, Absorptive capacity	Transfer accomplished	
Levin (2000)	Experience, Knowledge sharing	Product quality	Dependent variable measured by number of repairs to the product
Tsai (2000)	Strategic relatedness, Perceived trustworthyness, Network centrality	Transfer accomplished	
Stein & Ridderstråle (2001)	Socialization, Education, Compensation Documentation, Toleration, Motivation, Communication, Rotation, Reflection, Correction, Selection, Standardization	Transfer accomplished	Independent variables to solve different types of socio-cognitive obstacles to disseminations of skills
Tsai (2001)	Network centrlity, Absorptive capacity	Rate of innovation, Performance (ROI)	
Foss & Pedersen (2002)	Sources, Context specificity	Transfer accomplished	
McEvily & Chakravarthy (2002)	Complexity, Tacitness, Specificity	Product quality	

One of the most comprehensive studies of internal knowledge sharing was conducted by Szulanski (1996, 2000), who used *successful transfer*, within budget and time limits and with satisfied recipients, as a dependent variable. Szulanski (1996) found that the three most important factors, or "origins of stickiness", were *absorptive capacity at the recipient, causal ambiguity* and *arduous relationships* between sources and recipients of knowledge. Causal ambiguity is denoting the inability to map the relationship between a capability and a performance outcome (Lippman & Rumelt, 1982), and is thus an effect of the characteristics of the knowledge. Absorptive capacity (Cohen &

Levinthal, 1990) refers to the ability to absorb knowledge from the outside, and is driven by existing stocks of knowledge and manifested in an ability to evaluate, assimilate and apply knowledge. It is a characteristic of the recipient of knowledge in a transfer situation. Relationships are arduous if there is a lack of intimacy, i.e. if it is difficult or costly to communicate between individuals in different units. The character of relationships is an effect of the organizational context.

In another study of the relationship between the character of the knowledge sharing and the *success of transfer*, Foss and Pedersen (2002) found evidence that *the source of the knowledge* as well as *the context specificity of the knowledge* were key success factors. Simonin (1999) discusses the role of causal ambiguity in knowledge sharing in alliances, and, unsurprisingly, finds that ambiguity is negatively associated with accomplished transfer, but he also identifies, empirically, some of the drivers of ambiguity. *Tacitness*, referred to as the implicit and uncodifiable accumulation of skills resulting from experience (cf. Reed & DeFillippi, 1990), is one such driver, as is *complexity* (referring to the number of interdependent technologies, routines and individuals linked to the knowledge). Consequently, *experience* was found to be negatively correlated with ambiguity.

In a detailed account of the social and cognitive factors critical to the dissemination of competencies, Stein and Ridderstråle (2001) discuss transfer problems and strategies to solve them. Drawing on Polanyi (1958), three aspects of dissemination need to be dealt with. Firstly, situations where the source of knowledge "knows more than he can say" may be caused by problems of articulation (tacit knowledge, inability to articulate), monopolization (unwillingness to share), retaliation (fear to share due to uncomfortable consequences) and restriction (lack of physical proximity or appropriate infrastructure). Strategies to resolve such problems include *socialization, education, compensation, documentation, toleration, motivation, communication* and *rotation*. Secondly, when the source "says more than he knows", extrapolation or reduction, as well as manipulation and exaggeration may occur. Such problems can be dealt with through *communication, reflection, correction* and careful *selection* (of employees). Thirdly, recipients of knowledge may "hear things different from what is said", again causing extrapolation and reduction of "facts". *Socialization* and *standardization* can correct such behaviour.

Furthermore, the value of the stocks of knowledge at the source is a potential factor. The more valuable it is, the more likely it is that the recipient will attempt to use it (Gupta & Govindarajan, 2000). The absorptive capacity will determine whether or not it will work. Another factor, related to whether competitive advantage is achieved, is the uniqueness and inimitability of the knowledge. If knowledge transferred internally can also be transferred externally to competitors, for instance through personnel migration or intelligence activities, there is a risk that the effects, on costs say, will be duplicated by competitors. Here, the commonality of knowledge between actors will determine the risks of failure (Zander & Kogut, 1996). Another risk refers to the downsides accompanying the articulation of the knowledge necessary to be able to transfer it. Articulation requires simplification, which means that aspects of knowledge might be overlooked (Boisot et al., 1997). Some argue that the risks associated with articulating and transferring tacit knowledge are so high that it is more effective to accept the higher costs for coordinating a diverse set of organizational skills (Grant, 1996). However, others argue that organizations must try to spread knowledge, otherwise it will be difficult to reap the leveraged benefits of knowledge at all (Sanchez, 1997). It is worthwhile to note the content-oriented view of knowledge: it is an entity, potentially partly obscure, that can be passed around between individuals, with a certain degree of difficulty, and with varying degrees of communicational success.

Organizational Context

Apart from the direct features of cognition, the role of the organizational context is often referred to as a factor in sharing ventures. Simonin (1999) suggested that *cultural distance* (differences in the view of collaboration) and *organizational distance* (differences in business practices, institutional heritage and organizational culture) are positively associated with causal ambiguity.

An early study by Epple et al. (1991) reported that knowledge on one production shift can be transferred to another. But knowledge is not completely embodied in technology, meaning that knowledge is not entirely possible to transfer just via technology, human interaction is necessary as well. Epple et al. (1991) singled out two factors, *training* and *geographical proximity* between the source and the recipient of knowledge, as important for successful knowledge transfer. The dependent variable in their study was *transfer*, measured in terms of direct labour hours per unit of output. In a subsequent study, Epple et al. (1996) conjecture that the *managerial and engineering attention* paid to the recipient of knowledge is an important factor. Darr et al. (1996) studied knowledge transfer between franchise pizza stores within a corporation and found that transfer was more likely to occur between stores within a given franchisee firm, than across franchisees, even though part of the same corporation. Geography is thus again a factor, but also "perceived" proximity. Darr et al. do not explain the reason behind the more intensive transfer between units within franchisees, other than stating that *the level of communication* (phone calls, meetings and personal acquaintances) is more intensive within than across groups of franchise stores.

In their study of hotels in Manhattan during the period 1898 to 1980, Ingram and Baum (1997) used *survival* as a dependent variable, without explicating the factors that drive knowledge sharing. They found that, among those hotels that had survived, many were part of hotel chains and had survived partly because of their access to knowledge elsewhere within the chain. Although it was stated that chain affiliation was not always directly linked to survival, this enabled chain hotels to learn more than independent competitors about operating matters and strategic responses to changes in the environment. One such example was accounting routines, which are very important, not just for reporting but also for internal cost control within the hotel industry. It was also an area where the industry was constantly underperforming, resulting in very poor knowledge of how a particular business was operating financially. Apparently, chains were leading the sophistication of accounting routines within the hotel industry (Ingram & Baum, 1997).

Argote and Ingram (2000), adopting a socio-cognitive approach, conclude that *social subnetworks* of individuals are a major factor in sharing knowledge. Achieving compatibility between subnetworks is highly difficult and their status determines whether it is at all suitable to transfer knowledge. In their study of product development projects, Hoopes and Postrel (1999) suggested that intraorganizational *integration*, i.e. the sharing of knowledge, cooperation and coordination, helps to prevent so-called *glitches*, i.e. project errors caused "by a lack of interfunctional or interspecialty knowledge about problem constraints" (Hoopes and Postrel, 1999: 843). Knowledge sharing, one of the independent variables, is stimulated by *intensive integrative practices* such as cross-functional meetings, the early development of specifications and the broad participation of multiple functions.

Along the same lines as Szulanski's discussion on arduous relationships, Gupta and Govindarajan (2000) suggest that the *richness of transmission channels* (formal and informal integrative mechanisms such as liaison positions, task forces, permanent committees, interpersonal familiarity, personal affinity and convergence in cognitive maps; cf. Galbraith, 1973; Edstrom & Galbraith, 1977) is equally valid in explaining successful intraorganizational knowledge flow. Similar conclusions are drawn in two studies by Tsai (2000, 2001), which identify *absorptive capacity, strategic relatedness*, so-called *network centrality* (number of firm-internal linkages to a unit) and *perceived trustworthiness* as independent variables.

Motivation

A third group of factors falls under motivation (e.g. May, Korczynski & Frenkel, 2002). However, the role of motivation appears debatable and is less clear, according to research. Relatively few empirical studies actually study motivation, and even fewer claim that motivation is important. Motivation has been found to drive source units to share knowledge (cf. Gupta & Govindarajan, 2000), but not all studies have been able to corroborate this, either because they have not studied it, or because they found it to be unimportant.

Szulanski (1996) studied the link between accomplished transfer and a range of factors and found no link between motivation and transfer accomplishments. Cognitive and relational factors were more important and thus, suggested Szulanski, it is better to stimulate learning capacities and relationships than incentives. In a subsequent paper (Szulanski, 2000), the downsides to motivation were elaborated upon. Szulanski suggested that highly motivated adopters might;

> exacerbate problems of implementation by prematurely dismissing outside help, expanding seemingly straightforward modifications into major projects, making unnecessary modifications to preserve pride of ownership and status or to let out hidden resentment […], or switching to new practices at a suboptimal moment because of unchecked enthusiasm (Szulanski, 2000: 24).

The so-called *not-invented-here* syndrome (Katz & Allen, 1982, Hayes & Clark, 1985) has occasionally been referred to, concerning instances where obtained knowledge is not used, due to a lack of will. This lack of motivation might emanate from a range of different factors, including distrust, lack of will to change and a perception of knowledge as unproven. It can result in sluggish implementation and even direct rejection.

Motivation can be important on the "source" side, too. In framing the independent variables behind accomplished knowledge sharing, Szulanski (1996) hypothesized that sources of knowledge may be reluctant to share important knowledge, because of the perceived risks of losing ownership or even internal uniqueness and superiority, or because of a lack of willingness to devote time and costs for the benefit of others. This has been elaborated upon by Prahalad and Hamel (1990), in the discussion on the "tyranny of the SBU". This tyranny refers to the unwillingness of individuals and units to share their resources and knowledge with sister units, and is a matter partly caused by organizational context. In an organization structure where local units have profit centre status and enjoy autonomy, motivation to allocate costs and efforts in order to stimulate the business of others can be low, if there is no reward system in place to compensate. Although part of the same corporation, straightforward SBUs might not acknowledge a shared identity.

Similar issues are discussed by Stein and Ridderstråle (2001) who claim that motivation can be important on both "sides" of the transfer venture. When the source of the knowledge "knows more than he can say", problems may arise because of "monopolization", i.e. an unwillingness to share knowledge. Fear of sharing may also be a factor, for instance when organizational units are vertically integrated, i.e. transacting with each other. Stein and Ridderstråle (2001) suggest that socialization, toleration and communication can serve to improve the motivation to change under such circumstances. On the contrary, situations in which the source "says more than he knows" potentially signal an exaggerated commitment to disseminating knowledge.

Despite the above references to literature that address motivation, the view of the role of motivation is ambiguous. Many empirical studies do not discuss it, the reason for this being difficult to assess. One reason could be difficulties measuring motivation in a quantified sense; and quantification has proved to be important in most empirical knowledge sharing research.

Concluding Remarks

Based on this literature review, we can conclude that knowledge transfer theory rests on theories emphasizing the nature of the knowledge shared, the cognitive abilities of those "receiving" knowledge, the organizational and social context within which transfer occurs, and, to a lesser extent, the motivation to share and receive knowledge. There is no unanimous explanation across studies; different studies espouse different factors. Theory is also heterogeneous in its view of the dependent variable. To a great extent, accomplished sharing is used as the dependent variable, but there are exceptions.

This connects back to our initial point that understanding knowledge transfer requires a broader approach than simply discussing knowledge *per se*. Knowledge is always much more than an objective "matter of fact"; it is always contextual, subjective, situational, social, and if the circumstances are right, it might even be of economic importance. While the stream of empirical research certainly provides an extensive input to the factors that make or break sharing projects, we still do not know much about the organizational and managerial obstacles and issues *ex post* the accomplished sharing, after organizational learning has occurred. It appears to be an assumption that sharing and learning in themselves are good, or as Argote et al (2000: 2) put it: "organizations that are able to transfer knowledge effectively from one unit to another are more productive and more likely to survive than organizations that are less adept at knowledge transfer".

For someone who studies strategic management, this narrow definition of the dependent variable opens up a range of research issues on the immediate context of transfer ventures. The link between knowledge, sharing and strategic measures such as competitive advantage or profit is not given, far from it. Knowledge can be unsuited, too idiosyncratic (even in the most homogeneous of organizations), too unproven, and motivation may be low for a number of reasons. The reasons why sharing does not automatically generate economic value (or any other measurement of rationality, e.g. self-fulfilment or individual emancipation), is that it is not a universal, objective, generic "thing", that it is laden with norms and values, that it is difficult to define, and that the humans involved are not able or willing to teach and learn.

In the two cases reported in this book, SCA Packaging and AstraZeneca, we will show that knowledge transfer and sharing may be arranged in a number of different ways, and we will highlight the heterogeneity and pluralism of knowledge sharing, both in terms of content and processes. Knowledge sharing occurs on a daily basis in organizations, but what is truly interesting is seeing the implications, effects, of sharing. Both cases provide evidence of the magnitude of ways in which sharing can be facilitated and consequences managed.

Summary and Conclusion

The construct of knowledge is generally regarded as being subject to data and information processes and interpretation. However, there is no straight linearity between data, information and knowledge, these three constructs instead being implied in one another. Therefore, knowledge (as well as data and information) is a complex concept that cannot fully be captured in functionalist and instrumental knowledge-sharing models and tools. Still, knowledge may be shared in practices. In this chapter, two generic approaches have been sketched, e.g. the writing of codified knowledge and the communication (e.g. talking, showing, modelling) of uncodified or tacit knowledge. The review of the literature on knowledge sharing suggests that there is a great diversity in the field and that at least three aspects of knowledge sharing have been examined: cognitive factors, organizational context, and motivation. In the following two chapters, two different knowledge-sharing projects or initiatives will be examined. In Chapter Four, the Eurobest programme at SCA packaging will be discussed, while in Chapter Five the use of knowledge facilitation seminars at AstraZeneca will be examined. These two case studies point to the complexities of managing knowledge sharing within organizations. For

instance, the writing and communication of codified and uncodified knowledge is never isolated from the social context in which knowledge is constituted, enacted and employed. Therefore, knowledge sharing is always embedded in relationships between individuals and communities of practice in the
workplace. The two cases studies are intended to serve as illustrations (or
"thick descriptions") of the more theoretical arguments put forth in Chapters
One, Two and Three.

Chapter 4

Knowledge Sharing at SCA Packaging

Introduction

SCA (Svenska Cellulosa AB) is a Swedish forestry company, founded in 1929. They make hygiene products such as diapers and tissue, forest products like publication paper, solid wood products and pulp, and packaging, such as containerboard and corrugated paper boxes. The group has an annual sales turnover of more than € 9 billion (2002), which breaks down into Hygiene Products at € 4 billion, Packaging at € 3 billion and Forest Products at € 1.5 billion. On top of that, a separate unit catering for the North American market (and producing hygiene products and packaging) has an annual sales turnover of approximately € 1 billion. The group has grown steadily over the last decade, almost exclusively based on acquisitions, and has trebled its sales turnover since 1993. SCA employs some 42,000 people in over 40 countries.

One of the strategic logics of the SCA Group is the value added strategy. Refining wood fibre has been a central strategic issue, which has also stimulated vertical integration. Historically, this has been driven by SCA as a means of securing capacity utilization, more recently as a way to exit the fairly cyclical forest industry, and to create value from fibre. Today, SCA is quite explicit in its focus on "value-added products" such as hygiene products and corrugated paper packaging. Nonetheless, SCA owns more than 2 million hectares of forestland in Sweden. They are listed on the Stockholm and London stock exchanges.

The study referred to in this chapter concerns the SCA Packaging business unit (SCAP), which has its headquarters in Brussels, Belgium. SCAP principally supplies two lines of vertically-integrated products: containerboard, for the production of corrugated boxes; and corrugated boxes. The two product lines form independent divisions within SCAP. The Corrugated Division, which is the focal point of this study, has an annual sales turnover of approximately € 2.5 billion, and employs some 18,000 people at over 200 sites in 22 European countries. Hence, the Corrugated Division is far larger than the Containerboard Division.

SCA has been in the packaging business since the early 1960s, but it was not until the late 1980s that its business started to grow, primarily through acquisitions. It became a formal business unit in 1991. Since 1987, the unit has grown from an operation with less than ten units in France and Sweden, producing some 300 million square metres of corrugated board, to one producing 4,500 million square metres. In terms of sales turnover, Germany, Italy, France and the UK are the largest markets for SCAP boxes, but the company is present on a number of other markets as well.

The box industry is undergoing a period of consolidation, but markets are still fragmented. In terms of market share, SCAP is among the top five in the world, surpassed by, for instance, Smurfit (IRE), International Paper (US), and Weyerhaeuser (US). On European markets, they are part of the big three, with Smurfit and Kappa (NL). Together, the three represent approximately one third of the European market. All three are the result of aggressive acquisition strategies. Taking into account that there are more than 400 companies producing corrugated boxes in Europe, it is still a fragmented market.

Part of the reason that the market is fragmented has to do with transportation costs. Shipping corrugated paper is expensive due to the large proportion of air in the product. Using a logic in which suppliers take responsibility for delivery, this becomes increasingly expensive the further away from customers the box is produced. Being subject to market prices (derived from pulp and paper prices), excess transport costs will destroy profit on the supply side. A sediment taken-for-granted "truth" is that a box plant cannot be profitable on shipments to addresses more than 250 kilometres away from the production site. This is not entirely true, because certain offerings, which require a certain degree of physical or service quality, may generate price premiums.

The Corrugated Division of SCAP supplies five lines of packaging products, roughly speaking; conventional boxes, for instance ones that contain food and vegetables, beer and other beverages; heavy duty boxes, for instance ones that contain chemical or industrial products; cushioning products, including protective packaging such as moulded and fabricated foam plastics and thermoformable plastics; display products, for instance advertising displays in supermarkets; and commercial operations, including selling (but not producing) peripheral material required to pack and dispatch products, for instance, tapes, plastic wraps and marker pens. Conventional boxes are by far the largest product in terms of sales turnover, but the other products are growing rapidly.

Food-related producers, for instance producers of processed foods, fresh foods and beverages, form one important target segment, but consumer durables and industrial goods are expanding their share. The electronics industry is becoming an increasingly important segment to the corrugated industry.

In terms of organization, the SCAP Corrugated Division is divided into five European regions: the Nordic Region (Sweden, Denmark, Finland, and Russia among others), Middle Europe (Germany, Austria and Poland among others), Western Europe (including France, Belgium, The Netherlands and Switzerland), Southern Europe (Spain, Italy and Greece among others) and the UK & Ireland. Each region is managed by a managing director (MD), and supplies conventional box products, but the other four product groups are not marketed in all five regions. Like the regional level, each unit within a region is run as a profit centre, with a general manager (GM) responsible. Local units can differ in character. Making a corrugated box requires principally two vertically integrated production processes, including corrugation (paper reels of containerboard are converted into corrugated sheets) and conversion (corrugated sheets are cut and printed according to customer requirements). This means that a "conventional" unit in the SCAP Corrugated Division can either be a "sheet feeder" (a unit specializing in corrugation), a "sheet plant" (specializing in conversion) or a "box plant" (both processes included). In parallel, certain units specialize in making displays, heavy duty boxes, cushioning products and in selling packing devices. By far the most common unit types are box plants and sheet plants.

As stated, each unit is a profit centre, responsible both for costs and sales and profits. This, plus the fact that a unit cannot normally supply customers located far away, emphasizes the local character of the business. Each unit enjoys a significant degree of autonomy. Control mechanisms vary, but in general, units are measured on one or more of return on operating capital, profit margin and cash-flow, compared to budget, on a monthly and annual basis. Investments and capital expenditures have to pass rigid and extensive application reviews, thus increasing the possibilities of head office to exercise control. The head office in Brussels has 50 or so people working on technology (machinery utilization and investments), information technology, pan-European sales coordination and design development.

According to SCAP respondents, the deep decentralization of the organization has some advantages in terms of, for instance, local ownership and commitment, but disadvantages when it comes to realizing synergies and collaboration between units. Due to the fact that machinery is fairly homogeneous across the entire industry, and customers are becoming increasingly pan-European, many respondents feel that more effort has to be put into materialising synergies created, for instance, in IS implementation, design solutions, sales and marketing – and knowledge-sharing in all parts of the value chain.

Given the local nature of operations, it is of course important to realize the impact of the local market when it comes to the issue of strategy. One important factor is the connection between packaging and paper prices, which frames what sort of prices a plant can normally attract (this concerns conventional boxes and to some extent heavy-duty products too; prices for cushioning display and products, and merchant services render different and higher prices more independent in relation to paper prices). To some extent, the conventional box-making business is subject to cost-plus pricing. Price premiums exist for small orders, just-in-time deliveries, short order cycles, printing qualities and clever structural designs, for instance. On a higher-order level, the integration of different packaging solutions, such as cushioning and conventional packaging, can be bundled to provide a more holistic solution. Certain SCAP units also provide packing and logistics services at customer sites. For instance, one unit takes charge of the kitting of manuals and guarantees, and the packing and distribution of the computers the customer produces and sells. So, there are clearly windows of opportunity for price premiums. Nonetheless, cost management is a key issue in the industry. Resources applied to this include more formal matters such as scale (created through acquisitions and globalization) and financial management control principles. Other than that, the sharing of resources such as information systems, an increasing number of e-business solutions with key customers, the continuous rationalization of work processes, joint sales campaigns either within segments or within geographic markets, common technical solutions (so that the number of machine suppliers can be reduced and maintenance efforts kept down), the benchmarking of a range of activities, and other efforts, are striving towards cutting costs at local units. The latter efforts tend to be orchestrated by head office staff. There do not appear to be any stuck-in-the-middle problems; the most profitable units tend to have slightly higher prices and slightly lower costs than their sister units.

On the divisional level, SCAP has no formal strategy, but it communicates a vision as well as values. The vision is partly formulated as a set of tasks, but some of these are oriented towards objectives, ends. Those that refer to actions, means, include "concentration on differentiated, high value-added products", "operating with the highest standard of ethics in all respects" and "with the highest standards of employee safety", and "complying with and supporting environmental and product safety legislation". Five more or less explicit values stipulate that the company focuses on, among other things, "performance not politics", "openness: sharing information and problems", being "ambassadors not barons". Other than that, one central concern is continued geographical expansion, within Europe and overseas.

In the following section, we shall discuss knowledge sharing within the Corrugated Division of SCAP. As previously mentioned, one core issue, especially given the increasing magnitude and multitude of the operations provided by the growth strategy, and the fairly homogeneous technical base (machinery and work routines are similar from plant to plant, regardless of geographical location), has been to share knowledge in areas related to production. With such a number of comparable units, but unique and partly isolated historical heritages, the opportunities to improve results, based on sharing knowledge about how to maximize machines, grow tempting. This is what the remainder of this chapter will focus on. But production knowledge is not the only field where SCAP shares knowledge. These processes are also evolving in the fields of sales, marketing, design, logistics and supply-chain management, accounting, and research and development on machines and raw material, only not at all with the same level of infrastructure, scale, scope and formal attention as the field of production knowledge.

The ambition of this chapter is to discuss production knowledge sharing in terms of cause and effect, actually, financial effect, and what it means to an organization to attempt to manage its utilization of knowledge in a way that helps to improve financial performance. We will do this by discussing the Eurobest programme, which is a knowledge sharing programme designed to make sure that machines used in conventional box plants are optimized. We will focus on so-called "box plants", which have been part of the programme since its start in late 1996. We will discuss, initially, its history and objectives, management and types of knowledge included. Subsequently, we will focus on the link between knowledge and performance (or, to put it differently, whether and how knowledge is strategic) and the drivers of and obstacles to this link.

The Eurobest Programme

In this section, we will briefly discuss the history and background, and the distinct features of, the Eurobest programme. In the next section, we will focus on the result of the programme, and review links between Eurobest and performance indicators, as well as track factors helping or hindering learning and performance improvements based on knowledge sharing.

History and Background

The concept of the Eurobest programme dates back to late 1996 and the appointment of a new vice president of manufacturing, recruited from an American partner with whom SCAP had had an alliance for some years. The outgoing VP, who was also an American, left the job stating that one of his most valuable experiences gained from SCAP and Europe was "to learn ten new ways of doing the same thing", implying that the SCAP network displayed a certain degree of heterogeneity in its work routines. This idea was carried forward by the new VP, and one of his first priorities was to focus on "manufacturing excellence".

In late 1996, a programme was devised, with the overall objective of improving productivity through the detailed measuring of production performance (productivity definitions such as unit of output produced per minute, direct labour hours per unit of output and raw material waste levels), interplant and intermachine benchmarking and knowledge sharing. A lot of effort was made at the office of the VP of Manufacturing to document texts regarding methods and advice, to create training courses, to set definitions and methods of measurement, to prepare the planning and reporting of documents, to work out mechanisms for instigating improvements and to create an organization throughout the network to facilitate the implementation and monitoring of progress, and to market the programme. From early 1997 and onwards, the programme was described exhaustively in group communications (such as staff magazines) and in dialogue between top management and subordinate line managers.

In terms of communicating the launch of the programme, the CEO of SCAP stated in March 1997 that "Eurobest will have the highest priority in 1997 and it will be an excellent support for us in making continuous improvement. Simply put, we have to increase our productivity and avoid unnecessary costs". The VP of Manufacturing said "Between two identical machines, acquired at the same time and sharing the same configuration, there can be a performance difference of 15%. Imagine a 15% difference in productivity and in production downtime. That is an enormous difference which should not exist if we could share methods between plants". In a keynote speech made at a selling-in venture at a manufacturing managers' meeting in the UK in May 1997, the context and logic of the programme was reemphasized by the VP:

> I am here today to briefly share with you some of the challenges SCA will face in the future and what strategies we plan to follow to offset these challenges. The world is acting a lot smaller with improvements in communication and

transport. We know about world events almost as they happen. The same is true for business, with open markets the options for supply are no longer limited to a small geographical area. Our customers now have many options for different styles of packaging from all over the world. This results in a customer base that is more vulnerable to seeking other more cost effective solutions. What must we do to meet this challenge? Use the leverage of being a large company to share successes in performance improvement, management style changes and newly acquired skills. The future will demand several things of us. Better quality, better service and better value from the products we supply. To meet this challenge we must develop an organization capable of the following: First, 3 sigma quality levels or 99.97% usable product, anything less will leave us vulnerable to alternate products. Second, lead times of 48 hours or less, delivered on time and at the exact count. Customers are no longer willing to accept large inventories to accommodate our inability to respond quickly and accurately. Third, we must be the lowest cost producer of the products we manufacture. Remaining the lowest cost producer is the only way to ensure we will be competitive in the future. And by the way, these three challenges are exactly why we have developed Eurobest to create more reliable capacity within our organization. [...] We need to leverage our size to raise our performance in quality service and costs. It is now up to us to use the tools we have and to share our learning's so we can raise the performance.

Since then, Eurobest has been a high-profile item on the agenda for SCAP. Almost every new issue of the staff magazine has a section on it. It is communicated in annual reports, award ceremonies are held, results are discussed in management meetings, performance measures and plans are recorded in a substantial data warehouse accessible on the group intranet, training is formalized for key personnel, and the body of articulated knowledge is accumulating. In terms of contents, the character of knowledge, programme organization and routines, incentives and benchmarking, and knowledge sharing are important features.

The Character of Knowledge

The measuring of productivity is based on machine type, including the corrugator and a host of converting machines such as so-called diecutters (machines that cut and print sheets) and flexo-folding machines (machines that print and crease sheets). Some of the knowledge regarding production routines communicated through the programme is linked to individual machine categories, whereas other pieces of knowledge and advice are generic, potentially referring to the principles of production.

It is not possible by any means to provide a list of all the articulated and recorded knowledge artefacts, there are simply too many. SCAP themselves distinguish between "work practices" and "methods", where the former are considered elements or principles of the way a plant operates, and the latter are treated as specific ways of performing a task or improvement process. Among work practices, SCAP has a record of knowledge and advice in fields related to crew size, work hours per shift or day, product mix selection (whereby the variety of the raw material used can be reduced), standardization of procedures, goal setting and feedback routines, targeting machine speed, continuous runs (minimizing machine downtime), training frequency and contents and pedagogics, job rotation, plant maintenance routines, team meetings (a team can be a team of 2-4 people working together on machine on a shift basis) where all members get a chance to propose improvements, routines for visiting sister plants, alliance partner plants or customers, as well as educating trainers.

In terms of methods, the knowledge-base is very broad, containing, at one end of the spectrum, methods that are extremely short and concise (see the "Pickie Stick" example in Figure 4.1, adopted from an American alliance partner), and at the other end, fairly complex methods of executing lengthy maintenance checks and operations. "Methods" include a range of routines that help improve machine tool changeovers, tool setups, reducing overruns, order runs, machine settings and configuration, preventive and predictive maintenance, temperature checks, production scheduling, housekeeping, and downtime tracking and analysis. In addition, a range of devices is introduced to help certain tasks. A "book of ideas" is also available, in which clever ideas like the Pickie Stick are compiled. On top of that, advice is also available on how to use devices such as video cameras to document routines.

The origins of these practices and methods are both internal and external. Some are based on common knowledge regarding production and manufacturing, others emanate from alliance partners, and still others originate internally, from a plant that has been proactive and clever, or simply lucky in local tinkering.

Programme Organization

The programme is administered from the office of the VP of Manufacturing. Since the start in 1996, there have been several people in this position, but the Eurobest programme has progressed strongly and become well-rooted in the company. From late 1997 through to early 2002, the project was managed and represented by Frank Linnerz, a group manufacturing engineer, aided by colleagues in the manufacturing department. Technical experts, specializing in different machines, cooperate with units and make sure that new wisdom is absorbed in external areas such as consulting, management, and science. One colleague keeps track of and reports results submitted by local units on the intranet.

PICKIE STICK
Corrugator 15

Problem: Removing waste (i.e. loose back, start up, splice waste) between the cut-off and down-stacker requires walking on the top belt and crawling on the bottom belt.

Solution: Use a "Pickie Stick" to remove scrap sheets.

Process: Construct a "Pickie Stick" from a 54" piece of electrical conduit with a 2" long bolt attached to one end. Grind the bolt to a point — this becomes the "Pickie".

Cost: Less than $10.00

Benefits: Safety improvement — using the stick eliminates the need for employees walking or climbing on a moving conveyor, thus eliminating a potential safety hazard.

Contact: XYZ
           Chicopee, MA
           413-123-4567

Figure 4.1. The "Pickie Stick": An explicit piece of production knowledge

On lower organizational levels, regional manufacturing directors are responsible for helping and supporting local units in implementing new methods and practices and improving production performance, and for managing regional networks of unit manufacturing managers. On the unit, or plant, level, the manufacturing manager is formally responsible for planning and supporting the annual work of individual machine centres in implementing new methods, monitoring progress and setting targets. Supervisors and machine operators are informed with varying regularity, depending on the plant routines. Some plants feed back information about performance on a daily basis, while others simply refrain from informing about results. Key operators and supervisors are sent on training courses and are responsible for making sure they have knowledge of, and apply, accurate methods. This in turn requires active interaction with the accumulating body of the methods available on the intranet, and a dialogue with sister plants that can serve as benchmarks.

Each machine centre sets annual targets for the different measures, including actions to be taken to ensure targets are achieved. Actions, in this case, refer to methods and practices to be adopted and applied. These results are then followed up at a frequency that depends on the ambitions of the unit, but ultimately this is monitored by head office at least once a year. The reason is partly to be able to identify the machine centres that have made the largest relative improvement in relation to last year and in relation to plan. Those who "win" are awarded, at a dinner held somewhere in a European capital, to which three (i.e. including two runners-up) machine teams per machine are invited. The dinner is attended by top management, who hand out prizes. Award ceremonies are also held in certain regions as well, and in some case even at plants.

Apart from awards, Eurobest performance is not a formal metric for units. Line units are measured using a few items, closely linked to financial performance. This does not, of course, stop MDs and GMs, and even the CEO, from using Eurobest metrics in the overall assessment of performance and in the dialogue with subordinates.

The performance of each machine centre is available for anybody to view, on a month-by-month basis, on the group intranet. The idea of benchmarking, i.e. using the measurements to track benchmarks in order to be able to study them and/or exchange knowledge with them, is part of the core of the programme. The other part is the actual knowledge sharing.

Knowledge Sharing

Knowledge is shared in a variety of ways, including interaction, cooperation, training and the distribution of texts on methods and practices that have been successful elsewhere. A number of things can trigger the ambition to absorb knowledge. Within the Eurobest programme, one obvious trigger is poor performance, either in relation to comparable units or in relation to set plans and targets. Another trigger in its own right is the regular events that head office initiates.

Interaction can, for instance, take the form of visiting one or more successful plants for a period of time. Some plants have used this opportunity, and sent one of their own machine experts to visit peers at other plants for a couple of weeks spread out over a long period. In other cases, plants invite representatives or experts from other plants to come to visit and help work out problems or under-achievements. Another aspect of interaction refers to working together with corporate experts, for instance members of the Manufacturing department at the head office. This force spends part of its time leading or taking part in specific, technical projects in local or regional units. Plants can also draw on resources at regional levels.

Collaboration refers to situations whereby plants actually hire or exchange, with some permanency, key staff from other plants, or run joint development projects over a long time period. This happens with some regularity, and in some regions, formal experts are appointed for each machine category to make sure that new methods are understood and applied and machines are optimized.

Training is a third, obvious, way of sharing knowledge. SCAP provides courses for all types of staff. "Prospect employees" or "high potentials" take part in a one-year (part time) course on technical development training, including education in methods and technologies using a broad approach. Students could number staff throughout the network, for instance machine operators and even GMs. Other than that, specific courses centred upon individual machine types are also offered. Here, SCAP may cooperate with machine suppliers or other external organizations, e.g. industry trade organizations and technical education institutes. Any kind of machine worker can be invited to take part in this type of training. The extent to which they actually get a chance to do this depends on the local GM; being fully-fledged profit centres, they have to carry all the educational costs, and spending on education is not mandatory.

Perhaps the key means by which SCAP tries to spread knowledge is through the distribution of texts about production routines or about technical devices that could help improve certain production tasks. As discussed earlier, the character of the texts varies, from very explicit and detailed advice, tips, on how to improve certain tasks, to more abstract descriptions of work-practice "philosophies". These are available, physically, at head office, in files and folders and books etc, and they are updated and distributed to plants. New or revised methods are distributed regularly. The documents are also accessible via the intranet in a handy format. The problem is that not all people have access to computers or the basic skills required to run a computer or browse the net. Furthermore, again because of the cost issue, local plants may not even have computers for the production corps to use. In a general sense, any plant or individual that is interested in finding out more can do so, either by searching the intranet or by requesting material from his or her subordinates. However, someone who cannot operate a computer and has a subordinate who will not let him or her spend time reading the books will have a problem taking in new knowledge. Thus, it takes a willing and computer-literate employee and a supportive local management for knowledge to be shared. This "voluntarist" arrangement appears logical to a decentralized organization such as SCAP. We will discuss knowledge sharing in more detail in the following section.

So far we have discussed the history, the background, the character of the shared knowledge, programme organization and knowledge-sharing approaches. However, a key question is, of course, whether this knowledge-sharing arrangement has had any effect on the organization and the local units, and, if so, why.

Eurobest and Performance

There are many ways to define and analyse "effects" on performance. Of course, SCAP has made its own assessments over the years, but they have not been very detailed as regards the finer effects. Here, we have taken a causal-sequential approach, meaning we measure, stepwise, 1) whether there has been any sharing of knowledge, i.e. whether local units have improved the performance indicators being measured; 2) whether any learning has contributed to efficiency (or other proxies for profit); and 3) whether any efficiency improvements have contributed to profit. Subsequent to the quantitative assessment, we conducted qualitative case studies at six plants in order to work out *why* different types of plants achieve certain effects highlighted in the quantitative study.

The magnitude of machine types means we will be focusing the discussion below on corrugating machines. All machine types have been studied through the logic just described above, and the results replicate those found for corrugators, only with less statistical clarity. There are few "significances" connected with converting machines, even though the statistical patterns are similar to those of corrugators. This is because some of them are short in supply at SCAP (one particular machine only exists at five plants), but also because each converting machine at a plant plays a more insignificant role, being one of several options – most plants have between eight and 15 converting machines with overlapping and partly identical capabilities. On the other hand, corrugators come in ones, unless a plant is in the process of changing machine. Moreover, any box has to pass the corrugator, while this is not the case for a given converting machine.

Quantitative Assessments

This section is divided into three parts, including descriptive statistics, correlation studies, interpretations and process sequences.

Knowledge Sharing – Descriptive Statistics The first question, whether transfer had occurred, was operationalised as regards whether the measured production performance had been improved. Figures 4.2 and 4.3 indicate that there were improvements, both in machine speed and productivity. They also show the differences between plants that were at SCAP in 1996, and those that were acquired during the process. "Average, Old plants" refers to the average annual machine speed at 32 plants already in SCAP at the start of the programme in 1997. "Average, Acquired plants", refers to 6 plants that were part of a number of acquisitions made in 1998 and 1999. Overall, older plants improved machine speed by 16% between 1996 and 2001, while acquirees managed to increase machine speed by 7.5% between 1999 and 2001. In terms of labour hours per unit of output, older plants increased their productivity by 16%. Acquired plants managed a 2% reduction. Figure 4.4 also shows that waste levels have been reduced between 1996 – and 2001.

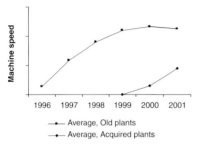

Figure 4.1. Machine speed evolution (y axis not crossed at zero)

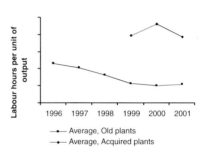

Figure 4.2. Productivity evolution (y axis not crossed at zero)

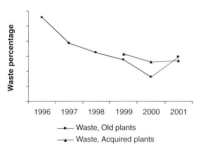

Figure 4.3. Machine speed evolution (y axis not crossed at zero

These descriptive statistics indicate that some progress had been made in the three areas targeted for improvement, as a consequence of the knowledge transfer programme (the same patterns were also apparent for converting machines). If we allow performance metrics like this to be indicative of learning (see for instance Epple et al., 1991), we can argue that knowledge sharing or transfer, learning, has taken place. It is also noteworthy that veteran SCAP plants have been highly successful in relation to competitors, such as those that were acquired during the process. In terms of machine speed, acquirees were principally three years behind old SCAP plants. The gap is even higher in productivity, but smaller for waste performance. In fact, in 2001, the acquired plants outperform the older ones. It is also noteworthy that there seems to be a limit to the improvement. All three measures indicate a decreasing rate of learning for plants involved in the exercise longer.

Knowledge Sharing and Financial Performance. What, then, are the implications for financial performance? The correlations between the manufacturing performance indicators and profit and loss data are exhibited in Table 4.1, which only includes data from 2001. The findings are more or less identical for each year between 1997 and 2001 and for the entire period.

The correlations show some important features. Looking at the independent variables, it turns out that machine speed seems to impact costs. A higher machine speed correlates negatively with raw material costs, labour costs and, logically, with the total cost. Maintaining machine speed reduces machine downtime and increases output at lower cost. The same tendency is true for direct productivity, only not as statistically strong. This implies that the better the direct productivity (number of staff at the machine in relation to output), the lower the overall labour costs (including all staff at a plant), material costs and total costs per unit of output.

But none of these variables are associated with margin, implying that there is no connection between machine speed or direct productivity and profit. As it turns out, this is because cost reductions are offset by price reductions. The correlations indicate that high speed and productivity are also associated with lower price levels, hence no correlation with margin. Waste levels, however, seem to have a different kind of impact on performance. Low waste levels are strongly correlated with margin. There is no correlation between machine speed or direct productivity and waste performance.

Table 4.1. Simple correlations, significance. Absolute levels

	WASTE	SPEED	DIRPROD	MARGIN	PRICE	TOTCOST	RAWMTRL
SPEED	-0,119						
DIRPROD	0,129	-0,683 ***					
MARGIN	-0,573 ***	0,063	0,040				
PRICE	0,112	-0,644 ***	0,461 **	0,059			
TOTCOST	0,290	-0,649 ***	0,438 **	-0,287	0,938 ***		
RAWMTRL	0,076	-0,568 ***	0,361 *	-0,157	0,801 **	0,827 ***	
LABOUR	0,562 **	-0,534 ***	0,417 **	-0,333 *	0,716 **	0,798 ***	0,402 *

*N=38. * Significant on 0.05 level. ** 0.01 level. *** 0.001 level.*

To check on the evolution longitudinally over the entire time span, we studied the correlations between the relative changes, 2001 vis-à-vis 1996, in terms of speed, direct productivity and waste levels on the one hand, as well as relative changes in price, total costs, raw material costs, labour costs (the latter four adjusted for currency rates and inflation) and margin, also in terms of relative changes between 1996 and 2001 (see Table 4.2). That comparison supported, albeit not with a strong statistical significance, the propositions made regarding the relationship between speed, direct productivity and waste improvements and implications regarding costs, prices and margins. These findings seem to signal that, while there might be successful knowledge transfer, this does not necessarily mean that performance is improved. For instance, as indicated by the study of the effects of speed increases, costs may well go down, but prices may decrease as well, entailing there is no effect on margin.

Table 4.2. Selected simple correlations, significance. Relative levels

	WASTE	SPEED	DIRPROD
MARGIN	0,423 *	0,283	0,318
PRICE	-0,147	-0,068	-0,202
TOTCOST	-0,263	-0,137	-0,262
RAWMTRL	-0,273	-0,223	-0,265
LABOUR	-0,228	-0,217	-0,341

*N=28. * Significant on 0.05 level. ** 0.01 level.*

One can study financial impact in other ways than regression analysis, for instance by analyzing the trend for certain financial performance indicators. One such measurement is the Labour cost to Sales ratio, which improved relatively strongly between 1996 and 2001. The average Labour cost per produced unit of output increased slightly, but was below inflation levels for the EU countries. Raw material costs increased due to higher paper prices, further raising prices for customers. However, nothing significant happened to the division's margin during this time period. Which, in a sense, confirms the pattern that became visible in the regression analyses. In addition, a range of factors influence the Profit & Loss statement, not just the results of the Eurobest programme.

Interpretations. In principal, two groups of explanations or interpretations of the relationship between Eurobest performance and financial performance can be made on the basis of the statistics. One focuses on internal factors while the other assumes that causalities are reversed and that external factors drive performance development.

Assuming causality in the sequence discussed, i.e. that Eurobest performance drives costs down, is perhaps not radical. What is more surprising is that reduced costs then appear to drive prices down, and there are two potential *plant-internal* factors that could be in play. We received evidence of both in the qualitative study (see below). One explanation could be that plants striving to improve Eurobest performance narrow their product mix, i.e. the range of box products offered. Or, plants may simply reduce the quality of their products, for instance by reducing the range of colours and other tasks that potentially trigger machine downtime. Furthermore, in their quest to run machines faster, plants may encounter problems with the physical quality of boxes, i.e. damaged goods and so on. However, a second explanation could simply be that the sales force reduces prices, incrementally, as it becomes aware of cost savings achieved in production. A salesperson, whose performance is measured in sales volumes, for instance, will be tempted to sell a larger volume at a slightly lower price. He or she can do this to a certain extent without jeopardizing profit, but if done extensively, profit may actually decline. This way, cost benefits accruing from knowledge sharing (and other) efforts are handed over to, and appropriated by, customers.

A second category of explanation is simply that causalities are reversed, meaning that it is price reductions, generated by markets where supply capacity is in abundance and where customers rigorously negotiate and buy on prices, that trigger cost-cutting exercises. These, in turn, might direct plants to emphasize their efforts to improve their Eurobest, among other things. Hence, price reductions stimulate Eurobest efforts which in turn reduce costs. This *plant-external* explanation holds true for many plants on more competitive markets (as indicated earlier, there is a difference in competition intensity across the markets which SCAP are active on).

Both the internal and external explanations for the possible link between Eurobest and financial performance can be in play. However, generally, for a given plant, the character of the link is explained by only one of the two explanations. At some plants studied in depth, respondents signalled, quite correctly, that the dividing line is unclear between a negotiation situation where a salesman is being "soft" and is cutting prices and one where the customer is being strong and fierce regarding price reductions.

Knowledge Sharing and Performance: Sequences

Regardless of the factors, the statistics indicate that the sequence of events leading up to financially successful knowledge sharing faces a set of organizational challenges:

1. *Transfer of knowledge.* As measured here, it was evident that SCAP, on a corporate level, was successful in improving its average waste performance, machine speed and direct productivity. However, not *all* units were successful in absorbing and implementing new methods. So, an initial issue to deal with concerns the management of the sharing *per se.*

2. *Cost or Price improvements.* Overall, in cases where production performance was improved (sharing had occurred), there was an improvement in certain cost items. However, not all plants were successful in this respect. Thus a second managerial issue concerns the conversion of successful sharing, learning, into improved cost items or product quality (manifest in increased prices or sales volume).

3. *Profit improvements.* However, as indicated by the statistical findings, even if individual profit proxies such as labour cost per unit of output are improved, this does not necessarily mean that the margin will improve. This implies that a third managerial issue concerns the conversion of individual cost or price improvements into profit.

So, as the statistics have implied that knowledge transfer is not automatically "good", the factors that influence this process needed to be understood, hence the six onsite case studies.

Onsite Case Studies

Given the different problems associated with various phases of the sequence between knowledge and profit discussed above, six plants were singled out for case studies. As it happened, the plants differed from each other in terms of success in the knowledge-sharing programme. Plants 1 and 2 did not improve their production performance at all throughout the period. Plant 3 did improve, but failed to convert into costs or sales improvements. Plant 4 improved some costs, but not its profit margin. Plants 5 and 6 actually managed to improve margins.

As derived empirically from plant case studies, eight factors appear to make a difference regarding success and failure when transferring knowledge and converting it into financial performance: 1) the local perception of Eurobest, 2) aspirations and strategic ambitions, 3) the view of internal competition, 4) the view of the nature of the knowledge being transferred, 5) programme management and control, 6) local communication, 7) the ability to manage the strategic implications of learning, and 8) corporate control mechanisms. The eight factors can be attributed to the three different phases in the following manner: Factors 1-6 appear to be valid for plants that do not even succeed in improving their production performance indicators, i.e. plants which cannot argue that they have absorbed and applied new knowledge and routines. Factors 2 and 8 are characteristics of plants that are unable to convert knowledge into improved costs or prices, while factors 7 and 8 appear to be linked with plants that absorb and apply knowledge successfully and make cost improvements, but fail to make a profit because prices are cut as well. The factors will be discussed in accordance with each of the three sequence phases.

Managing Knowledge Sharing

The first issue, making sure that knowledge is transferred and converted into improved production performance, appeared to be affected by factors 1 to 6. Plants 1 and 2, which failed, indicated difficulties in these areas, while the other plants did not.

For instance, the local perception of Eurobest varied. Out of the ten respondents, none expressed a positive attitude to the programme, or argued that it had, or could have, a positive impact. Representatives claimed that the transfer programme; "does not sufficiently address the different local circumstances" (general manager), that it has been "misunderstood and misused", and that "it is merely a section of the annual productivity budget" (production manager). One manager stated; "we are not ready for it yet, but it fits our volume strategy well". Emphasizing the slightly alienated perception of the programme, one respondent made it known that; "the worker of the year approach doesn't fit our culture". In contrast, the successful plants indicated a slightly different perception. They focused on the knowledge provided by the programme, and the possibilities of the benchmarking arrangement. "It is a knowledge base that has helped us survive over these years" (general manager). "It is a library of methods" (production manager). "The concept of sharing knowledge is very good, and we also try to use it when communicating with our customers" (sales manager). Respondents also indicate that the programme has become integrated into day-to-day routines. "Generally, the initial buzz is gone. It is institutionalized now. It is not just a tool, it is a way of life" (production manager). "It has helped us develop a team spirit, it is in the minds of the workforce" (operator).

The second factor, referring to local aspirations and strategic ambitions, also appears to differ from plant to plant. As described by one general manager:

> We have other priorities here at the moment, like developing our customer base. The advice is important, but obviously I am not familiar with it. I don't think we need that production knowledge today.

Another general manager said; "We don't have time. We are not active enough, definitely not." A supervisor: "Whenever we try to change things here, there are obstacles prolonging implementation. Things simply die, and so does motivation". "I don't know of anybody who has been trained in how to use the intranet" (supervisor). Representatives of the more successful plants give a slightly different picture. "Even with the knowledge and experience that I have, I sometimes find radical solutions in the programme. It surprises you, and you can never get too much" (production manager). "I am deeply involved in working on assimilating new methods" (general manager). "We now have screens by each of the machines, where the intranet can be accessed. Each team also has formal gatherings at which they exchange knowledge".

A third factor refers to internal competition. Because the programme included databases including both methods and performance results, and because there were annual awards, a sense of competition emerged. This existed previously as well, locally, between shifts at the plants. The weaker plants did not see competition as an incentive, partly because they were too far from being the best in the corporation at the outset. "Playing in Division Three you don't really think about the Premier League". "Many of our guys have given up competing" (production manager), partly because they claim to have interests outside winning competitions: "We're not driven by being best, we have to produce good results, period" (general manager). "There is always someone somewhere with better opportunities and knowledge than us" (supervisor). On the positive side, an operator stated that;

> Competition is good in the sense that it makes people here want to avoid being the worst

More successful plants appear to thrive on internal competition. "The people's perception of competition is important, and here it is not so strong that it brings negative effects" (general manager). "The transfer programme means we can now compete on a constructive basis across the company" (supervisor). However, plant-internal competition is still important: "We compete with ourselves in relation to last year and we compete between shifts" (supervisor). "We have made great use of the internal competition, between shifts and so on" (general manager). Underlining the ease with which certain units approach competition, one worker at a plant located in the former East Germany said:

> In Eastern Germany we are used to socialistic competition. We are used to being benchmarked and compared, and to setting targets and making plans. It is not new to us, we did it in the old days as well.

The fourth organizational issue, referring to the view of the nature of the shared knowledge, shows some interesting differences. Part of the purpose of the transfer programme is to articulate, make explicit, knowledge about certain work routines. However, it appears that less successful plants perceive production knowledge as more tacit and difficult to articulate, than do more successful plants – they do not trust the articulated knowledge to be the only means of deciding work routines. "There is a large proportion of tacit knowledge that cannot be taught or transferred" (supervisor). "There are many variables, each machine has its own quirky bits" (operator). "We have a complex process that we cannot write down. There are many parameters to think of. We once tried to list all the parameters to consider but it is impossible" (general manager). Successful plants take a different view. "There is a certain tacit component but I want to break it down." (production manager).

> We wrongly believe it to be a form of art rather than bring it closer to science. Some of it is art but we overplay that (production manager).

"Quite a lot could be written down. We can improve by writing things down" (supervisor). Successful plants also address motivational factors. "Motivation drives learning here" (operator). "There is a tacit component, and then you need motivation to be able to take it in" (production manager).

The routines for programme management and control, a fifth factor, also differed between successful plants and those less so. The initial idea of Eurobest management was that, at minimum, plants should set one-year plans for each machine outlining waste, speed and productivity targets, then monitoring and feeding back progress with some regularity. Their ambition was that production managers should be involved in the local assessments, if not the general manager. The intention was also that local plants should have creative meetings and forums for discussing methods and ways to proceed. The less successful plants did do less, in this respect, than the others. "I am involved in the planning exercise only, once a year. I never discuss these figures explicitly with my boss but we do discuss productivity quarterly" (general manager). "We don't display performance figures on the notice board nowadays" (production manager). "I have meetings with key operators for an hour every three weeks where we might cover it" (production manager). "I look at the figures quarterly and focus on highlights. I go through them with the production manager then, too" (general manager). "We don't really discuss the figures explicitly, we used to but not anymore. The programme is on the backburner" (supervisor). Successful plants have managed it differently. "I follow it up on a daily basis and have meetings with key staff three times a week, when we discuss it. On a monthly basis, I go through it with all the staff" (production manager).

> I communicate on a daily basis with operators and they really react to it. I have daily meetings about downtime, overproduction and so on. The planning exercise is dealt with rigorously with shift leaders and the teams. We follow it up on a monthly basis, and we have broken down annual targets into quarterly ones to achieve better control (production manager).

"On the shifts, we talk about it when new data is displayed. All workers know about the performance" (operator). "I interact with operators on a daily basis" (general manager).

A sixth factor refers to the plant-internal communication of results and implications. It appears that the less successful plants sense the urge to improve the communication of what is being done and achieved in production to other stakeholders. Improvements in activities other than production appear to be perceived as potentially in conflict with productivity improvements. "Sometimes, the production figures are interpreted by people who do not have the whole picture" (production manager). "There is too much focus on productivity, you cannot forget the market side" (general manager). "We must communicate better with Sales". "We need to communicate better with customers" (sales manager). "We need to communicate better between plants" (supervisor). Production is also seen as lacking an understanding of the programme implications. "We must communicate better with the production people, they don't understand this very well here. They must understand that this is something that makes things easier for them" (supervisor). Communication is less of an issue at the more successful units. No one suggests that communication is a problem. "I am involved on a monthly basis, or if there is an *ad hoc* debate about something between sales and production" (sales manager). "We are informed about our production performance and, if it suits our purposes, we will make it known one way or another to our customers" (sales manager).

Converting Knowledge

Plant 3, successful in taking on new knowledge, actually failed to convert it into cost or sales improvements. Relating to the eight overarching managerial factors, aspirations and strategic ambitions, incentives and corporate control mechanisms seem to explain a large proportion of the plant differences.

In relation to aspirations and strategic ambitions, one issue at Plant 3 is that it lacks the incentive provided by a competitive market. Its profit levels have always (for decades) been high, albeit declining due to recent market entries and price cuts. Sales volume has declined as well. The plant's strategy has not been based on low prices and low costs, but on a higher degree of differentiation. "I try to make sure that we sell by helping our customers to serve their customers, rather than just offering a low price. But the market is changing and prices and margins are going down, so the limbo metaphor is clear. We need to improve costs in the near future, and we will have to do this without jeopardizing quality. If there is a price reduction, it is down to market conditions, not our quality. There is no relationship between production performance and quality". "It is not as competitive here as elsewhere, but the growing low-frills segment is driving price averages down. And we are not the best at that." (sales manager). "Our variable costs are high, and we are worse than some" (general manager). "The market change has forced us to look at business we are not so good at doing, in order to fill capacity" (production manager). Plant 3 has been relatively slow in cost reductions, e.g. material costs, rationalizations, and job redundancies, to cut labour costs.

> We have made a few people redundant over the years, but it has been through natural recession, which keeps the morale up. The market has been a bit difficult here over the last three years due to the declining economy. And people are aware that we will have to make changes to the cost base, but that we will do it in a natural way. They mustn't feel threatened, because then we will have morale problems. But if we don't improve, our competitors will take our jobs away (general manager).

Plants that did convert production performance into financial improvements were more focused on making the necessary changes. One general manager said; "we were in a position where we had to cause redundancies. There was no other way we could have survived. It is not nice. And we also had to make a lot of changes to our working capital base, cutting stock and so on".

As long as the market could be perceived as calm, there was no immediate hurry for plant 3 to cut its costs and improve its margin further. With high margin levels, much higher than most of its sister plants within the corporation, the incentives to work harder were less significant. One respondent claimed; "yes, the thermostat has been switched off here for years". Corporate head office, which controls business units mainly via one or two financial targets in relation to budget, felt no urge to alter or extend target variables, as long as the units delivered according to budget. There was no measurement of whether improved production performance was actually linked to cost reductions.

Improving Profit Margins

The third and final concern is being able to ensure that improvements in costs (or sales) are not offset by other costs, or by declining prices. Plant 4 was successful in keeping labour and other costs down, but it also experienced declining price levels. The ability to manage the strategic implications of learning, as well as corporate control mechanisms, is a factor explaining some of the differences between successful and unsuccessful plants.

While Plant 4 succeeded well in production performance and cost reductions, it also suffered from declining price levels. Three or four different explanations were offered by respondents. One explanation was that increased production performance not only reduced costs but also prices through reduced customer-perceived quality. Less physical and service quality, and a narrower product scope, could explain the lower price levels. However, the respondents claim that this is not the case at their plant, and they view cost and quality as completely independent of each other. "In fact, if anything, cost reduction and quality improvements are positively related" (production manager). "There is no connection with price" (sales manager). A second explanation could be that sales people "give away" cost cuts to customers through lowered prices. "If there is a fight on the market, you might give things away" (general manager).

> We give some things away. There is no connection at all between our production efficiency and bad quality. If the sales guys understand there is a cost reduction in anything, it is already in their heads and they start to talk about it and will give it away (sales manager).

For this particular plant, the market prices did not decline, indicating that price reductions were caused by "giveaways". "If there is a fight on the market, you might use a part of your cost savings to cut prices. But it has to be controlled within the strategy framework" (sales manager). Another potential explanation could be the leakage of knowledge to competitors, or that competitors, one way or another, are able to replicate the cost cuts. Although it is difficult to assess due to data access issues, SCAP respondents claim they know of no migration of personnel. Furthermore, they had not displayed the methods or performance information to outsiders such as consultants, even if there are obvious risks that certain customers inform competitors. "We made the same mistake some years ago, when we started to go public and give away productivity gains to selected customers" (sales manager).

The explanatory factors just presented could partly be described as an inability to manage the strategy implications of learning. The two plants that did not offset cost reductions saw the programme as part of the strategy, and used it to improve their product market performance. "Price implications is not an issue here. It could be both ways. But I don't see a conflict between the transfer programme and sales activities. That's why the whole plant has to work as one team, which we have taken care of by making sure that both sales and production have the same, interdependent objectives" (general manager). "We decide on quality first, and then we optimize speed and all the other stuff" (sales manager). "Price management is prioritized here, even if low-cost is our main priority" (sales manager). "We have grown our volume by twenty percent since 1996, and kept our price levels up while cutting over-all costs by ten percent. That would not have been possible without Eurobest" (general manager).

One factor that could stimulate the ability to deal with the strategic implications lies in the corporate control mechanisms. Extensions of the performance targets to include metrics comparing production improvements with profit improvements would have been welcome, according to some respondents. One general manager, of a plant successful in terms of profitability, said: "As some plants are not really forced to cut costs and so on, it could be a point. Some may have had too good a life. I can see some additional metrics being added to the measurements, as weights in the overall assessment of plants and managers". In the absence of such mechanisms, plant management uses its own incentives. "We have internal awards both for successful production people and sales people who manage to increase sales. Organizationally, sales and production have to be coordinated. Neither can benefit at the expense of the other, it is logically impossible. The coordination is absolutely core to the strategy" (sales manager).

Concluding Remarks

Many things could be said about knowledge sharing based on the SCAP case. One is that knowledge management can be a very basic, down-to-earth venture, with a pragmatist orientation. Knowledge is shared and transferred in many social settings, not just businesses that we normally link with "knowledge intensity", such as R&D, consulting and information technology. Straightforward blue-collar production type work can also be subject to formalized learning, albeit under slightly different forms, depending on the character of the knowledge and the business requirements. And of course, any human activity requires some sort of knowledge, applied consciously or subconsciously. In this particular setting, one interesting observation is the sport-like character that knowledge sharing can assume. Set up as a benchmarking exercise, competition becomes important. This is evident in the heavy use of sporting metaphors among workers. "Division one", "Champions League", "team spirit", "coaching", "award ceremonies" and "speed" are frequent concepts that can be linked to sport, particularly football. A third observation links back to the quote in the text made by a worker from the old Eastern Europe, about being used to planning and being measured. The Eurobest programme was imported from a US alliance partner and can be seen as integral to an American style of management, including benchmarking and a "worker-of-the-month approach". Perhaps surprisingly, this style of management appears to fit the view of workers from the old communist countries in Eastern Europe. Somewhere in between, we find the Western European worker, who is sceptical about being measured and put on a pedestal and awarded for having done what he or she is paid to do. Whether or not this is because the Western European working class requires independence in relation to state and corporation is a question requiring analysis outside the scope of this book.

Apart from the above observations, the interesting contributions from the SCAP case can be discussed on the basis of the statement that *knowledge is contextual.* One such remark connects with the view of the dependent variable in much research on knowledge sharing and transfer. Much of the research is concerned with transferring and sharing, and the factors that facilitate or hamper this – not whether sharing is beneficial and what it might additionally require to be beneficial. The data provided in the Eurobest case enabled a wider comparison with the financial results and, as discussed, it is not a given that learning effects financial performance. In order to facilitate the conversion and capitalization of learning, managerial and organizational efforts have to be applied.

Another aspect, evident in the plant case studies made here, is the importance of motivation and other incentives. The strong focus on motivational aspects is, perhaps, triggered by our focus, not just on learning, but also the wider implication regarding financial performance. If one is only interested in whether and how transfer and sharing initiatives stimulate knowledge transfer and sharing, it may well be in order to focus more on the cognitive factors. But as discussed here, when it comes to extending efforts to making organizational changes and reducing costs and managing prices, motivation becomes increasingly important. That is not addressed extensively in the knowledge-sharing literature, and may well be suitable in research other than on strategy. But, in a practical and contextual field such as strategy and strategic management, we cannot see how these issues can be effectively removed from the research agenda.

As previously mentioned, motivation was key in the Eurobest programme. The eight distinguishing factors discussed all concern motivational, noncognitive issues. This is a potentially uncontroversial proposition, but earlier knowledge transfer research has actually not addressed it as being particularly important. Those who have studied it have had mixed results in terms of the role of motivation. Here, it does become important, partly because we have "extended" the dependent variable, but partly also because we wish to emphasize that knowledge is a far "larger" phenomenon than, say, "data". As we discussed in the previous chapter, not only is knowledge contextual, it is also based on cognition and on beliefs and norms and values about how to perceive and do things. Of course, when it comes to sharing knowledge, i.e. attempting to learn, one's view of one's work may capsize, which is potentially distressing. With this broader view of knowledge and knowledge sharing, as subject to beliefs and norms and values, a feature such as motivation becomes completely logical – people are not programmed robots.

In addition to the suggestion that the dependent variable be extended and the conclusion that motivation is more important than theory might assume, there are some observations that associate directly with existing theory. One such thing is the role of the organizational context, including control mechanisms and incentives. Furthermore, the popular dichotomy between tacit and explicit knowledge, for instance, surfaces in this study too. Nothing in this study suggests that we can overlook the distinction between these two types of knowledge; in fact, as is made evident, much of the knowledge and information regarding methods and so forth discussed here is tacit in nature. Furthermore, no findings have signalled that it is easy to codify and transfer tacit knowledge. However, the findings do stress that knowledge may not be permanently tacit, and that some effort can help to turn "tacit" knowledge into workable and less tacit knowledge. Stating that a piece of information is tacit could partly be a way of obscuring the fact that one does not have the time or energy to try to codify, write down and sharing knowledge – hence motivation and prioritization are again part of the picture. SCAP will probably not be able to transfer methods, let alone transfer performance, completely across its network – but they want to try. And this circumstance has actually helped some plants turn red figures into black ones, to fend off increased industry competition, and others to improve performance, despite the fact that many plants cannot claim to have done much or benefited from the venture.

Chapter 5

Knowledge Sharing at AstraZeneca

Introduction

This chapter presents a study of knowledge-sharing activities at a pharmaceutical company, AstraZeneca, an Anglo-Swedish company which merged in 1998. While the knowledge transferred at the paper company SCA, presented in the previous chapter, was heavily dependent on the ability to code and decode operational knowledge aimed at more effective production activities, the knowledge being shared at AstraZeneca is of a more tacit nature. The pharmaceutical industry is subject to detailed regulations and work practices are thus developed on the basis of the recommendations and instructions of various authorities. As a consequence, most of the day-to-day practices are determined by so-called standard operations procedures (SOPs). Every new co-worker at AstraZeneca R&D is trained to work in accordance with the various SOPs, covering most domains of the new drug development process. But even though the SOPs are useful guidelines for day-to-day operations, they are unable to cover all aspects of work. What is not fully covered by the SOPs is what we refer to as experienced-based learning or tacit knowledge, i.e. not so extensive but important know-how regarding how day-to-day work functions reading between the lines. In Chapter One, we referred to what Garfinkel (1967) called the *etcetera principle*. This principle states that all practices are more detailed, context-dependent, and emergent than a written or codified account of such practices will ever be able to capture. There is always a residual category — the "etcetera" — that is outside of what can be formulated by any instruction. The experiences and know-how denoted by the residual category of the "etcetera" is what successful knowledge-sharing practices may be able to capture. Among knowledge management theorists, the notion of tacit knowledge is used as a general category denoting what cannot be formulated in written documents and speech. In this chapter, the notion of tacit knowledge is one single theoretical construct aimed at covering the knowledge that remains after everything else has been codified.

Near and Far Transfer of Knowledge

In their analysis of competencies in the pharmaceutical industry, Henderson and Cockburn (1994) distinguish between *component competence* and *architectural competence*. The former denotes the "the local abilities and knowledge that are fundamental to day-today problem solving" while the latter is "the ability to make use of these component competencies — to integrate them effectively and to develop fresh component competencies as they are required" (Henderson & Cockburn, 1994: 65). In the first place, companies need to have core competencies they can exploit, for instance, expertise in the relevant areas of discovery and new drug development in the pharmaceutical industry. Secondly, companies also need integrative mechanisms enabling the productive use of the component competencies — architectural competencies. Nancy Dixon (2000) writes: "Near transfer is applicable when a team has learned something from its experience that the organization would like to replicate in other teams that are doing very similar work. I call this Near Transfer not because of the geography involved but because of the similarity between the source team and the receiving team" (Dixon, 2000: 54). Dixon distinguishes between near and far transfer and writes of what she calls Far Transfer:

> Far Transfer is applicable when a team has learned something from its experience that the organization would like to make available to other teams that are doing similar work. If I stopped there, the description would sound no different than Near Transfer. There are, however, two important additional criteria, and the first relates to the nature of the task. The task that is subject to Far Transfer is nonroutine whereas the task in Near Transfer is routine ... The second significant difference between Near Transfer and Far Transfer is that Far Transfer is applicable when the knowledge that the source team has gained is largely tacit rather than explicit (Dixon, 2000: 80)

Dixon's two categories are useful because they distinguish between the sharing of routine-based and the sharing of non-routine knowledge. The notion of routine is however a problematic concept to employ when distinguishing between near and far transfer. Feldman and Rafaeli (2002), Feldman (2000) and Pentland and Rueter (1994) have suggested that routines are dynamic scripts that enable a broad variety of activities to be captured by the same routine. Therefore, there are no routines in terms of being static standard operation procedures, instead there are continuously changing practices that are derived from the same script (see also Callon, 2002). According to Dixon (2000), the Far Transfer concept is also characterized by its emphasis on tacit knowledge. Since tacit knowledge is a complex and highly elusive construct, we would like to suggest that tacit knowledge is also involved in Near Transfer. There are always tacit components involved in knowledge-based activities (Tsoukas, 1996: 14). In consequence, we would like to stress "geography" (in its broadest sense) as one of the distinguishing qualities between Near and Far Transfer. Near Transfer denotes knowledge sharing within a rather homogeneous environment while Far Transfer deals with knowledge sharing between more heterogeneous activities. In what follows, we will present knowledge sharing at AstraZeneca. The Near Transfer of knowledge here is the sharing of know-how and experiences between clinical study teams, i.e. an environment characterized by rather standardized processes, activities and events. The Far Transfer activities deal with the sharing of knowledge between different therapeutic areas (e.g. cardiovascular or cancer medicine) and between different project management levels in new drug development projects. While both transfers are set at the same pharmaceutical company, there is a difference, in terms of routinization, between the different decision-making processes. In the clinical study teams, the work was to a greater extent routine-based than the work done on the higher project management levels. In consequence of this, the knowledge shared needed less translation and contextualisation in between study teams than on the higher project levels. Thus, Dixon's dichotomization can help make sense out of the different practices of knowledge sharing at AstraZeneca.

The Pharmaceutical Industry

One of the trends in the pharmaceutical industry is expansion and consolidation. For the last five years, mergers, acquisitions or alliances have consolidated many pharmaceutical companies. Novartis, GlaxoSmithKline, and AstraZeneca are some examples of this recent restructuring of the industry. One of the reasons for such consolidation within the industry could be the need to manage substantial R&D budgets more effectively. For instance, in 2000, Pfizer had an R&D budget in excess of USD 5 billion and hosted an R&D organisation of more than 12,000 researchers (The Economist, 2000). The pharmaceutical industry is, thus, investing heavily in R&D. For instance, Jones (2000: 342) reports: "It is calculated that two companies, GlaxoSmith-

Kline and AstraZeneca now account for more than 25% of all business expenditure on R&D in the U.K.". R&D investment in the pharmaceutical industry in relation to other industries is illustrated in table 5.1.

Table 5.1. International R&D intensities (1998) (%).
Adapted from Jones (2000: 348)

Sectors	UK	International
Pharmaceuticals	15.0	13.5
Software/IT	4.9	13.6
Chemicals	1.7	6.1
Electronics	3.2	5.3
Engineering	1.6	3.3

Pisano (1997: 4) writes: "In many ways, the pharmaceutical industry is a classic high-tech industry: R&D intensity is high, product development is long, costly, and risky; and profitability depends critically on launching new products in timely fashion". To obtain optimum revenue, many large pharmaceutical companies are focusing more and more on products in the research pipeline which are expected to become blockbusters or "megabrands", i.e. a drug whose sales exceed USD 1 billion per annum. One reason for the focus on megabrands is the substantial costs involved in new drug development, caused by greater regulatory demands for documentation and extensive clinical trials. The tendency in the industry is thus to maintain a high focus on decreasing time to market and reducing bottlenecks in order to optimise the patent term of the product (Tranter, 2000). Another approach to making the drug discovery and development processes more effective is increasing the influence of technology on R&D programmes such as computer-aided drug design (CADD), combinatorial chemistry linked to high throughput screening (CC/HTS) and genomics (Horrobin, 2000). This entails that a great number of molecules can be tested. Thomke and Kuemmerle (2002) write: "Typically, for each successful drug that made it to the market, the firm began with roughly 10,000 starting compounds. Of these, only 1,000 would make it to the more extensive *in vitro* trials (i.e. outside a living organism in a setting such as a test tube), of which 20 would be tested even more extensively *in vivo* (i.e. in the body of a living organism such as a mouse) before 10 or fewer compounds made it to human trials" (Thomke and Kuemmerle, 2002: 622). However, such technical innovations are, by necessity, not regarded as something inherently positive. Many laboratory scientists are skeptical toward this "automatization" of work: "Field interviews revealed that traditional chemists felt threatened by the new technology [high throughput screening] that appeared to automate many of the tasks that they had so carefully learned and refined over many years" (Thomke and Kuemmerle, 2002: 631. See also Cardinal, 2001). The pharmaceutical industry has always been a knowledge-based industry and its profitability is based on its ability to create and exploit new scientific knowledge. The last decade has resulted in an unprecedented rate of information generation in almost every domain of science. This paves the way for many opportunities, but the challenge for the industry is to exploit scientific know-how and skills in a cost-effective and timely manner. One of the pronounced concerns or outcomes of these factors, in combination with large complex organizational structures and increasing demands for efficiency, decreased risk-taking during early research, is how to create a balance between creativity and economies of scale (The Economist, 2000).

The costliest part of the new drug development process is the clinical studies leading to regulatory approval. Koretz and Lee (1998: 53) writes that "the logistics and costs of these late stage trials can be daunting: one trial for a recently-approved drug involved 11,000 patients in 27 countries and 700 treatment centres ... This process is conducted under careful regulatory guidelines, covering everything from scientific and ethical standards to record keeping. The end product of this phase is an application for approval from regulatory agencies, such as the Food and Drug administration (FDA) in the USA." However, when able to provide the regulatory agencies with credible information leading to the registration of a new drug, substantial financial effects could be expected by the focal company, although only one out of ten products make it on to the market, and out of those reaching the market, only two out of three will break even. This makes the pharmaceutical industry a risky business. Roberts (1999) points out that "the profits earned within the pharmaceutical industry are consistently well above those earned in the next highest earning industry" (Roberts, 1999: 668). Koretz and Lee (1998) remark: "A modestly successful drug can easily have annual revenues of $200 millions and the 'blockbusters' will go even higher — Prozac sold $2.56 billion in 1997." In consequence, the ability to undertake quick, rule-governed, reasonably low-cost, and credible clinical studies is a major organizational capability and a source of sustainable competitive advantage in the pharmaceutical industry (Yeoh & Roth, 1999; Roberts, 1999). Since the entire industry is, as Koretz and Lee (1998) point out, under detailed scrutiny and subject to audits, the clinical testing process includes a number of different kinds of knowledge, know-how, skills, and experiences.

The pharmaceutical industry is heavily based on scientific knowledge in the various life sciences. Representatives of the industry take great pride in serving as an intermediate link between science and the market, speculative thinking and applied science. Several studies of such industries and health care organizations testify to scepticism among medical experts toward management in various forms. Scientists and clinicians maintain an anti-management position at times to reinforce their own role as beyond the trite matters of management. In a study of a health care organization, Newell (2001) found such willingness to keep managerial issues at arm's length. "Clinicians have regarded management as the other", Newell (2001: 601) writes. She continues: "Any clinician taking up a management position — even within the medical establishment — risks loss of respect and clinical visibility. Perceptions of the secondary status of managers are deep in a medical culture that has not esteemed management work" (Newell, 2001: 604). In a similar study of Britain's National Health Service, Parker quotes a General Manager:

> Many medical staff still see ... management as threatening. I think many see it as being irrelevant to their day-to-day jobs and I also see that a number of them think that even if it's not threatening it just isn't going to be of any help to them. (General Manager, National Health Service (NHS), UK, cited by Parker, 2000: 116)

The distance between management and scientific and clinical practice is maintained within the industry. In comparison to the sciences, management concerns have a relatively low status within the industry.

AstraZeneca

AstraZeneca is a provider of medicines in many therapeutic areas but the three largest are cancer, cardiovascular and gastrointestinal medicine. The R&D centres are located in Europe (in Sweden at Södertälje, Lund and Mölndal and in the UK at Charnwood and Alderly Park) and in the U.S., employing more than 12,000 R&D personnel. In 2002, its R&D budget exceeded USD 3 billion. Today, following the merger of two large pharmaceutical companies, AstraZeneca employs more than 58,000 co-workers worldwide. In the following sections, we will examine the use of a knowledge facilitation method using what Dixon (2000) calls near and far transfer. In order to understand the difference between near and far transfer, some basic understanding of AstraZeneca's organization is required. All drug development is organized by means of different therapeutic areas. One therapeutic area may be, for instance, cardiovascular medicine, i.e. medicine that treats heart and blood system diseases. Within each therapeutic area, there are a number of Global Project Teams (GPTs). These teams are responsible for a portfolio of projects within one therapeutic area. The Global Project Director (GPD) leads the GPT and is the strategic director of the team, while the Global Project Manager (GPM) is the true project manager, managing the more operational parts of the GPT. Reporting to the GPT are a number of satellite teams, e.g. the regulatory, marketing, pharmaceutical R&D and clinical development teams. During the later phases, the Clinical Development Team (CDT) is responsible for managing a programme of clinical studies within one indication in the therapeutic area. The Clinical Development Leader (CDL) leads the CDT. The CDT consists of a number of experts (medical, regulatory, marketing etc) as does the GPT, and has Clinical Study Teams (CSTs) reporting to the CDL. CSTs conduct specific studies wherein, for example, the requirements of the regulatory authorities are met or competitor comparisons are clinically evaluated. The CST is the lowest level of the project hierarchy and the most operational level of the project organization. Even though the model gives the impression of a project hierarchy, the different project sub-teams grow and diminish over time in a dynamic manner as the demand for that particular sub-team goes up or down. Figure 5.1 shows a model of the organization.

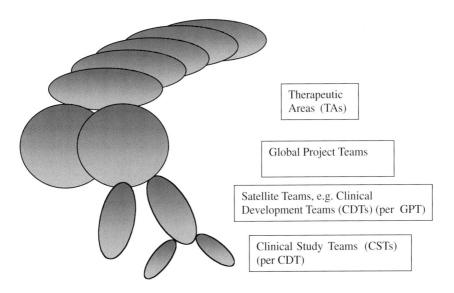

Figure 5.1. The project organization of AstraZeneca

The New Product Development Process

The research process of the modern pharmaceutical industry involves a large number of different scientific disciplines. The development of a pharmaceutical product can be generalised by dividing research into three major processes, (1) Discovery (2) Development, and (3) Product support and life-cycle management.

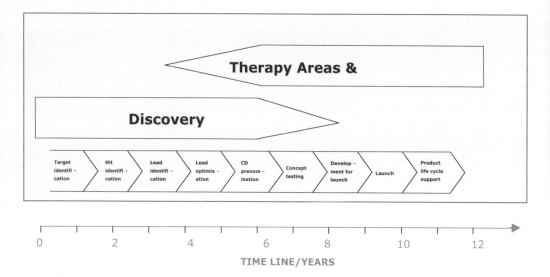

Figure 5.2. Overview of the drug research process

Discovery (Experimental medicine)

The primary objective for the Discovery or the pre-clinical organisation is to bring forward either ideas for disease relief modification of symptoms, or in the best case, a cure for a disease using a new chemical entity (NCE). The drug discovery process, Phase 0, begins by defining a disease area and a target to manipulate. This target should have the potential to alter the disease or its symptoms in the desired way. The target may, for example, be a receptor or an enzyme. The medicinal chemists synthesise substances that are tested in the relevant in vitro systems or biological models by biochemists and pharmacologists respectively (Lesko, Rowland, Peck & Blaschke, 2000). The aim is to establish a chemical structure to a biological activity relationship, which in a successful project leads to a candidate drug (CD). The CD is then further tested for putative toxicity and, if found safe, an application for approval for testing on humans is filed (Investigation of a New Drug, IND) with the drug regulatory authorities and Ethical Committees. The discovery process is complex and involves many factors that could influence a successful outcome. It normally takes three to five years to produce a CD.

Development (Clinical R&D)

Once authorities have approved the IND, the first studies are started in male, usually healthy, volunteers. The aim of these studies is to investigate the tolerability of the drug and its pharmaco-dynamic and pharmaco-kinetic properties, i.e. how the drug affects the body and how the drug is affected by the body, respectively. Furthermore, if possible, the dose effect and time effect-relationship should be studied during Phase 1. Subsequently, the new drug is administered to patients for the first time, Phase 2. The aim of these studies is to clarify whether the drug has the desired therapeutic effect and dose-effect relationship, i.e. proof of concept. The main aim during Phase 3 studies, which are large-scale studies, is to establish the role of the new drug in the current therapy state-of-the-art arsenal. In doing so, the effect of the new drug is compared with reference substances and often with a placebo. During all phases and following approval of the drug for launch, any adverse effects are followed in a meticulous way. Following approval of the drug, the clinical effects of the drug are studied further during Phase 4 studies, which can be quite extensive. The clinical programme often takes four to six years to carry out. The clinical research programme continues after product launch by collecting data from outcome research and epidemiology data from patients and may lead to new indications for the product.

Development (Pharmaceutics)

In conjunction with the CD nomination, appropriate drug delivery systems for further toxicological and clinical studies are often required. The pharmaceutics organisation is responsible for developing the appropriate pharmaceutical formulations of the drug together with the relevant analytical technology in order to document the finished product. Many drug molecules often display properties or characteristics making it complicated to acquire an optimum therapy and methods of administration. Examples are the low bioavailability, stability or low solubility of the drug. These factors, in combination with marketing and compliance demands such as patient-friendly design and once daily administration, often require highly sophisticated drug delivery technologies in order to produce a competitive pharmaceutical product. Formulation development often runs in parallel with the clinical programme during a period of several years prior to launch. The pharmaceutics organisation is also responsible for developing appropriate methods for large-scale manufacture of the product.

In summary, the R&D process is an extended task often running more than ten years and is not only a complex and expensive endeavour, it also includes a certain factor of unpredictability. For example, new scientific data arising from toxicology or clinical studies, can, at any time during development, jeopardise a project. Or, using Pisano's (1997) description of the industry: "R&D intensity is high; product development is long, costly, and risky; and profitability depends critically on launching new products in a timely fashion."

I. Near Transfer: Knowledge Sharing in Clinical Study Teams

Knowledge Sharing and Transfer in Clinical Study teams

A major pharmaceutical company such as AstraZeneca employs a great number of knowledge sharing mechanisms and tools in its multiplicity of activities and undertakings. What we call the near transfer of knowledge focuses on knowledge sharing within and between clinical study teams during the later phases of the new product development process. The clinical development process at AstraZeneca is, as described earlier, organized via project teams that work on a detailed sub-study within the overarching research programme. Each team consists of a number of experts, e.g., Clinical Research Leaders, Clinical Research Assistants, Medical Advisers, Data Coordinators, and Study Administrators. One single sub-study may, in extreme cases, include up to 25,000 patients in up to 30 countries, so clinical development studies are complex matters where the process has to be carefully monitored. Because of the high degree of regulation, both externally in terms of the auditing procedures in use (see Power, 1994; Pentland, 2000) and the internal use of standard operation procedures (SOPs), the day-to-day work of clinical development project teams is very regulated and standardized. In addition, as a consequence of the complexity of the process in terms of data compiled and processed, clinical development project teams tend to become rather isolated from one another. One of the perennial issues among clinical development co-workers was the need for more joint learning between clinical project teams. Even though the everyday practices were rather standardized, there was always room for interpretations and idiosyncratic practices developed locally. Clinical development co-workers wanted to know about all those small-scale inventions and solutions contrived within each team in order to adopt the best solutions in their own work. However, the demand for an arena where such aspects of the work could be discussed and examined had not been dealt with at the company. In 2000, what is here referred to as the *knowledge facilitation method* was designed by Jonas Roth and Lena Berg at AstraZeneca R&D, Mölndal Sweden. The intention behind the knowledge facilitation method was to provide an arena where clinical development project teams could learn from one another. All projects that are finalized, that are entering a new phase (passing a milestone or a tollgate), or are starting a new project are invited to go through the knowledge facilitation method in order to obtain knowledge or provide and share insight into how the project deals with various issues during the clinical development process.

The knowledge facilitation method discussed in this section is referred to as a mechanism for the near transfer of knowledge because, although all clinical development projects have their own specific challenges and conditions depending on the substance being clinically evaluated, there are still a great number of generic activities and practices that are shared between all clinical development projects. For instance, one of the recurring themes of the interviewees with the clinical development team co-workers was the issue of how to communicate with the various authorities evaluating the work. For instance, medical authorities such as America's Food and Drug Administration (FDA) are very important for pharmaceutical companies because they make the final decision as regards whether the particular drug will be accepted and registered. Therefore, communicating with the authorities was considered an important area of competence and a complicated part of the work. For instance, how should one formulate an application to the FDA? Another domain often discussed as an important skill within the team was communication: How should one communicate effectively without overloading all the team members with all sorts of information? These kinds of generic activities were shared between the clinical development projects teams thus allowing the knowledge facilitation method to serve as a mechanism for paving the way for knowledge sharing and transfer between project teams.

The Knowledge Facilitation Method

The intention of initiating knowledge facilitation in the clinical project environment was to develop a method that could increase knowledge sharing between, for example, clinical project teams within the organization. The knowledge facilitation method consists of three steps that will be described below; all steps were facilitated by two colleagues working together who were outsiders as regards the project involved in the method. In order to make the sharing of knowledge effective, a few key prerequisites were jointly identified with the management of the clinical unit. Taking into consideration the focus on effectiveness in the R&D organization, the knowledge facilitation method had to be time and cost-effective and, above all, the time spent by project members on knowledge sharing should not jeopardize the chance to meet the project objectives, rather the other way round. In order to legitimize the knowledge facilitation initiative, this was given the assurance of having full management support. Moreover, the facilitators had broad experience of the organization being studied, as well as lengthy experience in the clinical R&D unit, and an extensive personal network. The profile of the facilitators was important as regards increasing trust when initially approaching the various projects. The major steps of the knowledge facilitating method are set out in Table 1 and described further on.

	1.	2.	3.
Context	Team leader (1,5 h)	The team (2 h x ~3)	Teams (1 h
Content	Interview/dialog	Brainstorming sessions Structure content	Interactive seminar with target groups
Output	Output • Facilitator gets insight into the team • Team leader obtains time for reflection • Mutual sharing of network • Legitimacy to continue	Output ¥ Articulation of tacit knowledge ¥ Creating collective knowledge ¥ Production of knowledge in a sharable form	Output ¥ Sharing experience across team boundaries ¥ Creating new knowledge ¥ Building of dynamic micro-communities ¥ Creating personal networks
Facilitator role	Lead the discussion Documents Scheduling meeting with the team	Facilitate the meeting Build an open climate Structure experiences Provide focus	Introduce and close the session Facilitating the dialog Documentation

Table 5.2: The basic elements of the knowledge facilitating method at AstraZeneca

Step 1: Legitimize and Familiarize

The first step is to have a structured interview with the project leader. This step will familiarize the knowledge facilitators with the project and provide an idea of the activities the project leader thinks are important, the things that are positive or problematic and the experiences that could be worth sharing. If the project is in an early phase, the project leader will express the knowledge requirement and the challenges the project will face. During this first step, the project leader will have a chance to reflect and to put into words what he/she already knows. During the interview, the facilitators can share their experiences of facilitation in other projects with the project leader and, in so doing, directly add value to the project leader or more indirectly, point to a person having the knowledge that the project leader is seeking. The interview is documented and takes 1-2 hours. At this initial meeting, the facilitators reach agreement with the project leader regarding how to continue and whom to contact within the project.

Step 2: Unlock the Tacit Knowledge – Structure Explicit Knowledge

The second step usually consists of more than one session. The core group of the project gathers in the same room for a two-hour brainstorming session. The outcome is "knowledge on every wall", as one project member put it, referring to what was captured from the meeting on flipcharts and whiteboards. Usually, an additional session is needed subsequent to the information from the first brainstorming session having been structured. The time between the sessions gives the project members a chance to reflect on the material, which often leads to additional experiences from the first session being added. The facilitators lead the sessions and structure the information, while the project members actively and jointly reflect upon their experiences and create a common view of these experiences or knowledge gaps. The result is often a mind-map containing the common knowledge gained from all the sessions and occasionally a draft set of slides jointly produced for a workshop or seminar. The facilitators document all sessions, and the total time spent together with the project members is between two to six hours. The facilitators continuously switch roles during the brainstorming sessions. One poses questions, facilitates the dialogue, and directs attention to common interests in the group. The other listens, captures the process in writing, and prepares to switch roles with his/her colleague.

Step 3: Sharing with the Organization

Step three is when the experiences from earlier steps are shared with other members of the organization. This could be via a workshop, a meeting, a seminar or any other preferred alternative for sharing experience and knowledge. The important thing is that it is interactive, with peers asking questions and commenting on what is being said on the basis of on their own experience. If, during step 2, one or two specific issues are of particular interest to the team, step 3 could be aimed at developing a collective understanding of that phenomenon in the two groups. One example of an issue is how to boost patient recruitment when this does not go according to plan, or how best to collaborate with the regulatory department internally during the phase of regulatory submission. In order to obtain a more dynamic encounter between the teams, both the "receiving" and the "giving away" team would often go through steps 1 and 2 in parallel. In doing so, both teams are givers and takers and have a collective view of their experiences or needs.

Step 3 is, then, an encounter between two teams when common experiences from earlier collective actions are shared, resulting in a high absorptive capacity in both teams (Cohen and Levinthal, 1990). Using Nonaka and Takeuchi's (1995) terminology, both teams *externalize* their tacit knowledge and, through *combination* and *socialization*, share what is of joint interest. In addition, new knowledge is created when the two teams collectively visualize their tacit and explicit knowledge in the interactive social process taking place. This last step (step 3) usually takes about two hours, but could be extended into a one-day workshop. The facilitators play a relatively minor role here, simply coordinating the meeting and facilitating the dialogue.

Even though the knowledge facilitating method consists of three steps as it is written, it is flexible and can be adjusted to the requirements of the projects and practical constraints such as time and the availability of people in the teams. For example, the interview with the project leader could be done by phone or even by e-mail, if no other way is possible. The second step with the team could be skipped, if time does not allow this or if the team has carried out project reviews itself. In this case, the third step will take longer and demand more from the facilitator to create a team view and not just individual views of what really took place during the project.

Outcomes from the Knowledge Facilitation Method

"Good luck, but as far as I know, nobody will come and attend those seminars," one executive manager argued before the initiation of knowledge facilitation activities at AstraZeneca. Another former manager at the company was sceptical for other reasons: "Nobody will tell you what went wrong, you will only hear success stories". Despite such remarks, seventeen project leaders from different projects being conducted at the Clinical R&D unit have been interviewed, with nineteen action learning workshops, thus far leading to eight sharing sessions across project boundaries, having been held, all in all involving more than ten projects and more than one hundred and fifty people. Contrary to the senior manager's negative predictions, the project leaders and members had a positive view of the knowledge sharing initiative. One of the participants at one of the seminars argued: "It is crucial for us to be able to improve the innovative climate, our working routines and the flexibility within our organization". Other voices said: "I wish more people in my team could have attended the meeting today" and "This sharing session was excellent, but the first step [step 2 of the method] with our team was something we never take time to do ourselves".

The outcomes of the facilitating action are tied to the different steps of the process. *Step 1:* During the interview with the project leaders, they expressed appreciation about the time to reflect on what had really happened in their projects. One project leader argued: "It is nice to talk to someone who is so interested, it gives me the time to articulate my thoughts – sometimes thoughts new to me as well". The interview gave the project leaders a chance to focus on what was important in their projects when questions like, "What is the most crucial thing in your project right now?" or "What experiences do you think other project leaders want your project to share with them?" were raised and became the subject of reflection.

Step 2: At the initial meetings with project members, a typical brainstorming session would start with very stressed and half-interested, though slightly intrigued, individuals. At one of the sessions, one of the project members was reluctant to join in at all: "I have a dental appointment in 45 minutes, so maybe there's no point in being here." A colleague of hers argued: "I will not be presenting anything to anybody after today, I have so many other things to do in the coming weeks, but I can sit here and listen." After 45 minutes of intensive work with a good dialogue underway and a whiteboard full of shared experienced, the first woman had to be reminded not to miss her appointment. Her colleague, who was only there to listen, was deeply involved in the discussions and was making plans for the next step.

Once the initial tension had worn off, the groups usually had positive opinion about the sessions. "This is very interesting; it gives us time to reflect on what is central to the work we have been doing," one project assistant reflected. Another member of the project expressed surprise: "Look at how much we have produced in two hours, I am impressed." They also reflected on things that had not crossed their minds before. For instance, one project group jointly drew a very complex map of its lines of communication between different collaborators and outsourcing partners, with dependencies that included their technical organization. One sub-project leader contended: "This picture is something that we have always needed but have never drawn." A few weeks later, the same person told us: "The shared picture that we drew of the project organization gave us a boost in our current reorganization of the project." The picture was later used in the seminar when explaining to colleagues how communication was organized within the project.

Regarding the facilitator's role and the method used, they mentioned the importance "of having a facilitator from outside who knows the clinical process." It was also a method of collectively reflecting upon what had actually been done and structuring such information and knowledge. "You made us see the big picture together", a project co-worker remarked after one session.

Step 3: The sharing sessions have sometimes been of the more traditional seminar type, where the project members take turns in telling their colleagues their stories, one by one, or as a panel essentially discussing what they came up with during the brainstorming sessions. A more common approach uses the workshop style whereby teams meet around a topic of shared interest and share experiences, or whereby an experienced team from a late phase of the drug development process meets with a team that is at a very early stage of the process to share experiences, very much driven by the needs of the team starting up the project. One example is a study team, that had been working for many years with a large complex clinical study, meeting another study team in the throes of starting a similar study, but in a different disease area. The starting team had actually been trying to find a spot in the calendar for quite some time with the other team, but had never succeeded in finding the time or the incentive to match up. With the facilitators running the method, a meeting was arranged in less than two weeks, resulting in spin-off meetings after the first without a facilitator present. One of these spin-offs was a meeting when team members actually sat down peer-to-peer and worked through the data collection forms (called Case Record Forms) in detail, which is one of the major documents in a clinical study and which can have a major impact on the results and efficiency of the entire project. Another example, more representative of the seminar type of sharing, is a group that talked about how important it is to choose the right people for the different external expert committees (such as the Ethical Committee) working with the project group. After the seminar, it was clear to everyone that choosing members for these committees was, in fact, a form of knowledge which this group had gained from working with different committees for a long time. "I am very glad that I went to this [seminar]. Now I know whom to contact when it comes to committees," said one participant.

Knowledge Facilitation in Clinical Project Teams: Summary and Conclusion

The near transfer of knowledge at AstraZeneca aimed to create an arena wherein project experiences and learning could be articulated among team members and then shared with other team members. The method proved to be a rather effective way of dealing with the need for an institutionalised form of organized refection on project work learning within the clinical development function. Prior to using the knowledge facilitation method, there were very few opportunities for knowledge sharing between project teams. The knowledge facilitation method thus provided one arena of discussion between teams. Not only did the team members believe it was valuable to discuss their own experiences and learning within the project team, they also appreciated being able to have the opportunity to learn something from their fellow clinical development co-workers. Even though the knowledge facilitation method does not rely on the use of advanced technology, or resource-demanding consultancy services, and is primarily to be regarded as a rather easy to use method of knowledge sharing among co-workers, it has proven capable of serving its purpose. The clinical project team co-workers appreciated the method and claimed they learned something during the joint seminars.

II. Far transfer: Knowledge Sharing between Clinical Development Teams

Project Management Support at AstraZeneca

The second type of knowledge sharing and transfer we will be examining in this chapter deals with what Dixon (2000) calls *far transfer*. To put it simply, far transfer aims to share knowledge of non-routine activities in an organization. As we noted in the previous section, clinical development work is largely determined by externally imposed regulations and internally-enacted standard operation procedures (SOPs). On the other hand, there are always opportunities for making individual decisions about how activities should be organized and carried out. Clinical development work is rather predictable and standardized in comparison with other phases of the new drug development process. The near transfer of knowledge is always located within communities of practice undertaking similar work. Far transfer, on the other hand, deals with knowledge sharing within heterogeneous communities or environments characterized by a greater degree of uncertainty, in comparison with the near transfer milieu.

One of the most important competencies of pharmaceutical companies is their project management skill. Since most new drug development processes are organized in the form of temporal organizations, a project, project management skills are of great importance to the time-to-market performance and the level of cost in new product development projects. In early

2000, AstraZeneca started a *Project Management Support Office* (PMSO) in order to enhance the project management capabilities and competence of the company. The PMSO is supposed to serve as a support function for all sorts of project management issues in drug discovery and development R&D. Among other things, the PMSO, which is a global function responsible for all six sites in Sweden, the UK, and the USA, established a knowledge management position. The PMSO's knowledge management vision stated that the function should "enhance Knowledge Management activities that increase the knowledge flow within the company" and "foster a culture of collaboration between units and employees" and "create a more effective and productive project environment". The PMSO function thus aimed to serve as an integrative mechanism between the great variety of projects at AstraZeneca. The PMSO is developing a number of project management guidelines on how to conduct projects, and provide training and facilitation in project management, tools for project managers, an extensive intranet service for project management information, and a helpdesk for the project management centre of excellence. The Global Project Directors (GPDs) and Global Project Managers (GPMs) responsible for running a portfolio of projects within one therapeutic area, run so-called GPD forums and GPM forums, sponsored by the PMSO, where experiences and learning can be exchanged between different therapeutic areas and global projects. The PMSO web service caters, among other things, for the requirements of the GPDs and GPMs. The PMSO identifies and develops the guidelines for how project work should be undertaken. These guidelines are based on know-how, expertise and the needs of the firm and are built around existing best practice project management such as the PMI's, body of knowledge. The Project Management Institute is a global project management association. (Project Management Institute (2000) A Guide to the Project Management Body of Knowledge (PMBoK® Guide) (http://www.pmi.org)).

The guidelines address facets of project management work like risk management, management control, value management, knowledge management, leadership and group dynamics, and other human resource management issues. When developing the guidelines, a reference group of experienced project managers and functional managers are involved who will subsequently form a community of practice around the specific area of interests manifested in the guideline. These communities of practice not only develop the guidelines in association with the PMSO, they are also responsible for the further development of the guidelines and keeping up-to-date in the specific area of expertise. In addition, the PMSO arranges an internal project management conference where people across the R&D organization can come together and listen to lectures highlighting important aspects of project work, to share learning, listen to case stories from projects and to network.

In the remainder of this chapter, we will be addressing the activities of the knowledge management initiative at the PMSO. The guiding principle for knowledge management work at the PMSO was that there existed substantial demand within the organization to discuss, examine and visualize the different processes and activities within the various projects, and that this examination would very much evolve around the notion of knowledge. Similar to near transfer within the clinical development function, the projects of the different Therapeutic Areas (TAs), e.g. gastrointestinal, cardiovascular and cancer medicine, were also in need of an arena for knowledge sharing and transfer. While a clinical study team is responsible for a single sub-study within the broader trial of one substance, i.e. there are, after all, a considerable number of fixed parameters in the process, the project portfolio on the higher project management organisational levels is broader and includes more decision-making under uncertain or ambiguous conditions. Thus, there is a greater demand for different competencies and know-how regarding the GPTs and CDTs than in the clinical study teams. In the next section, knowledge sharing and transfer between the so-called Clinical Development Teams (CDT) is examined, using the knowledge facilitation method as described earlier.

Working with Knowledge Transfer

Types of Far Transfer

When the notion of far transfer is used in this section, it denotes at least four different types of knowledge sharing. First, knowledge is shared between sites at AstraZeneca. Although the organization is global, there are still specific competencies and experiences at the local sites. Therefore, the co-workers at certain sites benefit from meeting co-workers from other sites on the team level to discuss practical problems. Second, far transfer denotes learning between sites in different countries. At AstraZeneca, there are major sites in Sweden, the UK, and the USA, and numerous market companies all over the world. Knowledge sharing between sites located in different countries is an important part of far transfer. Third, far transfer is used when knowledge is shared between therapeutic areas of the company. AstraZeneca operates in seven different therapeutic areas. These different therapeutic areas are based on different scientific know-how, skills, and competencies and are very different from one another. Therefore, knowledge sharing and learning between therapeutic areas is useful. There are generic processes in new drug development but there are also different opportunities for conducting, for instance, clinical research in different therapeutic areas, hence the potential for learning across TA boundaries. Fourth, and finally, far transfer is used here to denote knowledge sharing concerning matters that Dixon (2000) refers to as non-routine work, but what is more adequately thought of as work characterized by a high degree of abstraction and uncertainty, for instance how to make decisions under uncertain conditions. When planning a clinical development programme, one of the key activities of the clinical development team, a series of studies, has to be designed. Because one cannot fully anticipate the outcome of the earlier phases of the clinical trials, it is complicated to make decisions about how the studies during the latter phases should be conducted. Yet, the clinical development plan needs to clearly state how such studies are to be conducted. Thus, the clinical development team is put in the position where it has to make decisions under bounded rationality (Simon, 1957). To make a decision for an entire clinical development plan, prior to having access to the relevant information, is therefore less uncertain if one has experience of conducting similar studies. In consequence, joint knowledge sharing between clinical development teams is a most important strategic capability for the company.

In summary, far transfer represents here a number of different types of knowledge sharing activities. In comparison with near transfer in the relatively homogeneous clinical study teams, sharing many of their concerns, the domain of far transfer includes more abstract processes and uncertainty.

Topics of Discussion in Far Transfer

The clinical development teams are responsible for the entire clinical development programme of a particular candidate drug, delivered from the Discovery phases. Such a clinical development programme includes all sorts of *in vivo* studies, i.e. when the substance is tested on human beings. The first phase, Phase One, is undertaken by the Experimental Medicine department. During Phase One, it is important that the individual testing the substance is carefully evaluated and that the researchers have significant scientific training in the relevant areas. These studies include voluntary participants such as students and are conducted in order to obtain the pharmacological and pharmacokinetic profiles of the substance in human beings and to see if the findings from pre-clinical studies are translatable to the clinical setting. Phase two studies are similar trials on a very limited number of patients with the disease targeted for cure, and are conducted to confirm that the substance in fact provides the desired effects and does not have any obvious side effects. Experimental medicine thus hosts the expertise needed to conduct confirmatory studies that will enable the candidate drug to be subjected to full-scale clinical studies. Phase Three studies are conducted by the Clinical Operations Department. During this later phase, scientific confirmation of the substance should be safeguarded and the studies should instead aim to provide evidence in favour of the substance in larger populations than those used during the Phase Two studies. In consequence, the key competence of Clinical Operations is the management and logistics of large-scale studies. The discovery phase is founded on competencies in synthesis chemistry, different areas of expertise in medicine and biochemistry. The early phases of the development process are based on competencies in clinical medicine, pharmacology and pharmakinetics, as well as other domains of expertise dealing with the distribution of the medicine. The latter phases of the development process make use of clinical trial competencies in terms of the management and logistics of such large-scale studies. Since there is a sequential division of labour throughout the new drug development process, there are several points at which the interest and competencies of the different phases may interfere. For instance, the discovery department is rewarded for the number of candidate drugs it is able to deliver during the fiscal year, which is also an important parameter for performance evaluation of the portfolio, aimed at shareholders and analysts. During the development phases, the candidate drugs provided by the discovery department are processed in order to become finalized new drugs. Resourcing all of these candidate drug projects is a tough job, since experience shows that only a few of the candidate drugs will meet the requirements for further development and thus also require resources. Sometimes, all candidate drugs pass the early tests and suddenly there is more work to do than there are resources available during the early development phases. Thus, there is at times, at least according to representatives of the development phases, a mismatch between the discovery and the development phases. Another domain of controversy is the shift between Experimental Medicine and Clinical Operations. The competencies of Experimental Medicine and Clinical Operations are different and thus there may be discussions about how a new candidate drug should be taken from a small-scale Phase Two study to the significantly larger Phase Three study. There is, to some extent, a qualitative leap between Phase Two and Phase Three studies, i.e. Phase Three studies are not Phase Two studies writ large, but are instead based on a different logic. In consequence, representatives of Experimental Medicine and Clinical Operations may have different opinions about how to run clinical studies requiring competencies from both functions, e.g. large phase two studies.

Another topic of discussion was development of the so-called *Clinical Development Plan* (CDP). The CDP is the main document for the entire series of studies that will turn the candidate drug into a new drug application and a new registered drug. Since not all events can be anticipated at the point in time when the plan is written, there are great opportunities for enhancing the CDP by discussing it with more experienced researchers. One thing the CDT members found puzzling was what kind of internal and external committees were expected to evaluate the CDP. In new drug development, different ethical and scientific advisors are involved as reviewers of the different documents in order to safeguard the meeting of ethical and scientific requirements. However, the roles and responsibilities of these committees were not clear to everyone and there was a discussion about where the team was empowered to make its own decisions and where a governing body would have to be consulted. In addition to the compulsory committee reviews, there are a number of internal committees that make the more strategic decisions for the company. For the CDT members, these decision-making processes were rather complicated to grasp fully. Another area of discussion in terms of the CDP was which experts in the form of pharmacologists, medical doctors or statisticians should be involved in the process of writing the CDP and in the review of the document. In other words, the division of labour between the different stakeholders should be managed. Taken together, the *formal procedures* for producing the CDP constituted one important area of joint learning between CDTs.

The CDTs also expressed an interest in what could be called team building and project management issues, i.e. how to run these large scale project portfolios and maintain a sense of commitment and involvement among CDT co-workers. This challenge comprised a number of more specific topics. One evolved around how to manage and lead multi-skilled teams. Another addressed how to deal with ethnic and cultural differences in the team, for instance how to relate to the American co-workers, their role in the global team and their accountability within their own organisation. Another cultural challenge was collaborating with Japanese colleagues and authorities, something that was generally held to be something of an experience for the Swedish co-workers. A third topic of discussion was how to attract and maintain the critical competencies in the CDT. For instance, medical doctors with expertise in new drug development were highlighted as being in short supply at one of the seminars. Several of the CDT members expressed their concern about the company's inability to offer adequate training in this respect for its medical advisors. In addition, how to detect and hire dedicated team co-workers was discussed as one of the major challenges of the CDT's activities.

Another area attracting great interest at the CDT seminars was how to engage successfully in company politics, i.e. how to affect strategic decision-making in the therapeutic areas. For instance, the reward system based on the number of candidate drugs delivered by the discovery department put significant pressure on the development organization. Therefore, the representatives of the development organization wanted to bring this issue into the debate. Another political issue is how to enhance the transparency of the decision-making process. For instance, which committees are supposed to have an influence on the Clinical Development Plan. Such highly political matters were treated as complicated areas to deal with by the CDT members. When meeting one another during seminars, there was a great deal of interest in addressing company politics.

By and large, the Clinical Development Teams had to take care of a multiplicity of problems and challenges. The teams were culturally diverse, in most cases geographically distributed, comprising a range of expertise and competence, and had to make a number of pivotal decisions on the basis of bounded rationality. In consequence, there are great opportunities for joint knowledge sharing and discussions about experiences from different new drug development projects. Here, the knowledge facilitation method served a purpose in terms of bringing different individuals and teams together and providing an arena for discussions about these challenges. Because the environment of the Clinical Development Teams was different, e.g. more ambiguous, complex and politically contested than the study team level in the near transfer setting, the knowledge facilitation method had to be adapted to these novel conditions. Next, we will discuss how the knowledge facilitation method is used in the far transfer setting.

Working with Knowledge Sharing in Far Transfer

In comparison to the more homogeneous clinical study teams, the CDTs were more composed of a number of different expert areas, often distributed between sites and even countries. In addition, the CDTs handle more complex research programmes wherein not all parameters are known in advance. In consequence, the demands placed on the knowledge facilitator role are more pronounced. For instance, before the CDT seminars, at which all members of two or more CDTs meet to discuss relevant topics, the knowledge facilitators arrange for interviews with Clinical Development members, not just with the Clinical Development Leader (CDL), and brainstorming sessions where relevant topics are discussed and examined. These sessions placed more demands on the knowledge facilitators because they had to delve into more complex and contextual sets of problems in order to understand the CDT's work. During the seminars, the knowledge facilitators thought of the CDT members as more demanding than the seminar participants in the clinical study teams. For instance, expectations were higher and the seminar participants have more diverse perspectives regarding the team than in the near transfer setting. Since the CDT is less homogeneous than clinical study teams, a greater variety of perspectives and topics are addressed among the members. In these teams, each individual represents a sub-team or their function and is therefore a spokesperson and a leader for another team or function. Therefore, more time is allotted to making sense of CDT work than during the near transfer seminars. There is, in brief, more need to develop a common ground for the participants. Even though the need for collective sense-making is more pronounced in far transfer, problem solving remains one of the key outputs from the seminars. A couple of examples of important issues addressed in the workshops were; how to organize and manage databases throughout the clinical research process as well as how and where diseases and adverse events and reactions should be coded, for instance, at one or several sites. Another, often addressed issue was how to cooperate and make commitments (write contracts) with the local market company regarding the delivery of patients or data. Related to the marketing company issue was how to deal with personnel changes and loss of the personnel doing the local work. The loss of skill and the time to train new personnel posed a real problem for the project team. All these issues were discussed and examples of how to solve them were often given by one team to another. Discussions about how to translate the experiences from one project setting to another were intriguing for all the participants. It often meant translating not just from one project to another, but from one project located in a different part of the country with a different local company culture, in a different therapeutic area and at a different stage of the drug development process.

In general, the generic knowledge facilitation method was useful in the far transfer setting. Some of the activities and mechanisms had to be fine-tuned but most the time, the method worked as intended. For instance, executive summaries were provided from every seminar. In order to make these executive summaries available within the company, they were published on the intranet PMSO homepage. Because the knowledge facilitation method proved itself capable of working as intended, new knowledge facilitators were trained in conducting similar seminars at other sites of the company. During 2002, three new knowledge facilitators were trained at the Clinical Project Management Department at Mölndal and four in Pharmaceutical R&D at the same site. In Södertälje, one of three Swedish sites, two new knowledge facilitators were trained at the Clinical Project Management Department.

Knowledge Management as Practice at AstraZeneca

This chapter only addresses, of course, a fraction of all the knowledge sharing activities that a major global pharmaceutical company makes use of. For instance, we do not examine the multiplicity of knowledge sharing mechanisms during the laboratory-based discovery phase preceding the development activities or database information sharing systems or personnel changes, functional meetings etc. However, it was never our intention to cover all of the activities, rather to provide some insight into using what we call the knowledge facilitation method. The knowledge facilitation method has been employed in a similar manner in two settings, the Clinical Study Team (CST) and the Clinical Development Team (CDT). Although these two levels of the organization deal with similar problems and challenges, there are important differences between them which need to be taken into account when working with the knowledge facilitation method. The CST undertakes more routine work, the teams are more homogeneous, there are fewer ambiguities needing to be sorted out and the issues addressed are primarily practical. In the CDTs, there is less routine work, teams are heterogeneous and culturally diverse, politics and ambiguities are part of day-to-day work and decisions need to be made under bounded rationality. There is, in brief, more standardized and codified knowledge in use in the CST, while the CDTs operate in a more politicized and complex environment. This makes the knowledge facilitation method different in the near transfer and the far transfer settings. In the near transfer setting, it is much easier to anticipate and predict what kind of issues and concerns will be addressed and thus the knowledge facilitator will, to a greater extent, be able to control the knowledge sharing seminars. In the far transfer setting, knowledge facilitators tend to serve more as discussants in the seminars, helping the participants to sort out what kind of problems and challenges are important to deal with. In the near transfer setting, the knowledge facilitators serve as both the integrating mechanisms between different CSTs and as experienced co-workers who have organizational tenure and experience of the specific domain, and who can thus be used to provide answers to inquiries. In the far transfer setting, the knowledge facilitator's role is more oriented towards a discussant's role, offering seminars where shared worries and concerns can be ventilated, but is also a start to orchestrate more contacts between the members of the different teams. In both cases, knowledge facilitation seminars serve as an arena where the various challenges facing the project teams can be addressed. Knowledge facilitation seminars are thus what Nonaka, Toyama and Konno (2002), using a Japanese concept, call a Ba, a physical as well as mental place where knowledge can be shared between individuals and project teams: "*Ba* is a place where information is interpreted to become knowledge" (Nonaka, Toyama and Konno, 2002: 49).

In comparison with the more technically advanced mechanisms and arenas for knowledge sharing, e.g. intranets (Newell, Scarboroguh, Swan and Hislop, 2000), e-mail (Brown and Lightfoot, 2002), or the computerization of activities (Gunge, 2000), the knowledge facilitation method uses "old fashioned" approaches like face-to-face discussions and a few whiteboard illustrations. In brief, the technological content of the method is rather low. Nevertheless, such "low key" approaches may fill an important gap in-between the array of technology-based knowledge sharing approaches that are being initiated in companies today. Thus, the main strength of the knowledge facilitation method is not the *amount* of knowledge shared or the *speed* of such sharing, rather its ability to anchor various individuals' problems and concerns in a discussion about *practices*, in day-to-day activities. The knowledge facilitation method — and here we are talking about both near and far transfer — in short enables for *thick descriptions* (see Ryle, 1971) of knowledge-based problems. Since thick descriptions require "thick analyses" and "thick solutions", knowledge facilitation workshops serve as opportunities to grapple with the practice-based problems that intranets and database information cannot effectively deal with. Thus, the knowledge facilitation workshops' aim, in Nonaka, Yoyama and Konno's (2002) phrase, is not only to share information but also to make it "become knowledge". Databases and other technology-based knowledge management tools are excellent aids when handling large amounts of information, there is no doubt about that. But the epistemological break between information and knowledge cannot be easily bridged with some computer-based application. It needs thoughtful reflection and discussions embedded in experiences originating from practice, and the joint sharing of such experiences among colleagues. Thus, the knowledge facilitation method is not a substitute for the more traditional knowledge management approaches, but is instead a complement to the set of knowledge-sharing practices within the firm. It is what enables the leap from information sharing to knowledge sharing.

Summary and Conclusion

This chapter has presented the second case study on knowledge sharing practices in organizations. The pharmaceutical industry is based on the application of scientific knowledge in the life sciences of biochemistry, pharmacology, medicine, and microbiology, but it also has an advanced level of competence in managing the logistics of large-scale clinical development work. This chapter has examined how the knowledge facilitation method, as it has been referred to, reinforces and supports the sharing of know-how and experiences during clinical development work. As has been suggested, the knowledge facilitation method in fact serves as a complementary method to all the computer-based knowledge management systems that have been in vogue recently. The knowledge facilitation method is not primarily aimed at sharing information, rather at producing and sharing knowledge through bringing people together and making them share their know-how and experiences with one another.

Chapter 6:

Knowledge Sharing in Organizations

Introduction

In this sixth and final chapter of the book, the two cases will be examined and related to the corpus of texts on knowledge sharing in organizations. The first of two points of departure for the analysis is that knowledge sharing in organizations, in itself a most diverse and polymorphous activity, is a key strategic capability in organizations in the so-called knowledge society, the second being that such a capability is always to be regarded as a practice. The two cases featured in this book, the SCA case (Chapter Four) and the AstraZeneca case (Chapter Five) represent two different industries and different types of activities. In consequence, the knowledge sharing practices of these two companies place different demands on the firm's knowledge sharing capabilities. Even though very different and highly specialized intellectual resources are employed at the two firms in the two industries, the possibilities still exist to treat them as though they were subject to knowledge management practices. Knowledge management is a broad management category comprising a rich variety of activities and processes aimed at exploiting and extending the firm's intellectual resources and capabilities. In order to attain the status of a theory, knowledge management techniques, models and concepts must be employable in different settings: It needs to be general. Therefore, one of the objectives of this chapter is to show that knowledge management theory does not just draw on strategic management theory, and what Schatzki, Knorr Cetina and Savigny (2001) call the practice turn in social theory, but that it is also possible to apply it to relatively heterogeneous cases. In addition, we argue that knowledge management theory needs to make use of detailed case studies of organizational practices rather than merely addressing theoretical concerns and conceptual discussions, something that is in many cases favoured in the strategic management literature, thereby resulting in long-standing discussions on the meaning and use of concepts such as capabilities, resources, rents, and so forth. Rather than adhering to what Astely (1985) calls *literature-based research*, knowledge management theory would benefit from conducting more *problem-based research*, i.e. research that is rooted in the everyday working life practices of organizations. The SCA and AstraZeneca cases explicitly address the challenges these two companies are facing in terms of knowledge sharing in their respective industries; the need for greater productivity in corrugated paperboard production and the more effective use of expertise in new drug development in the pharmaceutical industry. These are two challenges which, in various ways, entail implications for knowledge theory.

The chapter is structured as follows: First, the debate about knowledge sharing will be recapitulated. Second, the two cases will be examined. Third, we revisit the literature on knowledge management and critically examine how the two cases may contribute to a more elaborated analysis of knowledge management. Fourth, a framework for knowledge sharing will be presented. Finally, some implications are discussed.

Knowledge Sharing

The emerging knowledge management literature shares one basic assumption: In contemporary society, it is no longer resources such as land (as in agriculture) or technology and machinery (as in large-scale mass production), but intellectual resources such as knowledge, that are becoming the single most important production factor. This does not mean that technology and other production factors are to be neglected, rather that they are no longer the *primus motor* in economic growth. This argument is by no means uncontroversial and, in consequence, there has been an animated discussion on the validity of the arguments put forth by the protagonists of a "knowledge economy". It may be possible here to discern two positions. On the one hand, there is what one may call a radical camp claiming that we are moving into a wholly symbol-based, post-modern economy where the classical production factors are only of limited importance. On the other hand, there is a more modest (for a lack of a better concept) camp arguing that knowledge and other intellectual resources are of great importance but that such resources can never be isolated from other resources in practice. Knowledge is always inextricably entangled with what we may call the material (for an extended argument see Pickering, 1995; Hacking, 1992). For instance, the most advanced form of laboratory research is always dependent upon the use of state-of-the-art technology (Knorr Cetina, 1999; Lynch, 1985). The radical camp makes the claim that knowledge and the use of symbols represents a break with previous economic regimes, the modest camp argues that it is accurate to make claims that intellectual resources are becoming increasingly important to economic growth but that such intellectual resources are never employed as such, rather they are always becoming productive within a system of integrated and highly heterogeneous resources and capabilities. In our analysis of the two cases, we maintain that empirical research provides support for a modest stance. The radical camp hosts "speculative" sociologists such as Touraine and Bell and social theorists such as Baudrillard, while the modest camp includes researchers oriented towards empirical studies of "knowledge in use".

In more detailed terms, knowledge is treated here as a somewhat ambiguous construct, being manifested in embodied practices and emotionality as well as being entangled with the material. In the so-called knowledge economy, services such as higher education, or expertise in various forms, are never just knowledge per se but are always communicated, shared or used in specific settings. Such settings are always what make knowledge become knowledge. For instance, in his study of barristers' work, a most specialized form of juridical expertise, Harris (2002) shows that one of the key competencies of barristers was being capable of separating individual emotions from particular cases and relating to these cases as objectively and professionally as possible. In this case, the expertise or competence of the barrister is not solely a matter of formal training and previous experiences, but very much related to the management — the autosurveillance (Du Gay, 1996) of emotions — of the barrister's emotions and affects (see also Korczynski, 2003; Hodgson, 2003; Deery, Iversen and Walsh, 2002; Sutton, 1991). The highly specialized skills of the barrister are thus both intellectual and emotional, both when acquired as formal knowledge but equally as the skills of dealing with particular cases. It is the setting (e.g. the barrister's current brief) that makes his or her know-how become *knowledge-in-practice* or, to use a shorter formulation, a *skill*.

In addition, knowledge is never a coherent entity but is always distributed throughout organizations or sub-sets of organizations such as communities of practice. In consequence, there is a continuous need to integrate various knowledge resources. The ability to make use of intellectual resources is what makes knowledge a strategic asset. Knowledge sharing is thus a strategic capability enabling sustainable competitive advantage when handled properly. In day-to-day work, the strategic capability of knowledge sharing is manifested in practices at organizations: in meetings, shop-floor discussions, joint work, and in a multiplicity of different activities which take place in organizations and which are aimed at sharing know-how, an insight, or an idea (see Orr, 1996; Boden, 1994; Leidner, 1993). Taken together, the sharing of knowledge in organizations is far from trivial even though the idea is simple. Numerous hurdles and roadblocks may reduce the ability to make use of "what the organization knows" (to borrow Davenport and Prusak's, 1998, formulation).

Knowledge Sharing in the Two Cases

The SCA and AstraZeneca cases differ clearly from each other in a number of aspects. But both contribute to the understanding of knowledge-sharing routines at larger organizations. Below, we will analyze these cases in terms of their differences and similarities, and learning, both for practice and in relation to theory. We start off by summarizing the key observations.

Knowledge sharing at SCA and the Eurobest programme are closely linked to the strategy of the company. Having grown extensively throughout the 1990s and 2000s, one important means of generating synergies and a logic for the expansion strategy has been stimulating the sharing of knowledge between units along a broad range of dimensions, including production. It is obvious that a company such as SCA needs to estimate the value of its acquisitions based on some sort of knowledge exchange taking place. Plants share the same technology and even machinery, and in many cases they share customers as well. So, in a sense, the physical resource-base is similar from unit to unit, country to country. The differences lie in the routines via which the physical resources are utilized. And, when there is heterogeneity, there are windows of opportunity for dialogue and exchange. Another strategy-related factor is connected with the character of the industry that SCA belongs to. Being fairly mature and, on certain markets, a segment suffering from over-capacity, the pressure on prices is constant. Moreover, when there is an inability to innovate and escape such a situation, cost-cutting becomes imperative. To that end, the Eurobest programme fitted excellently — and it delivered. Apart from these two strategic logics of the knowledge sharing programme, it also helped the company to focus on and stimulate the work of shop-floor personnel by making them feel directly linked to something that top management marketed as particularly important, even strategic. In that sense, the management of Eurobest can be seen as a strategic capability, i.e. the skills and structure that help to utilize a core resource, the competence of the production functions. This statement underlines the situational character of knowledge.

The impact or effect of Eurobest was generally positive, with productivity increasing and costs being cut. But the weak correlations between knowledge sharing and profit operationalizations (such as EBIT) indicate a set of potential obstacles on the causal track between knowledge and financial performance. They also indicate that, on the local site level, the use and impact of Eurobest varied. There were several types of success and failure factors. Looking at the organization of the programme, it was probably important that this type of programme was orchestrated centrally. With extensive decentralization and local autonomy and profit centre status, the incentives for allocating resources and energy to projects like this are perhaps not as strong as they could have been within a different structure. The "corporate highlighting" of progress, which ensues when creating such a visible and well documented programme, can serve as a catalyst to activate units and individuals. The efforts made by the corporate team to stimulate learning have obviously been instrumental. Training, method documentation, award ceremonies, monitoring and measuring were important. The programme was aggressively communicated internally, which quickly generated an awareness of the meaning and purpose of the venture. The identification that followed helped individuals better understand what was expected of them and what they should expect of the other instances in the network. The support that ventures like this can obtain from using information technology is also worth mentioning. When knowledge is explicit enough to be communicated as written methods or procedures, and when the results of knowledge sharing are presented as numerically as they were at SCA, then information technology is an efficient tool. Database management and intranet linkups, as well as network and other hardware assets, are important. The rigorous documentation of performance, on a monthly basis dating back to 1996, has helped the company carry out serious data mining and extensive, statistical analyses involving production-related issues.

Looking at the results of the programme, the overall effect on profit appears limited. On the whole, there is a link between attempts to share knowledge and productivity and cost reduction, but no link with profit. Taking this whole chain of factors into account, one could conclude that there are three types of obstacles to the (financially) successful implementation of knowledge sharing programmes. Firstly, knowledge may not be transferred at all. Secondly, knowledge that is transferred might not lead to cost (or revenue) improvements on the plant level. Thirdly, improvements in costs (or revenues) might not lead to profit improvements. As we have said before, current research tends to focus on the first obstacle and reports, primarily, that organizational factors are key factors, along with cognitive factors such as absorptive capacity and causal ambiguity. However, in the SCA case, what appeared to be particularly important, assuming that financial performance is what counts, was the level of motivation at the local sites. The plants which saw Eurobest as a venture integral to their strategy, the plants which paid attention and applied energy to the task, the plants which tried to make explicit that which can be made explicit, the plants which had active plant managers, and the plants who dealt with costs and prices strategically (i.e. did not offset cost cuts with price cuts), did better than the others.

A key lesson from the SCA case is that learning and knowledge sharing probably require a lot more than the instrumental documentation of knowledge and the monitoring of performance. It is not sufficient, it would appear, to assume a drive of hundred percent among staff. They will take advice under consideration, fit it to their own frames of reference and their own agendas and act accordingly. If they do not understand or like what they hear, the planner's dream goes wrong. Under these circumstances, the only solution can be fitting the programme to the frameworks of the personnel and attempting to help them to want to modify or extend their frameworks. Anything else, including ordering people about, is pointless. Both strategies require efforts outside of the sharing itself. So, once again, we touch upon the contextual character of knowledge sharing.

The case of AstraZeneca suggests that knowledge sharing is not a self-organizing process but is instead something that benefits from being carefully managed and monitored. In the pharmaceutical industry, new drug development encompasses a broad variety of competencies and skills ranging from laboratory work during the discovery phases to the clinical trials that enable the new drug to be registered and launched on the market. Laboratory work of identifying the compound mobilizes disciplines and expertise in synthesis chemistry, microbiology and medicine. Development work on the candidate drug relies on pharmacology and disciplines in experimental medicine and the final, but costly, clinical trials make use of administrative and project management skills. Throughout the entire process, there are a number of highly specialized domains which overlap one another. In most cases, this works without problems, but at times, there are controversies between disciplines and functional departments which need to be dealt with. The knowledge facilitation model put to work at AstraZeneca has to date been employed during the development phases. One of the key skills of development work is conducting long-term and costly clinical trials. The four phases of new drug development, commencing with tests on laboratory animals during Phase 0 and ending with full-scale clinical trials during Phase 3, employ and integrate a large number of individuals representing different areas of expertise. The managers of Clinical Development Teams thus have to balance a number of interests and transformations in the movement from candidate drug to final drug application, the outcome of the Phase 3 study. For instance, the highly-scientific orientation and priorities of Experimental Medicine have to be harmonized with the objectives and competencies of the Clinical Research organization. In addition, the market organization is always represented in the Clinical Development Teams, bringing additional recommendations and concerns into the work. In consequence, managers of Clinical Development Teams have to manage rather complex processes. Their work relies on the use of tacit knowledge, previous experiences, communication skills and a range of know-how. The knowledge facilitation seminars serve to offer an arena wherein such different forms of knowledge can be shared between different actors in the Clinical Development Teams. As suggested in Chapter Five, the basic idea of the knowledge facilitation model is rather simple but its use in practice requires a number of different skills.

In terms of being a knowledge-sharing practice, the knowledge facilitation model is based on what Karl Weick (1995) calls *sense-making*. Managers in the development organization were often working under a significant workload and had to deal with a broad number of issues. They often expressed their concerns in terms of a lack of top management attention or their own shortcomings in balancing the different interests of the Clinical Development Teams. Thus, the knowledge facilitation seminars enabled Clinical Development Leaders (CDLs) to come together and discuss matters that they were concerned about. The knowledge-sharing model here is thus based on verbal communication — "talk" if you like — and the sharing of experiences and ways of dealing with different problems or challenges. Even if the knowledge-sharing model *per se* were not very "technical" in its outline, it would still require dedicated seminar leaders (the knowledge facilitators) whose research work, e.g. the interviews with CDLs and other relevant managers, was crucial for the seminars. Thus, the knowledge facilitation model is heavily dependent on local practices, i.e. the way new drug development works at that particular organization, AstraZeneca. Rather than adopting some ready-made management model and applying it to the local cases, the knowledge facilitation model emerged from within the practices of AstraZeneca. In addition, it fundamentally acknowledged the need for communicating experiences and concerns within communities of practice, and the strategic nature of such activities. Since new drug development in the pharmaceutical industry is a costly matter, especially in the later clinical trials, the knowledge facilitation seminars aimed to provide an arena enabling the improved sharing of knowledge which in turn would enable the company to save time and money. Thus, the knowledge facilitation model represents a model where strategic concerns as well as local practices are integrated and taken into account.

Differences

As is apparent, the two cases have clear differences, apart from supplying completely different products. The SCA case represents the manufacturing industry, which in this case is always partially oriented towards higher productivity and cost reduction. Here, knowledge sharing is, on the bottom line, aimed at eliminating non value-adding activities or making existing operations more cost-effective. To use a classic concept, knowledge sharing results in "single-loop" learning. In the case of AstraZeneca, knowledge sharing is not primarily aimed at reducing cost (at least not in the first place), but at making the new drug development process in its entirety less complicated and unpredictable — which may, over time, lead to cost reductions, but more importantly better products and a broader product range, and a faster time-to-market, if successful.

In the case of SCA, the main parameters of knowledge sharing activities were well known, while at AstraZeneca, the co-workers were operating under ambiguous conditions where one could not anticipate or foresee what would happen during the entire period of time when the new drug development process was underway. In the case of SCA, knowledge sharing was related to the effective use of the production machinery, i.e. various sorts of material and physical resources, while in the case of AstraZeneca, knowledge sharing dealt with experiences and know-how related to individuals who in turn represent different domains of expertise (such as experimental medicine or the market organization) at the company. Thus, the SCA case draws, one may argue, on *direct* or *material* relationships with machinery, while the AstraZeneca case addresses social relationships internal and external to the company (e.g., doctors in hospitals engaged in clinical trials). Therefore, the case of SCA represents one particular form of knowledge sharing characterized by, on the one hand, some knowledge or skill, and on the other, by a material resource such as a machine. This increases familiarity as well as individual and organizational awareness, and facilitates dialogue. Here, the knowledge is always entangled with the material resource. In the case of AstraZeneca, that relationship is much less pronounced because the knowledge sharing practices are not only located to particular machines, but are instead related to a variety of heterogeneous resources, in many cases the human capital embodied by different experts. This does not imply that knowledge sharing in the case of SCA is less complicated or more easily managed, but it does suggest that knowledge sharing evolves around the dual structure of knowledge-machinery. At AstraZeneca, knowledge is related to a complex structure of social relations and interactions. In fact, knowledge is not possible to separate from such a structure of social relations, but is instead its very outcome rather than external to it.

Another direct and connected difference relates to the character of the knowledge shared and the formal educational background of those sharing knowledge at the different companies. While the character of the knowledge shared at AstraZeneca is far more tacit and less codifiable (at least prior to successful discovery), production knowledge at SCA is easier to explicate. Throughout the Eurobest programme, SCA tried to make explicit different aspects of what was previously a knowledge field partially and fragmentally obscured by a lack of will to explore what could be made explicit through dialogue and interaction and through education. Using the knowledge facilitation model, AstraZeneca did something similar, only here it is less of a motivational barrier, more of a cognitive one, due to the advanced and sophisticated character of the knowledge, globally speaking. Advanced knowledge of pharmaceuticals requires more experience than it does to design the "pickie stick", for instance. Furthermore, the general level of education is higher in the pharmaceutical lab than in the box plant. While AstraZeneca employs scientists, SCA often employs production workers without an extensive education, other than elementary school. This affects and is affected by the more tacit character of the knowledge that AstraZeneca deals with. Nonetheless, both companies face the same principal objective, to share knowledge in order to improve their business. And, in relation to what is known by the personnel, both companies strive to explicate what, to some of their staff, is still tacit. In the case of AstraZeneca, the output from the knowledge-sharing activities is complicated to estimate with any statistical certainty. However, the sharing of experiences and know-how has contributed to shortening lead-times in new drug development and time to market, it has contributed to direct savings in the clinical research work through innovative solutions to practical problems and challenges, and through beneficial human resource management effects. Because most of the participants appreciated the knowledge facilitation initiative, the seminars provided an arena wherein common problems and challenges could be discussed. Providing hard evidence of the financial effects of such an arena requires highly econometrical sophistication, but it is likely that the seminars still made a difference to the co-workers at AstraZeneca.

In summary, there are significant differences between the two cases in terms of objectives, practices, output and assumptions. Yet, these two cases share the underlying notion that knowledge can be treated as an organizational resource that may further enhance competitive advantage.

Similarities

Notwithstanding their differences and similarities, both the pharmaceutical industry and the corrugated paper industry share the continuous pressure to enhance the value-adding activities in their processes, the shareholder value orientation, and an increasing pressure to make the activities more cost effective. Such is the situation in most industries in the contemporary economic regime and there is no proof that the situation will change radically during the coming period of time. The paper industry competes on a combination of quality and costs and, to some extent, on customized production, for instance, specific printing services. The pharmaceutical industry takes great pride in its track record in offering new and innovative drugs that have proved helpful to mankind. The pharmaceutical industry is fundamentally based on its ability to innovate and turn pharmaceutical innovations into marketable products, more so than SCA. To make a rather blunt generalization, one may argue that the pharmaceutical industry is dependent, to a greater extent than the corrugated paper industry, on its innovative and creative capacities. The pharmaceutical industry is, after all, a knowledge-based industries *par excellence*. Here, knowledge is patented and can directly form the basis of competitive advantages. In the packaging industry, there are certain product patents, but none with such a direct impact that a patented drug might give.

Looking at the knowledge sharing-routines of the two companies, there are some similarities as well. To start with, both SCA and AstraZeneca are deliberate in their approaches. The Eurobest programme and the knowledge facilitation model are two conscious, deliberate, reasonably well-planned ventures aimed at the same target, i.e. sharing different forms of knowledge internally. Although one could say different things about the rigidity of the two programmes, they both represent a strong strategic intent. This underlines the fact that much successful knowledge sharing is the result of conscious efforts and managerial intervention.

On the "architectural" level, both Eurobest and the knowledge facilitation model aim to create a forum for dialogue and exchange. And this is happening in an organizational context where anonymity and exclusivity might otherwise prevail. In the large MNC, which is bound to have a more or less decentralized character, it becomes increasingly difficult for senior managers to influence and communicate with lower level instances. Operative units might have to focus on their day-to-day business and not engage in costly knowledge-sharing exercises. Both Eurobest and the knowledge facilitation model serve to create this forum — or space — in a cost-effective manner.

In the same train of thought, both cases display the will to deal with potentially difficult matters. Facing the prospects of "managing" tacit knowledge, an organization can either refrain completely, or give it a try by enabling people to interact. Of course, for someone less energetic, the first option might be tempting. The latter is costly; it could potentially initiate an aggravated debate, and cause different types of problems in the organizational dialogue. Thus, we claim that making an attempt to see the extent to which things can be exchanged, shared, is bold. Perhaps this potentially risky decision is what triggers creativity. If energy and slack resources are not allocated for these sorts of ventures, the strategic evolution of firms will fall completely into the hands of chance.

The two cases show that it is the intellectual capital that underlies various competitive advantages. In the case of SCA, it is individuals who are capable of sharing what they know in terms of operations management, while at AstraZeneca, it is the co-workers who conduct the new drug development projects that make the difference between successful and unsuccessful projects.

Implications for Practice

Relating the two cases to practice, a set of key implications can be discussed. For instance, the SCA case underlines the importance of attempting to document not only methods but also the results of knowledge sharing. In direct connection with the results, one central concern has been coming up with and *agreeing* upon common definitions, across the network of plants. Earlier attempts ended in problems when plants disagreed upon the definition of, say, machine productivity. Was it related to labour hours or should it be related to labour costs? In order to reach consensus and make sure that plants actually use the metrics, the careful managing of definitions was central.

Of course, another highly important factor at SCA was the strong awareness rapidly created in the project. Top management supported the venture whole-heartedly, especially after the first improvements became visible. Resources were allocated, progress was discussed at board meetings and communicated, loudly one could say, in internal communications as well as in annual reports and other exchanges with the stock market. In terms of selling the venture, rhetorical efforts were made at launching the Eurobest as absolutely instrumental to surviving in today's turbulent market. There was no option, if SCA wanted to continue to beat the competition and keep its customers satisfied.

Looking at the organization of Eurobest, a key decision would make it a central programme, under the management of the Vice President of Manufacturing. This created a scalability that would not have been in place locally.

This way, production knowledge was made global, in a sense. Furthermore, the symbolic effects of arranging it on this level meant a proper degree of attention was being paid to it. In its logical extension, the competition that was evidently initiated created in itself an incentive for plants to start taking in, absorbing, new knowledge and methods. And the larger the cup you're in the more prestigious it becomes. Additionally, it was evident that the perception of European competition also initiated more local forms of competition. The quote that Eurobest is an incentive not to be the worst in the network indicates this. But other respondents also said that they were now more prone to comparing themselves — and communicating — across shifts and plants. In a way, the world grew larger for many of the teams and workers on the programme.

But Eurobest would not have continued if it had not been a complement to the monitoring and more mute forms of knowledge exchange with more interactive efforts, e.g. training staff and creating forums for exchange other than the ones each plant let their people attend. Courses and formal education, as well as visits to machine suppliers aimed partly, in parallel with the exchange itself, at creating a sort of forum for people with the same sorts of duties; a forum which would enable them to get to know each other and which would generate an atmosphere of trust and of being peers. The fact that SCA actively took on new methods suggested by their employees, together with knowledge absorbed externally, was one indirect way of rewarding their staff. Being recognized for having formalized a solution to a practical problem is, of course, an honour in any given profession. And, of course, despite the fact that some saw it as being put on a pedestal, the vast majority of the staff saw the formal, annual award ceremonies as evidence of the company's strong belief in them, and felt honoured about it. The same sort of award rituals were organized *ad hoc* and regularly at local or regional levels as well.

However, the most important practical implication from the SCA case is, perhaps, the indication that learning and knowledge transfer are not *automatically* linked to performance. Of course, this might sound obvious to some, but much of the empirical work that has been done in this field takes little notice of this fact. In the SCA case, the plants that succeeded did so by making a strong effort. By making sure they balanced the side effects, by visibly involving local management, by training people, by following up and giving feedback, by pegging up aspiration levels above satisfaction, by involving all local functions, and by fitting the venture into a coherent plant strategy, certain plants made financial use of it. These efforts have little to do with learning or with absorptive or retentive incapacities, and more to do with simple stuff such as individual character and motivation. We shall talk more about this below, but one key implication from the SCA case is that knowledge sharing is far more than sharing and transferring knowledge. It requires activity and it might require a change of the range of matters outside the application of "new" knowledge in a particular setting.

The AstraZeneca case suggests that communication between functional areas is of great importance. The new drug development process is constituted by a series of laboratory activities, testing of the compound in biological models, and various sorts of *in vivo* studies. The sequential movement from the work done in the synthesis chemist's laboratory until the final New Drug Application leaves the pharmaceutical company consists of many points where different expertise and communities of practice and "communities of knowledge" overlap. At these points, it is important that these different communities and groups are capable of communicating with one another. For instance, it is important that representatives from experimental medicine, clinical development leaders and market representatives are capable of seeing one another's interests and concerns. When laboratory sciences encounter market demands for profitability, shareholder value and other financial performance measures, it is sometimes claimed that one group overrates the scientific interest while the other primarily emphasises the financial performance of the firm. Such clashes of interests can be dealt with through more carefully designed communication between the different groups and interests within the firm.

The AstraZeneca case also suggests that communities of practice are an important carrier of knowledge and competence within the firm. During the knowledge facilitation seminars, different representatives of the Clinical Development Leaders and Clinical Study Leaders were brought together and given the opportunity to talk to one another on various matters. Because of the functional organization of the new drug development process, communities of practice are important arenas for knowledge sharing. At AstraZeneca, the Project Management Support Office (PMSO) explicitly works towards creating and reinforcing communities of practice that have vested interests in different organizational activities. Communities of practice are, by definition, groups of people who share day-to-day operations and have a particular interest in developing those operations. These communities are the primary entity for knowledge sharing within the organization and so knowledge management activities are, in many cases, directed towards such communities.

The case of AstraZeneca also suggests that knowledge management activities are always, on the bottom line, based on practices. In the knowledge facilitation model, aimed at sharing knowledge between individuals, the relevant information was collected via interviews with the project manager and seminar discussions with project members in the focal team, and later on with project team members from other projects. All these activities were practices aimed at enabling a more open-ended discussion of topics of great importance to day-to-day work within the organization. The knowledge facilitation model does not rely on any advanced information or communication technology and does not require a lengthy training programme or some other investment, but is instead based on the ability to create trust and an open and sharing culture within the organization (see Styhre, Roth & Ingelgård, 2002). Therefore, the knowledge-sharing practices are always based on practices; practices of interviewing, practices aimed at building commitment, practices or communication. Similar to certain Japanese management techniques and models such as Quality Circles or Kaizen (continuous improvements), the knowledge facilitation model is founded on the participation of the co-workers, rather than being an expert-driven model. The knowledge sharing that is produced during the knowledge facilitation seminars is always an outcome of the individual participants' interests, concerns and challenges. The knowledge facilitator (as the name suggests) serves merely to orchestrate such interactions.

Learning from the Cases

One of the persistent themes of research based on qualitative methods is the question of generalization. By generalization, we mean that the specific case examined would be representative of a wider set of companies, thereby containing some general insights and learning. Underlying the idea of generalization, we find the particular representing the universal, i.e. single cases gives access to a broader number of (in our case) companies than the two just studied. The notion of generalization is therefore an epistemological question: Can the world be examined by means of examining its single components? Another name for this question is the *problem of induction*. That is, can new knowledge be created based on a series of observations of individual entities and, if this is the case, where does that series end (see Popper, 1959, for a discussion on the problem of induction). Two companies are, of course, a bit short to make up a series of examinations, but the strength of the case study method employed here is not its ability to handle the problem of induction, rather it is to offer what Harding (1998) calls *standpoint theories* and Haraway (1991) calls *situational knowledge*, i.e. contextual, embedded theories of practice. To put it another way, the issue of generalization is not what is prioritized here because the methodology chosen in this study does not rely on a large number of observations, on the contrary, it relies on detailed and contextual observations of practices at two single companies. Therefore, the concept of generalization belongs to a verificationist tradition of thinking represented by, for instance, logical empiricists (see for instance Ayer, 1936) which is not adhered to in this study. Just because the concept of *generalization* is slightly misplaced here, this does not mean that the idea that there may be some general learning from the two cases is irrelevant. Quite the opposite: The case study method is employed when the object of study is complex and has a complicated relationship with its environment. Therefore, the case study methodology is applicable when examining entire social systems such as organizations. One of the benefits of an integrated analysis of social systems is that such an analysis may enable insights that would not otherwise be achieved. There is some general learning to be had from the cases of SCA and AstraZeneca.

Both cases show that knowledge management practices may be regarded to be what Karl Weick (2001) has called *small wins*. Small wins are thus not achieved through grand organizational change programmes or new corporate policies, but emerge instead from within the day-to-day practices, the small but significant amendments to operations, the small-scale improvements. Even though small wins may be triggered by the announcement of large-scale changes or long-term objectives, it is, on the bottom line, the day-to-day working life changes that change the small wins into competitive advantages. At SCA, the Eurobest programme was declared to be a long-term challenge for the company but it was in day-to-day operations and its small changes to the operations of the machinery that Eurobest actually made a difference. At AstraZeneca, the small wins were derived from the collaboration and communication between individuals representing different types of functional expertise. In consequence, knowledge-sharing practices benefit from being designed as a bottom-up process wherein the individual co-worker's activities and operations are the "drivers" of knowledge sharing. In consequence, knowledge management practices preferably take their starting point in actual needs and practical concerns, rather than being based on some abstract principle of, say, shareholder value. Knowledge management practices need to be embedded in the day-to-day practices of the organization. They should aim for small wins rather than serving as points of bifurcation for the organization.

In its logical extension, the concept of small wins can be positioned in relation to more significant forms of effect. It could be that small wins, incrementally evolving into something larger, are the way by which knowledge transfer materializes strategically. It does not appear to be completely unlikely that advantages based on knowledge transfer grow out of long term cultivation rather than radical change. Rather than being an organizational, top-down, commanded improvement, learning is bound to be individual, based on the efforts of individuals at local sites. Top managers can only create impetus (cf. Bower, 1970; Burgelman, 1983), facilitate, in order for the employees to take on board new knowledge. This method might take time, but the incremental, individual fit can also create something that is unique to the organization, and hence help to support uniqueness and competitive advantage over a longer time span. Thus the non-radical character of small wins might not be less important, strategically. On the contrary, it can be a source of uniqueness, creating not just competitive advantage but also, through the development of new knowledge and new practices, a stronger sense of identity and community.

Revisiting the Literature on Knowledge Sharing

The two cases examined in this book have implications for the literature within the field of knowledge management addressing the theory of knowledge sharing. In this section, this literature will be critically evaluated on the basis of the two cases presented.

Beyond Knowledge Per Se

One first trait of the knowledge sharing literature is that it makes the assumption that knowledge *per se* is always a good thing, both for the organization and for the individual. This contests the definition of the construct of knowledge. Organization studies offer numerous examples where management has to deal with different sorts of rigidities, outmoded ideas, resistance, irrelevant beliefs, and so forth. In a seminal paper, Hedberg, Nystrom & Starbuck (1976) discussed the notion of unlearning as an important organizational capability. Organizations need, the argument goes, to continually adapt to an increasingly changing external environment (see for instance D'Aveni, 1994, who represents the extreme position here). This adaptation puts pressure on the organization to continuously respond and take into account various stimuli (for lack of a better word) deriving from this supposedly changing environment. In consequence, knowledge needs to be continuously updated and is therefore always a highly contested organizational and individual resource. For some people, knowledge of a particular area may be highly valued, while for others such knowledge is of little importance. Therefore, it is complicated to argue that knowledge *per se* is always a good thing for the organization. This general approval of knowledge and intellectual capital underrates the antagonistic relationship between different communities of practice or functional departments or areas of an organization. The literature of knowledge sharing therefore makes the construct of knowledge an apolitical resource; it is not even *non*-political, i.e. kept outside political discussions, but *a*political, by nature something that transcends such everyday political discussions. To put it another way, the literature on knowledge sharing would benefit from a more critical view of the construct of knowledge and from acknowledging that what counts as knowledge (or non-knowledge) in organizations is a highly contested issue. This may be even more pronounced in times of rapid or radical organizational change where old business models are replaced by new ones and where certain knowledge is becoming obsolete. A more political view of knowledge would be capable of showing how different ideologies, interests, beliefs and objectives strongly influence the view of knowledge in organizations. A more political view of knowledge would also be able to critically evaluate the idea that knowledge *per se* is always a good thing by definition. Instead, knowledge is, alluding to Nietzsche, beyond good and evil, i.e. beyond "good" and "bad". It is intellectual capital that is useful or not useful, depending on a multiplicity of decisions and external conditions.

With this view of knowledge, one also escapes the more immediate risk of falling into the tautology trap which evidently accompanies ideas related to the "role of knowledge", "the knowledge society", and so forth. Of course, knowledge is important. It is inherent in much of the way we use the concept in the first place. If you have knowledge, that is logically good. And if you are worse off, you do not have knowledge. But, of course, that is an incomplete view of the world. You can never disregard the context of knowledge. If you could, how would we explain failure?

Reviewing the empirical work on knowledge sharing (see Chapter Three), it is clear that much of that line of research simply assumes that knowledge is good. Obviously, one reason for this could be that the methods applied frequently involve survey questionnaires containing Likert scale questions asking respondents to assess whether the knowledge transfer venture has been successful or not (cf. Szulanski, 1996, 2000; Simonin, 1999). Many researchers might lack access to data, and because there appears to be a problem with doing case studies, this limited access inhibits further reasoning. Or, despite having talked about knowledge and competitive advantage, it could be the case that many researchers do not reflect on the fact that they do not study these concepts other than through questions like "has the programme been successful". Those who do study what could at least be termed proxies for profit, e.g. labour cost per unit of output (cf. Epple et al, 1991; Darr et al, 1996), do not appear to realize either that they have not studied strategy. The SCA case shows that even if costs are cut, prices may be cut as well, leaving no room for increased profit. There are exceptions which do not assume that knowledge transfer is directly linked with performance, e.g. Ingram and Baum (1997) and Tsai (2001), who enquire about financial performance indicators such as long-term survival and return on investment.

The two cases reported here suggest that what counts as such "useful" (again for lack of a better word) knowledge is always dependent on local practices and the interests of communities of practices. At AstraZeneca, the Clinical Development Leaders were concerned that their medical advisors (generally Medical Doctors) had not been very well trained by the company. In the view of the Clinical Development Leaders, the medical advisors were, of course, legitimate team members with extensive skills, experience and know-how, but as long as they were not experienced in clinical development work, their full competence could not be fully exploited. In this case, what counts as legitimate knowledge is grounded in the practices of clinical development work. In consequence, there is, alluding to Kant, no knowledge per se but only knowledge *for us*, i.e. knowledge that we can make use of and exploit in a more or less effective or useful manner. The literature on knowledge sharing would therefore benefit from conducting more empirical research wherein the notion of knowledge is critically scrutinized and elaborated upon.

At SCA, the fact that knowledge is not something inherently positive was displayed through the fact that even among those plants that did learn, absorb shared knowledge and improved their productivity, not everybody managed to convert that improvement into increased profit. Instead, some of them either failed to realize cost improvements through redundancies or make the necessary improvements in planning and production runs. Or, if they did cut costs, some still failed to keep price levels up and hence transferred the rents accruing from cost cuts to customers via reduced price levels. Not all plants did this but enough did it to offset any correlations between learning and financial performance, on the whole. So, making sure people learn is only a partial victory, at best. Furthermore, the SCA case shows that it is a mistake to assume that people will always take on new knowledge or attempt to learn. It is, perhaps, more likely that they will not be motivated to do so, simply because they are comfortable with what they have and do, because what they have done over the years has proven successful enough, and because it requires effort other than the cognitive acceptance of new advice to attempt to do things differently. When it comes to converting learning into performance improvements, it should be made crystal clear that such things might, in the end, involve deeply unpleasant consequences like making people, colleagues, redundant. This is likely to concern colleagues who have worked hard in knowledge transfer as well. Of course, realizing these sorts of improvements might not involve making people redundant but, as in the SCA case, the knowledge transferred was related to improving productivity, and anybody who wants to cash in on productivity gains either has to grow his or her business (using economies of scale) or make people redundant. Again, human nature is not, perhaps, an ideal "instrument" in these types of managerial situations. Here, management theories taking into account "bounded rationality" (March & Simon, 1958) or the institutional norms and values on the organization or industry levels, but even more so on the individual level (cf. Meyer & Rowan, 1977; DiMaggio & Powell, 1983; Scott, 1995; Oliver, 1997), are absolutely necessary in order to be able to explain and understand these situations.

Knowledge is Interested and Embedded in Motivation

The second thing to note about the literature on knowledge sharing is that it does not take into account the incentives of individuals to share their knowledge and to absorb the knowledge of others. This lack of incentives and motivation is related to the underlying idea that knowledge *per se* is a good thing, which in turn implies that no incentives are needed when sharing knowledge. However, it is one thing getting access to relevant knowledge and another thing sharing one's own. Giving and receiving are not the same, even though they pre-require one another. Speaking of knowledge sharing, without taking into account the incentives of the individual taking part in such an "exchange", makes knowledge an abstract category. In this text, it has been argued that knowledge sharing is always embedded in and derives from practices. Practices are the standard operational procedures, routines or other activities constituting the individual's work and what gives this work its meaning for the individual. Practices are, then, the elementary form of organizations, organizations are constituted by a multiplicity of practices. The notion of incentive is immanent in the idea of practice; a practice is always founded on the incentive to carry out that practice in a proper manner. Incentives in organizations are, for instance, prestige, monetary rewards, shared ideologies, professionalism, opportunistic behaviours, and a great number of other intrinsic and extrinsic motivations that affect the individual's actions. An employee may strongly dislike a practice but may still want to keep his or her job and thus there is an incentive to carry out the routine. However, little is said about either the negative or positive incentives of knowledge sharing in this literature. The cases of SCA and AstraZeneca suggest that knowledge sharing is embedded in a number of social relationships which in themselves create incentives for the individual. The individual co-worker at SCA or AstraZeneca takes part in communications and exchanges, not because he or she believes that knowledge *per se*, or knowledge sharing, is necessarily a good thing, but primarily because he or she has an incentive to conduct operations in an effective manner. At AstraZeneca, co-workers engaged in new drug development processes regarded knowledge sharing as a means to an end, rather than the primary objective. Their incentive to distribute their experiences and know-how was to get the new drug registered and thus their day-to-day practices embodied such an incentive.

The role of incentives is also clear at the receiving end, so to speak. As we have argued previously, one should not, perhaps, assume that individuals are prepared to take on new knowledge just because it is there and because head office said so. Instead, as is evident in the SCA case, a whole range of incentives might be necessary in order to stimulate learning. In the SCA case, we said that the local perception of the transfer programme, local aspiration, the view of internal competition, the view of the nature of knowledge, local programme management and local communication were of central importance among those who appeared to be more efficient at taking in new knowledge. All of these factors are, more or less, related to motivational concepts, rather than cognition and the immediate character of knowledge. They are related to human, and not necessarily cognitive, qualities. When these variables were in place, people felt an incentive, even a desire, to do things. And of course, one might be tempted to believe that "well, why doesn't management make sure these things are in place, then?". We would argue, "can they?". They might be able to, but it is far from easy, we believe. In a sense, management can potentially *earn* it, by constantly taking into account individual preferences and by fitting knowledge sharing ventures into these local preferences. If we look at those plants which took on new methods and transferred their operations to the extent that performance was improved, incentives also played a part at these later stages. Then, incentives could be either in the form of a poor strategic position, or simply that the new knowledge is perceived as having a role in the strategy of the plant. For instance, most of the SCA plants that did better had low-costs as part of their strategic priorities. A few managers suggested that Eurobest performance could be added to the items that they and their plants were assessed on, in order to make sure that any improvements made were converted into performance improvements.

As we have said in previous chapters, incentives and motivation are often neglected in discussions about the factors stimulating successful knowledge sharing (there are exceptions). Few studies include motivation at all, and the ones that do find no support for its being a factor. Part of the reason for this could, in the first place, be that they only study the factors behind accomplished transfers. And in such cases it is more likely that, for instance, cognitive factors are more important than motivation. But, in later stages, when it comes to changing routines and making organizational changes, possibly, the relative importance of motivation and incentives is probably larger.

Knowledge is Situational, Local and Context-dependent

A third factor related to incentives and motivation is the organizational context within which the transfer takes place. This is a more popular variable in much empirical research, and it is frequently suggested that the aspects of organizational context that matter are related to geographical proximity (Epple et al, 1991; Darr et al, 1996; Szulanski, 1996), cultural and organizational distance (Simonin, 1999), social networks (Argote & Ingram, 2000) and network centrality (Tsai, 2000, 2001). Geographical proximity, social networks and organizational distance can be partly offset by electronic networks when knowledge is more explicit. Cultural distance is perhaps more difficult to resolve by means of intranets and the like. In the SCA case, however, the means by which participating units are controlled or encouraged to take part is perhaps the most important organizational factor. Because SCA is well decentralized, it runs a risk of having to deal with issues such as the tyranny of SBUs (Prahalad & Hamel, 1990) in cases like this. Units are controlled financially with limited intervention from programmes. A plant can refrain from doing anything to improve its Eurobest performance, as long as it is not interested in receiving any awards or as long as it delivers what it should in terms of return on capital, cash-flow, EBIT or whatever it is measured by. And, in such a setting, corporate managers have some delicate dilemmas to live with. Trying to force an optimization of metrics other than the financials can cause problems. Not trying to can do so, too. It could be worthwhile to consider ways of controlling activities in two dimensions, i.e. triggering financial performance while making sure that other ventures are optimized. Hopefully there is no trade-off between them.

Lack of Empirical Qualitative Studies

Fourth, one may argue that there is a sparse supply of detailed, empirical studies of knowledge sharing in organizations. In many cases, the literature offers a number of conceptual elaborations of a number of key concepts, or it provides some anecdotal evidence of *ex post facto* results that primarily serve to show that knowledge sharing is a good thing, rather than providing more detailed accounts of how such a process may happen. Even this may appear to be a sweeping formulation, the lack of empirical studies is cumbersome because it makes what is essentially practical — as has been argued in this book — appear to be a set of abstract principles. As has been pointed out above, there is a tendency to treat knowledge as an inherently productive organizational resource while, in fact, what counts as knowledge is always contested. Such propositional definitions of knowledge (i.e. knowledge is defined in lexical terms and not in terms of its practical use) are representative of this difference between empirical studies and conceptual frameworks. This lack of empirical studies is accentuated in the strategic management literature. In addition, those empirical studies provided are, in many cases, based on quantitative and statistical analyses of organizational activities. It would be helpful if more case studies were provided in the literature.

It could be the case that much of the criticism of the existing knowledge sharing theory that we have just drawn upon is directly linked to the state of the general strategy field. As stated in Chapter Two, the strategy field is fragmented, with the resource-based view (RBV) and the Industrial Organization (IO) perspectives dominating much of the content-oriented research. Both are concerned with performance in some form, either through resource-centred rent generation or through improved profit levels, or through competitive advantage, but they have different explanations for the relative success of firms. RBV claims it is down to valuable, unique and costly-to-imitate resources, whereas IO claims it is a matter of configuring the value-chain in a way that reduces cost or increases price in relation to industrial forces. If we compare the state of the theory on knowledge sharing, it is clear that this view is intellectually closer to the RBV (and, considering the more frequently referred RBV papers, a substantial part of them directly address knowledge as a strategic resource, cf. Amit & Schoemaker, 1993; Collis, 1996; Grant, 1996). Much of the theorizing is focused upon describing the character of knowledge and the attributes of knowledge which link up with performance, or make it strategic. As we have discussed in Chapter 2, the RBV has two distinct features: the view of the attributes required to be strategic, and the different resource typologies. We would argue that much of the knowledge sharing theories, or at least the empirical studies, fully takes in the typology-related discussion, but pays less attention to the mechanisms that make knowledge and learning valuable and unique, and so forth. Much of the work focuses instead on the character of knowledge, for instance, regarding whether knowledge is tacit or explicit and what sort of effect this might have on learning. Another example is whether knowledge is individual or organizational. And, as indicated, when researchers attempt to explain successful knowledge sharing, by far the most popular group of factors is related to absorptive capacity (an attribute of the recipient of knowledge) and causal ambiguity (an attribute of the knowledge transferred, and related to tacitness). These are factors that are very close to the resource in question, i.e. knowledge. Evidently, these are important factors. What we are saying is that there is a range of other factors, related to bounded rationality, norms, values, attitudes, beliefs, and, we would argue, the qualities and preferences of the people involved on either side of a transfer situation. If they do not have the will to take part, things will fail. If they do not want to, it might be that the transfer does not affect activities, practice (or the value-chain). If they do not want to, there might be no effects on costs or sales (the generic strategy choices), meaning there will be no effect on results. So, possibly, we need to combine the resource-based bias regarding current knowledge transfer and sharing theory with, at least, the language of the IO view — and of course all the social theories needed to understand why these concepts are, or are not, affected in a given situation.

What is also important about the RBV is its interest in resource uniqueness. Few of the empirical studies on knowledge transfer study the issue of uniqueness, other than stating that uniqueness, while being central to competitiveness, could be a barrier to successful knowledge transfer within the organization. A piece of knowledge could be unique due to its being tacit and difficult to codify, and so on. This means it is difficult for competitors to imitate, but it also means it is complex to deal with internally (cf. Grant, 1996; Boisot et al, 1997; Sanchez, 1997). Few empirical studies take this dilemma into account (notable exceptions include Kogut & Zander, 1995). We have not discussed this explicitly in this book, for methodological reasons. We could not get hold of comparable data from competitors, and so, in the SCA case for instance, we had to rely on the SCA respondents' view as regards whether the Eurobest programme was unique or not. None thought that production knowledge had leaked out to competitors, but nonetheless certain plants had to realize that their competitors were probably able to cut their costs as well (or lower their performance targets). This could naturally be explained by factors other than production knowledge improvements.

So, why all the talk about performance, finance, and profit? Why not just focus on the qualities and effects, vis-à-vis humans, created by taking part in a knowledge sharing arrangement? Well, for one thing, many ventures like this are framed, at least initially, so as to generate performance results. Furthermore, strategy is inherently related to changes in performance. Strategy has to do with what firms do, or experience, that alters their performance level, either in relation to their history or in relation to some sort of external benchmark, e.g. competitors or stock market expectations. One could have a range of views regarding this. Perhaps it is more convenient for researchers to neglect the performance variable and only talk about the resource in question: "this company has gone through a competence development programme", or "this organization has moved swiftly down the learning curve". We, however, think that knowledge management, from a strategy perspective, has to make the connection with whether or not the effort has paid off. This does not mean, of course, that concepts other than financial ones are uninteresting. On the contrary, organizational theories, sociological theories, theories about decision-making and strategic management, as well as knowledge-centred theories are needed in order to understand why certain financial outputs have been met or not. They are required as factors, independent variables, and they say more if they can be compared to strategic outputs. This, by the way, and if anybody should be in doubt, is not to say that knowledge sharing ventures are always aimed at improving performance. Some might be aimed at making staff happy, and that could, of course, be interesting from a range of perspectives – but the strategy researcher will probably not take heed, unless one could foresee or identify an effect on performance or competitiveness.

In terms of strategy processes, the emergent capability perspective probably has some merit in outlining the strategy context of knowledge sharing ventures. Clearly, the ability to manage knowledge sharing can be seen as a capability (cf. Leonard-Barton, 1992; Teece et al, 1997; Eisenhardt & Martin, 2000). They help us to see what sort of resources a capability can consist of, and what sort of impact these attributes might have. But as stated earlier, there is a potential risk in turning management capabilities into yet another form of resource or asset, in the broader sense. Perhaps we should instead view the management of knowledge transfer as a strategic process and follow the more longitudinal logics of Bower (1970), Burgelman (1983), Chakravarthy and Doz (1992) and process-oriented RBV work, like Amit and Schoemaker (1993), Schoemaker and Amit (1994), and Oliver (1997). The common thread among these references is their focus on the factors behind firm and organization characteristics affecting performance. Because they aim to understand, for instance, how certain resources evolve, the theoretical, explanatory framework has to be pluralistic, and include assumptions about bounded rationality, politics, power, language, cognition, culture, norms and values, and so forth. In any given empirical situation, one probably needs a battery of models and theories — a sophisticated framework, one could say — to be able to understand why transfer works, or not. So, in relation to the strategy field, we argue that not only do we need to combine RBV thinking and the IO language, we also need to include the process perspective, to account for all the managerial and organizational obstacles that one can encounter while trying to share knowledge in a way that improves the strategic position.

A Framework for Knowledge Sharing in Organizations

The main arguments put forth in this book can be captured in Figure 6.1 below.

Figure 6.1. A framework for knowledge sharing in organizations

On the one hand, the organization's knowledge sharing practices are always based on day-to-day practices on the shop-floor, in offices, laboratories and other relevant organizational spaces. It is here that knowledge is constituted and employed and thus where value is added to the organizational practices. On the other hand, such everyday working life practices are always related to and aligned with the organization's competitive strategies. Long-term objectives and competitive strategies, in terms of positioning and the development and use of organizational capabilities and resources, have significant effects on the organization's practices. This dual model draws on the perennial actor-structure discussion in social theory; strategy represents the structure - practices the actor. In between the firm level perspective and the shop-floor perspective, knowledge sharing takes place. Knowledge sharing simultaneously draws on organizational strategies and day-to-day practices; it is what bridges the long-term and the short-term perspective, the company with the individual, the abstract with the concrete and tangible. Knowledge sharing is thus dependent on a number of different variables, factors and conditions. Three factors have been identified: (1) Organizational context, (2) Cognitive factors, and (3) Norms, institutions, and incentives.

Organizational context refers to what parts of the organization are involved in knowledge sharing activities. For instance, knowledge sharing may involve sites, departments and functional units, communities of practice or individuals. Different knowledge-sharing activities may thus involve a variety of approaches and methods. For instance, as the SCA case suggests, the computer-based information technology system may be a useful tool when distributing codified knowledge between sites.

Cognitive factors denote the quality of the knowledge being shared. The causal ambiguities of knowledge imply that it may be complicated to identify and understand the relationship between various forms of knowledge and performance, therefore knowledge sharing is inhibited due to influences of bounded rationality. Absorptive capacity refers to the ability of the "recipient" of the knowledge to adopt and make use of the knowledge. For instance, in highly-specialized activities such as new drug development, individuals with different levels of formal training and education representing different functional departments may have a problem fully recognizing the problems identified by other co-workers in a cross-functional team. Therefore, absorptive capacities serve to delimit knowledge sharing in organizations.

Norms, institutions and incentives refer to a variety of social and sociopsychological factors influencing and affecting knowledge sharing in organizations. For instance, motivation, both extrinsic (e.g. monetary rewards) and intrinsic (e.g. personal commitment and interests), is an individual or group-based socially embedded factor that has implications for knowledge sharing. Institutions refer to a broad set of taken-for-granted or unreflected *modus operandi*, or worldviews, that make individuals behave in accordance with certain beliefs and ideas. The third group of factors integrates a great number of opportunities and obstacles that knowledge management programmes need to take into account in order to anticipate different reactions or resistances. For instance, as the AstraZeneca case suggests, the belief among some of the clinical study team members that they "had little to say" served as an initial threshold that needed to be passed before knowledge sharing seminars could be meaningful. When articulating the idea that experiences drawn from clinical studies could be of great help to newcomers and newly-started clinical studies, the initial scepticism turned into an affirmative attitude towards knowledge facilitation work.

The framework for knowledge sharing presented here thus recognizes that knowledge sharing is a strategic matter embedded in day-to-day practices. Knowledge sharing is also dependent on a number of social, cognitive, and culture-organizational aspects that need to be taken into account when running knowledge facilitation programmes. Knowledge is too elusive and ambiguous a construct to be captured by generic models and standardized procedures, but hopefully, the two cases have shown that knowledge-sharing activities are applicable — when carefully designed to serve specific interests and local organizational settings — to a number of highly heterogeneous environments. Needless to say, there are significant differences between corrugated paper manufacturing and new drug development, but the construct of knowledge sharing makes sense in both settings. Therefore, the framework for knowledge sharing is to be regarded as a mapping of what is inherently evolving and changing.

Summary and Conclusion

In this book, knowledge sharing has been approached from two different perspectives. On the one hand, all knowledge sharing occurs as *practices*, in conversations, operations, discussions and practical undertakings in everyday working life. One the other hand, knowledge sharing is a strategic management issue, aimed at creating sustainable competitive advantages. Treating knowledge sharing as a practice implies a bottom-up perspective of knowledge management; treating it as a strategic matter, makes knowledge sharing a top management priority. This dual nature of knowledge management is important to maintain when investing in knowledge management practices. Organizational resources and capabilities are always emerging from within practices but such practices need to be coordinated, monitored, and supported; in brief to become part of the firm's strategy. The two empirical studies, two cases representing two different industries and companies, suggest that knowledge sharing is a useful concept in various environments. The day-to-day practices of SCA and AstraZeneca comprise a great number of heterogeneous and specialized competencies and know-how, but in both cases, the idea of sharing such knowledge between individuals made sense and resulted in several practical undertakings. When scrutinizing the literature on knowledge management in general, and knowledge sharing, one may notice that there is an underlying assumption that knowledge is good *per se* and that knowledge is treated as a general construct applicable in all sorts of settings. In addition, the lack of detailed empirical studies makes it complicated to identify knowledge sharing practices which recognize the importance of a local, context-dependent and situational view of knowledge. The two cases presented in this book point to the local practices of knowledge sharing; the conversations, seminars, discussions and elaborations making up the knowledge-sharing process. Rather than thinking of knowledge sharing solely in instrumental and functionalist terms, it is important to acknowledge the fluid and social nature of knowledge. Therefore, it is important to think of knowledge sharing in terms of heterogeneous and polymorphous social interactions. For instance, the SCA case suggests that motivation and incentives are of great importance when conducting knowledge-sharing programmes. But motivation and incentives are always embedded in local and idiosyncratic conditions at the workplace, in the community of practice, or in a work team. Thus, knowledge sharing will always take place within social communities and can never be fully understood outside of such social relationships. This implies that the field of knowledge management would benefit from more detailed empirical studies wherein the context-dependent aspects of knowledge sharing are emphasized. In consequence, the predominant belief in the field that knowledge is always a good thing per se would be subject to criticism because day-to-day practices not only show how knowledge is constituted and employed, but also how certain knowledge is excluded and marginalized.

Hopefully, this book has contributed towards a more elaborated discussion on knowledge sharing within organizations. If nothing else, it points to the dual nature of knowledge sharing: it is both subject to corporate strategy decisions and is emerging from everyday work life practices. Effective knowledge sharing takes place on the macro-level and micro-level nexus. Furthermore, the two cases have pointed to the emergent and context-specific nature of knowledge. Similar studies in other industries and domains of social life would be beneficial to understanding how knowledge is constituted and shared in organizations and in society.

Appendix I: On Method

In this appendix, we will address some methodological issues. To start with, we will frame the two studies as being based on a collaborative research method, i.e. a research method that actively involves the members of the studied organization in practical research work. Then we will examine the data collection and analysis procedures used in the two cases.

Collaborative Research

In *The Nichomachean Ethics*, Aristotle writes (1996: 5): "[T]he end of science is not knowledge but action". Although this claim may appear modest, business school research has been criticized for not being exact followers of Aristotle in this respect. A more recent argument in the same vein is provided by Steve Fuller (1992): "Without succumbing to anti-intellectualism, a democratic society must always be suspicious of conceptions of knowledge in which the most valued forms of knowledge are the least accessible, or more sociologically, the most esteemed knowledge producers are the ones whose goods are accessible only to an elite set of consumers" (Fuller, 1992: 397).

Recently, there has been some debate over the lack of practical implications arising from business school research efforts. This discussion was initiated early on in the UK in the mid-1990s, influenced by Gibbons, et al.'s (1994) *The New Production of Knowledge* (see MacLean, MacIntosh and Grant, 2002; Tranfield and Starkey, 1998; Lilley, 1997) and has since then expanded overseas. Special issues dealing with the role of the university and the business school have been published by *Academy of Management Journal* (2001), *British Journal of Management* (2001) and *Organization* (2001). In addition, the corporate scandals in the US during 2002 further animated the discussion concerning the social role and purpose of business schools (Gioia, 2002; Adler, 2002).

To simplify things a bit, one may say that there are two different camps in this debate. On the one hand, there are the protagonists of a more practitioner-oriented research wherein practical problems are favoured over theoretical discussions. On the other hand, there are the defenders of the dominant paradigm. Starkey and Madan (2001) argue that there is a gap between the practitioners' interests and the business school researchers' endeavours. Rather than engaging in practical matters, researchers stick to what Astley (1985) calls literature-based research, i.e. theoretical problems, rather than problem-based research. Pfeffer and Fong (2002) argue that there is very little evidence that neither business school research nor business school graduate education makes any difference in terms of firm performance and bottom line results. For Pfeffer and Fong (2002), this implies that business schools need to critically evaluate the role they are intending to play in contemporary society. Similar concerns have been addressed by, for instance, Huff (2000) and Rynes, Bartunek and Daft (2001). On the other hand, business school research has been defended in terms of being a warrant for autonomous and critical researchers. For Grey (2001), the research done at business schools needs to be examined from a historical perspective. Grey writes:

> Business schools, more perhaps than any other part of universities, experience a curious dual insecurity. On the one hand, they fear, and have often experienced, the scorn of other, more traditional academic subjects. On the other hand, they often stand accused of being less relevant to business needs and concerns (Grey, 2001: S27).

The positivist and functionalist research paradigm generally dominated in business schools and social science departments until at least the 1970s (and this research tradition is still strong in many universities and business schools) because the natural sciences appeared to serve as a relevant, and above all legitimate, role model. While making claims of being able to offer practical useful knowledge, business schools have to deal with two, to some extent complementary, objectives: to conduct "rigorous" science while at the same time being able to promote it on the market. Grey (2001) believes that it is important that business school researchers maintain an independent role in society. Thus, one needs to accept a certain degree of autonomy in order to be able to deliver "useful knowledge":

> Much knowledge will ... only be used by other academics during the process of refining, testing, criticizing and discarding. This process is by no means self-indulgent or wasteful: it is central to the development of useable knowledge (Grey, 2001: S29).

In a similar manner, Kilduff and Kelemen (2001) express their deep concerns over business school research that is too entangled with practitioners' interests. They state their position quite explicitly: "To ask practitioners to play a major role in setting the research agenda is to risk condemning business-school research to a permanent triviality" (Kilduff and Keleman, 2001: S58).

The debate on the future of business school research serves as a background to the research methodology applied in the two cases. In both the SCA and AstraZeneca cases, we have elaborated closely with practicing managers and have enabled their interests to be reflected in the research methodology and outline. We refer to this research approach, following Adler, Shani and Styhre (2003), as a *collaborative research* method. Collaborative research shares many characteristics with action research methods (for an overview, see Reason & Bradbury 2001; Babüroglo & Ravn, 1992; Reason, 1999, 1994; Eden & Huxham, 1996; McNiff, 2000). To put it briefly, collaborative research and action research differs in terms of the degree of practitioner involvement; in action research, it is primarily the academic researcher that orchestrates the research process while in collaborative research, the entire research effort is the joint responsibility of the academic researchers and the participating practicing managers. Collaborative research implies here that we have not only attempted to enable research outcomes that appear in a published form in academic journals, we have also sought to provide knowledge (in its broadest sense) that could be of some help, in one way or another, to the participating companies. In addition, collaborative research is based on the active involvement of practicing managers. In the two studies, practicing managers were participating during the problem definition phase, the empirical work, and the analysis of the empirical material. The research also contributed to a discussion at the two firms.

Although we believe that there are several areas of research where an autonomous and independent researcher ensures the best relationship vis-à-vis the object of study, we think that business school research is, on the bottom line, aimed at producing practical knowledge (see Hatchuel, 2001). What is a source of discussion is, of course, using which time perspectives knowledge should attempt to be practical. Much knowledge produced by business school researchers, for instance more theoretical debates, may only be proven to be very practical after a substantial period of time. What appears to be the major source of concern for defenders of the dominant research paradigm is that all knowledge should be of immediate practical use. We believe that collaborative research may be a useful approach to enabling both qualified theoretical knowledge and knowledge that may be useful for organizational practices. We do not necessarily see a trade-off between academic rigour and practical relevance. In addition, the collaborative research method remains rather unexploited in business school research and thus — here we can talk in terms of the law of diminishing returns — there may be significant opportunities for new research findings and contributions.

Appendix II: Research Methods

SCA

Data Collection

All in all, SCAP has some 200 plants, but only 38 box plants (as of 2001) have a sufficiently homogeneous machine line-up and been part of the group long enough to be studied extensively. The 38 plants are spread across Ireland, the UK, France, Italy, Switzerland, Germany, Belgium, the Netherlands, Denmark and Sweden. Three basic outputs are measured per machine: average machine speed, direct productivity and waste; these results are reported monthly from the plants to the head office.

Data Analysis

The study is divided into two parts. The first is quantitative and aims to outline, generally at SCAP, 1) whether knowledge sharing (learning) has occurred, 2) the effects of sharing (learning) on cost items and price, and 3) the effects on profit. Here, we used reported data about machine speed (SPEED: average machine speed over the year), direct productivity (DIRPROD: average direct labour/unit of output over the year) and waste (WASTE: annual waste as proportion of purchased raw material) from the 38 plants between 1996 and 2001, for one type of machine (the only type existing at all plants). We then studied the correlations between these machine performance indicators and profit and loss data to check the relationships between achieved knowledge sharing and financial performance. The operating margin (MARGIN), and price (PRICE), total cost (TOTCOST), raw material cost (RAWMTRL), and labour cost (LABOUR) were selected, the latter four being measured in terms of the average per unit of output.

After having studied the general links between transfer success and financial performance, certain patterns became evident. In order to study them further, six plants experiencing different degrees of success were singled out for onsite case studies. The issue was then largely a matter of tracking the local success and failure factors, along different stages of the causal chain. At each plant, we interviewed the general manager, the production manager, the sales manager, a supervisor, and an operator. Interviews were semi-structured, including both closed and open questions to ensure exploration. Here, the factors given by theory (see Chapter 3) were enquired about, but we also enquired openly about other factors. We also conducted interviews with representatives of top management, including the programme manager. In total, 34 interviews were conducted.

AstraZeneca

The chapter on knowledge sharing at AstraZeneca is based on a research programme that has been running for a number of years within the Fenix Research Programme. Jonas Roth and Alexander Styhre conducted a study of how clinical project teams could share experiences and know-how in order to enable a more effective clinical research process at AstraZeneca. Eventually, Jonas Roth developed and implemented the knowledge facilitation model discussed in Chapter five, also in addition to presenting some of the learning and experiences in his doctoral thesis defended at Chalmers University of Technology. In 2002, Jonas Roth and Alexander Styhre embarked upon a study of how knowledge sharing could be organized between sites and projects. This study serves as the basis for the latter half of Chapter five (the section on far transfer).

Data Collection

Data was collected using a number of different methods and approaches over a four-year period. In the initial study, interviews were conducted with project co-workers in two clinical project teams comprising a variety of competencies. These interviews were semi-structured and lasted for approximately for 1.5 hours. Work on the knowledge facilitation model is discussed in Chapter five. This included numerous seminars and meetings with project co-workers in Clinical R&D at AstraZeneca.

Data Analysis

All interviews were transcribed by an independent bureau. The analysis of the material centred on finding categories that could capture recurrent themes in the material. The material was examined by three independent researchers and the final categories were negotiated among the participating researchers. After the initial analysis had finished, the results were reported back to the interviewees who were asked to provide remarks and comments on the analysis. This approach proved to be useful because it provided additional information on the practices in use at AstraZeneca.

References

Abrahamson, E. (1996a), Management fashion, *Academy of Management Review*, 21(1): 254–285.

Abrahamson, E. (1996b) Technical and aesthetic fashion, in Czarniawska, B. & Sévon, G., (eds.) *Translating Organizational Change*, Berlin: de Gruyter.

Abrahamson, E. & Fairchild, G. (1999) Management fashion: Lifecycles, triggers, and learning processes, *Administrative Science Quarterly*, 44: 708–740.

Adler, N., Shani, A.B. & Styhre, A. Eds., (2003), *Collaborative research in organizations*, London, Thousand Oaks & New Delhi: Sage.

Adler, P.S. (2001), Market, hierarchy, and trust: The knowledge economy and the future of capitalism, *Organization Science*, 12(2): 215–234.

Adler, P.S. (2002), Corporate scandals: It's time for reflection in business schools, *Academy of Management Executive*, 16(3): 148–149.

Alvesson, M. (2001), Knowledge work: Ambiguity, image and identity, *Human Relations*, 54(7): 863–886.

Ambrosini, V. & Bowman, C. (2002), Mapping successful organizational routines, in Huff, Anne S. & Jenkins, Mark, eds., (2002), *Mapping strategic knowledge*, London, Thousand Oaks & New Delhi: Sage.

Amit, R. & Schoemaker, P.J.H. (1993). Strategic assets and organizational rent. *Strategic Management Journal* 14(1): 33–46.

Andrews, K.R. (1971). *The concept of core strategy*. Homewood: Irwin.

Ansoff, H.I. (1965). *Corporate strategy: An analytical approach to business policy for growth and expansion*. New York: McGraw–Hill.

Argote, L. & Ingram, P. (2000). Knowledge transfer: A basis for competitive advantage in firms. *Organizational Behavior and Human Decision Processes*, 82(1): 150–169.

Arnoldi, J. (2001), Niklas Luhmann: An introduction, *Theory, Culture & Society*, 18(1): 1–13.

Aristotle, (1996),*The Nicomachean Ethics*, Ware: Wordsworth.

Arthur, W.B. (1994). *Increasing returns and path dependence in the economy*. Ann Arbor: The University of Michigan Press.

Astley, W. G. (1985), Administrative science as socially constructed truth, *Administrative Science Quarterly*, 30: 497–513.

Augier, M. & Thanning Vendelø, M. (1999), Networks, cognitions and management of tacit knowledge, *Journal of Knowledge Management*, 3(4): 252–261.

Babüroglo, O.N., & Ravn, I. (1992). Normative action research, *Organization Studies*, 13(1), 19–34.

Bakken, T. & Hernes, T. Eds., (2003), *Autopoetic organization theory: Drawing on Niklas Luhmann's social systems perspective*; Oslo: Abstrakt; Malmö: Liber; Copenhagen: Copenhagen Business School Press.

Bain, J.S. (1968). *Industrial organization*. New York: Wiley.

Barnard, C.I. (1938). *The functions of the executive*. Cambridge: Harvard University Press.

Barney, J.B. (1986). Strategic factor markets, expectations, luck and business strategy. *Management Science*, 42: 1231–1241.

Barney, J.B. (1991). Firm resources and sustained competitive advantage. *Journal of Management*, 17(1): 99–120.

Barney, J.B. (1994a). Bringing managers back in. In Barney, J., Spender, J.C. and T. Reve (eds), *Does management matter?* Lund: Lund University Press.

Barney, J.B. (1994b). Commentary: A hierarchy of corporate resources (A.L. Brumagim). In Shrivastava, P., A. Huff & J. Dutton (eds), *Advances in Strategic Management*. Greenwich: JAI Press.

Barney, J.B. (2001a). Resource-based theories of competitive advantage: A ten-year retrospective of the resource-based view. *Journal of Management*, 27: 643–650.

Barney, J.B., (2001b), Is the resource-based "view" a useful perspective for strategic management research? Yes, *Academy of Management Review*, 26(1): 41–56.

Barney, J.B. & Hesterly, W., (1999), Organizational Economics: Understanding the Relationship Between Organizations and Economic Analysis, in Clegg, S.R., Hardy, C. & Nord, W.R., Eds., (1999), *Studying Organizations: Theory and Method*, London: Sage.

Baudrillard, J. (1998), *The consumer society: Myths & Structures*, Thousand Oaks, London & New Delhi: Sage.

Bauman, Z., (1991) Modernity and the Holocaust, Cambridge: Polity Press.

Bauman, Z. (1999), *Culture as praxis*, London, Thousand Oaks & New Delhi: Sage.

Baumard, P. (1999), *Tacit knowledge in organizations*, London: Sage.

Becker, H.S., Geer, B., Highes, E.C., & Strauss, A.L., (1961), *Boys in white: Student culture in medical school,* Chicago: The University of Chicago Press.

Bell, D. (1973), *The coming post-industrial society,* New York: Basic Books.

Benders, J. & van Veen, K. (2001), What's in a fashion? Interpretative viability and management fashion, *Organization,* 8(1): 33–53.

Best, S. & Kellner, D. (2001), *The postmodern adventure: Science, technology, and cultural studies at the third millennium,* London & New York. Routledge.

Bettis, R. & Prahalad, C.K. (1995): The dominant logic: Retrospective and extension. *Strategic Management Journal,* 16(1): 5–14.

Black, J.A. & Boal, K.B. (1994). Strategic resources: Traits, configurations and paths to sustainable competitive advantage. *Strategic Management Journal* 15(2): 131–148.

Boden, D. (1994), *The business of talk: Organizations in action,* Cambridge: Polity Press.

Bogaert, I., Martens, R. & Van Cauwenbergh, A. (1994): Strategy as a situational puzzle: The fit of components. In G. Hamel & Heene A. (eds): *Competence-based competition.* Chichester: Wiley.

Boisot, M., Griffiths, D. & Moles, V. (1997). The dilemma of competence: Differentiation versus integration in the pursuit of learning. In Sanchez, R. & Heene, A. eds, (1997), *Strategic learning and knowledge management.* Chichester: Wiley.

Boisot, M.H. (1998), *Knowledge assets: Securing competitive advantage in the information economy,* Oxford: Oxford University Press.

Boje, D.M. (1991), The storytelling organization: a study of story performance in an office supply firm, *Administrative Science Quarterly,* 36: 106–126.

Boje, D.M., (2001), *Narrative methods for organization research & communication research,* London, Thousand Oaks & New Delhi: Sage.

Boland, R.J., Jr., et al (2001), Knowledge presentations and knowledge transfer, *Academy of Management Journal,* 44(2): 393–417.

Bourdieu, P. & Passeron, J-C, (1977), *Reproduction in education, society, and culture,* London: Sage.

Bourdieu, P., (1977), *Outline of a theory of practice,* Cambridge: Cambridge University Press.

Bourdieu, P., (1990), *The logic of practice,* Cambridge: Polity Press.

Bourdieu, P. et al., (1999), *The weight of the world: Social suffering in the contemporary society,* Cambridge: Polity Press.

Bower, J.L. (1970). *Managing the resource allocation process.* Cambridge: Harvard University Press.

Brandenburger, A. & Nalebuff, B. (1996). *Co-opetition*. New York, Doubleday.

Braudel, F. (1992), *The wheels of commerce: Civilization & capitalism 15th–18th century*, Vol.2, Berkeley & Los Angeles. The University of California Press.

Brief, A.P., (1998), *Attitudes in and Around Organizations*, London: Sage.

Brown, S.D. & Lightfoot, G. (2002), Presence, absence, and accountability: E-mail and the mediation of organizational memory, in Woolgar, Steve, ed., (2002), *Virtual society? Technology, cyberbole, reality*, Oxford & New York: Oxford University Press.

Brown, S.L. & Eisenhardt, K.M. (1998). *Competing on the edge: Strategy as structured chaos*. Cambridge: Harvard Business School Press.

Brusoni, S. & Prencipe, A. (2001), Managing knowledge in loosely coupled networks: Exploring the links between product and knowledge dynamics, *Journal of Management Studies*, 38(7): 1019–1035.

Brumagim, A.L. (1994). A hierarchy of corporate resources. In Shrivastava, P., Huff, A. & Dutton, J. (eds): *Advances in strategic management*, 10A, 81–112. Greenwich: JAI Press.

Burgelman, R.A. (1983). Corporate entrepreneurship and strategic management: Insights from a process study. *Management Science* 29(12): 1349–1364.

Burgelman, R.A. (1988). Strategy making as a social learning process: The case of internal corporate venturing. *Interfaces* 18(3): 74–85.

Callon, M. (2002), Writing and (re)writing devices as tools for managing complexity, in Law, J. & Mol, A., Eds., (2002), *Complexities: Social studies of knowledge practices*, Durham & London: Duke University Press.

Cardinal, L.B. (2001), Technological innovation in the pharmaceutical industry: The use of organizational control in managing research and development, *Organization Science*, 12(1): 19–36.

Castells, M., (1996), *The information age: Economy, society and culture*, Vol. 1: *The rise of the network society*, Oxford: Blackwell.

Castoriadis, C., (1987), *The imaginary institutions of society*, trans. by Kathleen Blamey, Cambridge. Polity Press.

Cavanaugh, J.M. & Prasad, P. (1994), Drug testing as symbolic managerial action: In response to 'A case against workplace drug testing', *Organization Science*, 5(2): 267–271.

de Certeau, M., Girard, L., Mayol, P., (1998), *Practices of everyday life*, Vol. 2, Minneapolis: University of Minnesota Press.

de Certeau, M. (1984), *Practices of everyday life*, Berkeley: University of California Press.

Chakravarthy, B.S. & Doz, Y. (1992). Strategy process research: Focusing on corporate self-renewal. *Strategic Management Journal* 13(1): 5–14.

Chandler, A.D. (1962). *Strategy and structure: Chapters in the history of industrial enterprise.* Cambridge: MIT Press.

Chatterjee, S. (1998). Delivering desired outcomes efficiently: The creative key to competitive strategy. *California Management Review*, 40(2): 78–95.

Chieza, V. & Manzini, R. (1997). Competence levels within firms: A static and dynamic analysis. In Heene, A. & Sanchez, R. (eds). *Competence-based Strategic Management.* Chichester: Wiley.

Chomsky, N., (1968), *Language and mind*, New York: Harcourt Brace Jovanovich.

Cillier, P. (1998), *Complexity and postmodernism*, London: Routledge.

Clegg, S.R., Viera de Cunha, J., Pina e Cunha, M. (20029, Management paradoxes. A relational view, *Human Relations*, 55(5): 483–503.

Cockburn, I.M. & Henderson, R.M., (1998), Absorptive Capacity, Co-authoring Behavior, and the Organization of Research in Drug Recovery, *The Journal of Industrial Economics*, 46(2): 157–182.

Cohen, W.M. & Levinthal, D. A. (1990). Absorptive Capacity: A new perspective on learning and innovation. *Administrative Science Quarterly* 35(1): 128–152.

Collins, D. (2000) *Management fads and buzzwords: Critical-practical perspectives*, London & New York: Routledge.

Collins, D. (2001), The fad motif in management scholarship, *Employee Relations*, 23(1): 26–37.

Collis, D.J. (1994). Research note: How valuable are organizational capabilities? *Strategic Management Journal*, 15(3): 143–152.

Collis, D.J. (1996). Organizational capability as a source of profit. In Moingeon, B. & Edmondson, A (eds). *Organizational learning and competitive advantage.* London: Sage.

Conner, K.R. (1991). A historical comparison of resource-based theory and five schools of thought within industrial organisation economics: Do we have a new theory of the firm? *Journal of Management* 17(1): 121–155.

Conner, K.R. & Prahalad, C.K. (1996). A resource-based theory of the firm: Knowledge vs opportunism. *Organization Science*, 6: 502–518.

Cool, K. & Dierickx, I (1994), Commentary: Investments in strategic assets: Industry and firm-level perspectives (P. Schoemaker & R. Amit). In Shrivastava, P., Huff, A. & Dutton, J. (eds): *Advances in Strategic Management*, 10A, 35–44. Greenwich: JAI Press.

Cyert, R.M. & March, J.G. (1963), *A behavioural theory the firm*, Englewood Cliffs: Prentice-Hall.

Czarniawska, B. (1998), *A narrative approach to organization studies*, Thousand Oaks, London & New Delhi: Sage.

D'Aveni, R. (1994). *Hypercompetition: The dynamics of strategic maneuvering*. New York. Free Press.

Daft, R.L. & Weick, K.E., (1984), Toward a model of organizations as interpretation systems, *Academy of Management Review*, 9(2): 284–295.

Darr, E.D., Argote, L. & Epple, D. (1996). The acquisition, transfer, and depreciation of knowledge in service organizations: Productivity in franchises. *Management Science*, 41(11): 1750–1762.

Davenport, T.H. & Prusak, L. (1998) *Working knowledge. How organizations manage what they know*, Boston: Harvard Business School Press.

Deal, T.E. and Kennedy, A.A., (1982), *Corporate culture*, Reading: Addison-Wesley.

Debord, G. (1977), *Society of the spectacle*, Detroit: Black & Red.

Deery, S., Iversen, R. & Walsh, J. (2002), Work relationships in telephone call centers: Understanding emotional exhaustion and employee withdrawal, *Journal of Management Studies*, 39(4): 471–496.

Deleuze, G., (1988), *Foucault*, Minneapolis: University of Minnesota Press.

De Long, D.W. & Fahey, L. (2000), Diagnosing cultural barriers to knowledge management, *Academy of Management Executive*, 14(4): 113–127.

Dewey, J. (1988), *The quest for certainty, The later works, 1925–1953: Volume 4: 1929*, Edited by J.A. Boydston, Carbondale & Edwardsville. Southern Illinois University Press.

Dierickx, I. & Cool, K. (1989). Asset stock accumulation and sustainability of competitive advantage. *Management Science*, 35(12): 1504–1511.

DiMaggio, P.J. & Powell, W.W. (1983). The iron cage revisited: Institutional isomorphism and collective rationality in organizational fields. *American Sociology Review*, 48(2): 147–160.

Dixon, N.M., (2000), *Common knowledge*, Cambridge: Harvard Business School Press.

Donaldson, G. (1969). *Strategy for financial mobility*. Boston: Harvard University Press.

Donnellon, A. (1996), *Team talk: Listening between the lines to improve team performance*, Boston: Harvard Business School Press.

Du Gay, P., (1996), *Consumption and identity at work*, London: Sage.

Durand, T. (1997). Strategizing for innovation: Competence analysis in assessing strategic change. In Heene, A. & Sanchez, R. (eds). *Competence-based strategic management.* , Chichester: Wiley.

Dyer, J.H, & Nobeoka, K. (2000), Creating and managing high-performance knowledge sharing networks: The Toyota case, *Strategic Management Journal*, 21: 345–367.

Eden C., & Huxham, C. (1996). Action research for the study of organizations. in *Handbook of Organization Studies,* Clegg S.R., Hardy C., &
Nord W.R. (Eds.); London, Thousand Oaks, & New Delhi: Sage.

Edstrom, A. & Galbraith, J.R. (1977). Transfer of managers as a coordination and control strategy in multinational organizations. *Administrative
Science Quarterly,* 22(2): 248–263.

Edwards, P., Collinson, M. & Rees, C., (1998), The determinants of employee responses to total quality management: Six case studies', *Organization Studies,* 19(3): 449–475.

Ehrenreich, B. (2001), *Nickel and dimed: Undercover in low-wage* USA, London: Granta.

Eisenhardt, K.M. & J.A. Martin (2000). Dynamic capabilities: What are
they? *Strategic Management Journal* 21(S): 1105–1121.

Empson, L. (2001), Fear of exploitation and fear of contamination: Impediments to knowledge transfer in mergers between professional service
firms, *Human Relations,* 54(7): 839–862.

Epple, D., Argote, L. & Devadas, R. (1991). Organisational learning curves:
a method for investigating intra-plant transfer of knowledge acquired
through learning by doing. *Organization Science,* 2(1): 58–70.

Epple, D., Argote, L. & Murphy, K. (1996). An empirical investigation of the
microstructure of knowledge acquisition and transfer through learning by
doing. *Operations Research,* 44(1), 77–86.

Etzioni, A. (1964), *Modern organizations,* Englewood Cliffs: Prentice-Hall.

Fayol, H. (1949). *General and industrial management.* London: Pitman.

Featherstone, M. & Burrows, R. (1995), Cultures of technological embodi-
ment: An introduction, in Featherstone, M. & Burrows, R., Eds., (1995),
*Cyberspace/cyberbodies/cyberpunk: Cultures of technological representa-
tions,* London: Sage.

Feldman, M.S. & Rafaeli, A. (2002), Organizational routines as sources of
connections and understandings, *Journal of Management Studies,* 39(3):
309–331.

Feldman, M.S., (2000), Organization routines as a source of continuous
change, *Organization Science,* 11(6): 611–629.

Fineman, S. (2001), Fashioning the environment, *Organization,* 8(1): 17–31.

Fineman, S., Ed. (1993), *Emotions in organizations,* London: Sage.

Foss, N.J. (1997): Resources and strategy: Resources and strategy: Problems,
open issues and ways ahead. In Foss, N.J. (ed): *Resources, firms and
strategies. A reader in the resource-based perspective.* 345–365. Oxford.
Oxford University Press.

Foss, N.J. & Pedersen, T. (2002). Transferring knowledge in MNCs: The role of sources of subsidiary knowledge and organisational context. *Journal of International Management*, 8(1): 49–67.

Foucault, M. (1972), *An archaeology of knowledge*, London: Routledge.

Foucault, M. (1973), *The Birth of the Clinic*, London: Routledge.

Fuller, S. (1992), Social epistemology and the research agenda of science studies, in Pickering, A., ed., (1992), *Science as practice and culture*, Chicago & London: The University of Chicago Press.

Gabriel, Y. (2000), *Storytelling in organizations: facts, fictions, and fantasies*, Oxford: Oxford University Press.

Galbraith, J.K., (1958), *The affluent society*, Boston: Houghton Mifflin.

Galbraith, J.R. (1973). *Designing complex organizations*. Reading: Addison-Wesley.

Garfinkel, H., (1967), *Studies in ethnomethodology*, Englewood Cliffs: Prentice-Hall.

Geertz, C. (2000), *Available light: Anthropological reflections on philosophical topics*, Princeton: Princeton University Press.

Gherardi, S. & Nicolini, D. (2000), To transfer is to transform: The circulation of safety knowledge, *Organization*, 7(2), 329–348.

Gherardi, S. & Nicolini, D. (2001), The sociological foundations of organizational learning, in Dierkes, M., Berthon, A., Child, J. & Nonaka, I., Eds., (2001), *Handbook of organizational learning & knowledge*, Oxford: Oxford University Press.

Gherardi, S. (2000), Practice-based theoretizing on learning and knowing in organizations, *Organization*, 7(2), 211–223.

Gibbons, M., et al, Eds., (1994), *The new production of knowledge*, London: Sage.

Gibson, J.W. & Tesone, D.V., (2001), Management fads: Emergence, evolution, and implications for managers, *Academy of Management Executive*, 15(4): 122–133

Giddens, A. (1990), *The consequences of modernity*, Cambridge: Polity Press.

Gilbreth, F.B. (1911). *Motion study: A method for increasing the efficiency of the workmen*. New York: Van Nostrand.

Ginsberg, A. (1994). Minding the competition: From mapping to mastery. *Strategic Management Journal* 15(S), 153–174.

Gioia, D.A., (2002), Business education's role in the crisis of corporate confidence, *Academy of Management Executive*, 16(3): 142–144.

Glaser, B.G. & Strauss, A.L. (1967). *The discovery of grounded theory: Strategies for qualitative research*. Chicago: Aldine.

Glover, L., (2000), Neither poison nor panacea: Shopfloor responses to TQM', *Employee Relations,* 22(2): 121–145.

Grant, R.M. (1991). The resource-based theory of competitive advantage. *California Management Review* 33(3): 114–135.

Grant, R.M. (1996). Toward a knowledge-based theory of the firm. *Strategic Management Journal* 17 (Winter Special Issue), 109–122.

Grey, C. (2001), Re-imaging relevance: A response to Starkey and Madan, *British Journal of Management,* 12, Special Issue, S27–S32.

Grint, K. (1997), *Fuzzy management: Contemporary ideas and practices at work,* Oxford. Oxford University Press.

Grosz, E. (1995), *Space, time, and perversion: Essays in the politics of bodies,* New York & London: Routledge.

Gupta, A.K. & Govindarajan, V. (2000). Knowledge flows within multinational corporations. *Strategic Management Journal,* 21: 473–496.

Guattari, F. (2000), *The three ecologies,* London & New Brunswick: The Athlone Press.

Gunge, S.P., (2000), Business process reengineering and the "new organization", in Knights, D. & Willmott, H. (eds.), (2000), *The reengineering revolution? Critical studies of corporate change,* London, Thousand Oaks & New Delhi: Sage.

Hacking, I. (1992), The self-vindicating of the laboratory sciences, in Pickering, A., ed., (1992), *Science as practice and culture,* Chicago & London: The University of Chicago Press.

Hackman, R.J. & Wageman, R., (1995), Total quality management: Empirical, conceptual, and practical issues, *Administrative Science Quarterly,* 40: 309–342.

Hall, R. (1993), A framework linking intangible resources and capabilities to sustainable competitive advantage. *Strategic Management Journal,* 14: 607–618.

Hall, R. (1994), A framework for identifying the intangible sources of sustainable competitive advantage. In Hamel, G. & Heene, A. (eds), *Competence-based competition.* Chichester: Wiley.

Hall, R. (1997), Complex systems, complex learning, and competence building." In Sanchez, R. & Heene, A. (eds), *Strategic learning and knowledge management.* Chichester, John Wiley.

Hamel, G. (1994). The concept of core competence. In Hamel, G. & Heene, A. (eds), *Competence-based competition.* Chichester, John Wiley.

Hamel, G. & Prahalad, C.K. (1995). *Competing for the future.* Cambridge, Harvard Business School Press.

Hansen, M.T. & Oetinger, von, B. (2001), Introducing the T-shaped managers: Knowledge management's next generation, *Harvard Business Review*, 79(3): 106–116.

Haraway, D.J., (1991), *Simians, cyborgs, and women: The reinvention of nature*, London: Free Association Books.

Hargadon, A.B., (1998), Firms as knowledge brokers: Lessons in pursuing continuous innovation, *California Management Review*, 40(3): 209–227.

Hargadon, A & Fanelli, A. (2002), Action and possibility: Reconciling dual perspectives of knowledge in organizations, *Organization Science*, 13(3): 290–302.

Harris, L.C., (2002), The emotional labour of barristers: An exploration of emotional labour by status professionals, *Journal of Management Studies*, 39(4), 553–584.

Hatch, M.J., (1996), The role of the researcher: An analysis of narrative position in organization theory, *Journal of Management Inquiry*, 5(4): 359–374.

Hatchuel, A. (2001), The two pillars of new management research, *British Journal of Management*, 12, Special Issue, S33–S39.

Hayes, J. & Allinson, C.W., (1998), Cognitive Style and the Theory and Practice of Individuals and Collective Learning in Organizations, Human Relations, 51(7): 847–871.

Hayes, R.H. & Clark, K.B. (1985), *Exploring sources of productivity differences at the factory level*. New York, Wiley.

Hedberg, B. & Holmquist, M. (2001), Learning in imaginary organizations, in Dierkes, M., Berthon, A., Child, J. & Nonaka, I., Eds., (2001), *Handbook of organizational learning & knowledge*, Oxford: Oxford University Press.

Hedberg, B.L.T., Nystrom, P.C. & Starbuck, W.H., (1976), Camping on seesaws: Prescription for a self-designing organization, *Administrative Science Quarterly*, 21: 41–65.

Henderson, R. & Cockburn, I, (1994), Measuring Competence? Exploring Firm effects in Pharmaceutical Research, *Strategic Management Journal*, 15:63–84.

Henderson, B.D. (1973). The experience curve-reviewed. IV. The growth share matrix of the product portfolio. *Perspectives*, 135. Boston: The Boston Consulting Group.

Henderson, B.D. (1984). The application and misapplication of the experience curve. *Journal of Business Strategy*, 4(3): 3–9.

Hertz, N. (2001), *The silent takeover: Global capitalism and the death of democracy*, London: Heineman.

von Hippel, E. (1994), 'Sticky' information and the locus of problem solving: implications for innovation. *Management Science*, 40(4): 429–439.

von Hippel, E. (1998), Economics of product development by users: the impact if "sticky" local information, *Management Science*, 44(5): 629–644

Hirst, P. & Zeitlin, J., (1991), Flexible specialization versus post-Fordism: Theory, evidence and policy implications, *Economy and Society*, 29(1).

Hochschild, A.R, (1983), *The managed heart*, Berkeley: University of California Press.

Hodgson, D. (2003), "Taking it like a man": masculinity, subjection and resistance in the selling of life assurances, *Gender, Work and Organization*, 19(1): 1–21.

Hoopes, D.G. & Postrel, S. (1999). Shared knowledge, 'glitches', and product development performance. *Strategic Management Journal*, 29: 837–865.

Horrobin, D.F., (2001), Innovation in the pharmaceutical industry, *Journal of the Royal Society of Medicine*

Huff, A.S. (1992): Mapping strategic thought. In Huff, A.S., ed., (1992), *Mapping strategic thought*, 11–49.

Huff, A. (2000). Presidential address: changes in organizational knowledge production, *Academy of Management Review*, 25(2), 288–293.

Huczynski, A.A. (1996), *Management gurus: What makes them and how to become one*, London: Routledge.

Huizinga, J. (1949), *Homo ludens: A study of the play-element in culture*, London: Routledge & Kegan Paul.

Ingram, P. & Baum, J.A.C. (1997), Chain affiliation and the failure of Manhattan hotels, 1898–1980. *Administrative Science Quarterly*, 42(1): 68–102.

Itami, H., (1987), *Mobilizing invisible assets*, Cambridge: Harvard University Press.

Jackson, B. (2001), *Management gurus and management fashions: A dramatistic inquiry*, London & New York: Routledge.

Johnson, G. (1987): *Strategic change and the management process*. Oxford: Blackwell.

Jones, O. (2000), Innovation management as a post-modern phenomenon: The outsourcing of pharmaceutical R&D, *British Journal of Management*, 11: 341–356.

Kalling, T. & Styhre, A. (1999), Management as text: Deconstruction and the language of the resource-based view on strategy. Paper presented at the Strategic Management Society's 19th annual conference, Berlin, Germany, October 3–6, 1999.

Kallinikos, J. (1996a), *Organizations in an age of information*, Lund: Academia Adacta.

Kallinikos, J. (1996b), Predictable worlds: On writing, accountability and other things, *Scandinavian Journal of Management*, 12(1): 7–24.

Katz R. & Allen T.J. (1982). Investigating the Not Invented Here (NIH) syndrome: A look at the performance, tenure, and communication patterns of 50 R&D project groups. *R&D Management,* 12(1), 7–19.

Kazanjian, R.K. & Rao, H. (1999): Research note: The creation of capabilities in new ventures – a longitudinal study. *Organization Studies*, 20(1): 125–142.

Kilduff, M. & Keleman, M. (2001), The consolation of organization theory, *British Journal of Management*, 12, Special Issue, S55–S59.

Kim, W.C. & Mauborgne, R.A. (1997). Value innovation. The strategic logic of high growth. *Harvard Business Review,* 75(1).

Knights, D. & McCabe, D., (1999), '"Are There No Limits to Authority?" TQM and Organizational Power', *Organization Studies*, 20(2): 197–224.

Knights, D. & Willmott, H. (eds.), (2000), *The reengineering revolution: Critical studies of corporate change*, London, Thousand Oaks & New Delhi: Sage.

Knorr Cetina, K. (2001), Objectual practice, in Schatzki, T.R., Knorr Cetina, K. & Savigny, E. von, Eds., (2001), *The practice turn in contemporary theory*, London & New York. Routledge.

Kogut, B. & Zander, U. (1992), Knowledge of the firm, combinative capabilities, and the replication of technology. *Organization Science*, 3: 383–397.

Kor, Y.Y. & Mahoney, J.T., (2000), Penrose's resource-based approach: The process and product of research creativity, *Journal of Management Studies*, 37(1): 109–139.

Korczynski, M. (2003), Communities of coping: Collective emotional labour in service work, *Organization* 10(1): 55–79.

Koretz, S. & Lee, G. (1998), Knowledge management and drug development, *Journal of Knowledge Management*, 2(2): 53–58.

Kotha, S., (1995), Mass customization : Implementing the emerging paradigm for competitive advantage, *Strategic Management Journal*, 16:21–42.

Kreiner, K. (2002), Tacit knowledge management: The role of artifacts, *Journal of Knowledge Management*, 6(2): 112–123.

Kreiner, K. & Mouritsen, J. (2003), Knowledge management as technology: Making knowledge manageable, in Czarniawska, B. & Sevón, G., eds., (2003), *The northern lights: Organization theory in Scandinavia*, Malmö: Liber; Oslo: Abstrakt; Copenhagen: Copenhagen Business School Press.

von Krogh, G. & Roos, J. (1995), *Organizational epistemology.* London: Macmillan Press.

Lado, A.A., Boyd, N.G. & Wright, P. (1992), A competency-based model of sustainable competitive advantage: Toward a conceptual integration. *Journal of Management* 18(1), 77–91.

Lam, A. (1997), Embedded firms, embedded knowledge: problems of collaboration and knowledge transfer in global cooperative ventures, *Organization Studies,* 18(6): 973–996.

Lam, A. (2000), Tacit knowledge, organizational learning and societal institutions: An integrated framework, *Organization Studies,* 21(3), 487–513.

Langlois, R.N. (1995). Capabilities and coherence in firms and markets. In Montgomery, C.A. (ed): *Resource-based and evolutionary theories of the firm. Towards a synthesis.* Boston: Kluwer Academic Publishers.

Lawrence, P.R. & Lorsch, J.W. (1967). *Organization and environment: Managing differentiation and integration.* Cambridge: Harvard University Graduate School of Business Administration.

Leidner, R. (1993), *Fast food, fast talk: Service work and the routinization of everyday life,* Berkeley: University of California Press.

Leonard-Barton, D. (1992), Core capabilities and core rigidities: A paradox in managing new product development. *Strategic Management Journal* 13(1): 111–125.

Leonard-Barton, D. (1995), *Wellspring of knowledge: Building and sustaining the sources of innovation,* Boston: Harvard Business School Press.

Lesko J.L, Rowland M., Peck C.C, and Blaschke T.F, (2000), Optimizing the science of drug development: Opportunities for better candidate selection and accelerated evaluation in humans, *Pharmaceutical Research,* 17(11): 1335–1341.

Levin, D.Z. (2000), Organisational learning and the transfer of knowledge: An investigation of quality improvement. *Organization Science,* 11(6): 630–647.

Lévi-Strauss, C. (1992), *Tristes tropiques,* London: Penguin.

Leydesdorff, L. (2000), Luhmann, Habermas and the theory of communication, *Systems Research and Behavioral Science,* 17:273–288.

Liebeskind, J.P. (1996), Knowledge, strategy and the theory of the firm. *Strategic Management Journal,* 17 (Winter Special Issue): 93–107.

Lilley, S. (1997), Stuck in the middle with you?, *British Journal of Management,* 8: 51–59.

Lippman, S.A. & Rumelt, R.P. (1982), Uncertain imitability: An analysis of interfirm differences in efficiency under competition. *The Bell Journal of Economics,* 13(2): 418–438.

Luhmann, N. (1982), *The differentiation of society,* New York: Columbia University Press.

Luhmann, N. (1995), *Social systems,* Stanford: Stanford University Press.

Luhmann, N. (2002), *Theories of distinction: Redescribing the descriptions of modernity,* Stanford: Stanford University Press.

Lynch, M. (1985), *Art and artifact in laboratory science. A study of shop work and shop talk in a research laboratory,* London: Routledge & Kegan Paul.

Lyotard, J.-F., (1984), *The postmodern condition: A report on knowledge,* Manchester: Manchester University Press.

Lyotard, J.-F., (1990) *Heidegger and the "jews",* Minneapolis: University of Minnesota Press.

MacLean, D., MacIntosh, R & Grant, S., (2002), Mode 2 management research, *British Journal of Management,* 13: 189–207.

Mahoney, J. & Pandian, J.R. (1992), The resource-based view within the conversation of strategic management. *Strategic Management Journal,* 13(5), 363–380.

March, J. & Simon, H. (1958). *Organisations.* New York: Wiley.

May, T.Y.-M., Korczynski, M. & Frenkel, S.J., (2002), Organizational and occupation commitment: Knowledge workers in large corporations, *Journal of Management Studies,* 39(6): 775–801.

Mazza, C. & Alvarez, J.L., (2000), *Haute Couture and Prêt-à-Porter:* The Popular Press and the Diffusion of Management Practices, *Organization Studies,* 21(3): 567–588.

McEvily, S.K. & Chakravarthy, B. (2002), The persistence of knowledge-based advantage: an empirical test for product performance and technological knowledge. *Strategic Management Journal,* 23: 285–305.

McLuhan, M. (1962), *The Gutenberg galaxy: The making of typographic man,* London: Routledge & Kegan Paul.

McNiff, J. (2000), *Action research in organizations,* London: Routledge.

Merton, R.K., (1957), *Social theory and social structure,* Glencoe: Free Press.

Meyer, J.W. & Rowan, B. (1977), Institutionalized organizations: Formal structure as myth and ceremony. *American Journal of Sociology,* 83(2): 340–363.

Miller, D. & Shamsie, J. (1996), The resource-based view of the firm in two environments: The Hollywood film studios from 1936 to 1965. *Academy of Management Journal,* 39: 519–543.

Mintzberg, H. (1978), Patterns in strategy formation. *Management Science,* 24(9): 934–948.

Mintzberg, H. (1994), *The rise and fall of strategic planning.* Englewood-Cliffs: Prentice Hall.

Moingeon, B. & Edmondson, A., eds, (1996), *Organizational learning and competitive advantage.* London, Sage.

Mol, A. (2002), Cutting surgeons and walking patients. Some components involved in comparing, in Law, J. & Mol, A., Eds., (2002), *Complexities: Social studies of knowledge practices*, Durham & London: Duke University Press.

Moore, F.C.:T. (1996), *Bergson: Thinking backwards,* Cambridge. Cambridge University Press.

Mosakowski, E. & McKelvey, B. (1997). Predicting rent generation in competence-based competition. In Heene, A. & Sanchez, R., eds, (1997), *Competence-based Strategic Management.* Chichester: Wiley.

Mouritsen, J. (2000), Valuing expressive organizations: Intellectual capital and the visualization of value creation, in Schultz, M., Hatch, M.J. & Larsen, M.H., eds, (2000), *The expressive organization: Linking identity, reputation, and the corporate brand,* Oxford: Oxford University Press.

Mouritsen, J., Larsen H.T. & Bukh, P.N.D. (2001), Intellectual capital and the 'capable firm': Narrating, visualising and numbering for management knowledge, *Accounting, Organization and Society,* 26: 735–762.

Munro, R. (2001), After knowledge: The language of information, in Westwood, R. & Linstead, S., eds. (2001), *The language of organization,* London, Thousand Oaks & New Delhi: Sage.

Nanda, A. (1996), Resources, capabilities and competencies. In Moingeon, B. & Edmondson, A., eds, (1996), *Organizational learning and competitive advantage.* 93–120. London: Sage.

Nelson, R.R. (1991), Why do firms differ and how does it matter? *Strategic Management Journal,* 12 (Winter Special Issue): 61–74.

Nelson, R.R. & Winter, S.G. (1982), *An evolutionary theory of economic change.* Cambridge: Harvard University Press.

Newell, S., Scarborough, H., Swan, J. & Hislop, D. (2000), Intranets and knowledge management: De-centred technologies and the limits of technological discourse, in Prichard, C., Hull, R., Chumer, M. & Willmott, H., eds., (2000), *Managing knowledge: Critical investigations of work and learning,* New York: St. Martin's Press.

Newman, W.H. (1951), *Administrative action: The techniques of organization and management.* Englewood Cliffs: Prentice-Hall.

Normann, R. & Wikström, S. (1994), *Knowledge and value.* London: Routledge.

Nonaka, I, Toyama, R. & Konno, N., (2002), SECI, Ba and leadership: A unified model of dynamic knowledge creation, in Little, S., Quintas, P. & Ray, T. eds. (2002), *Managing knowledge: An essential reader,* London, Thousand Oaks & New Delhi: Sage.

Oliver, A.L. & Montgomery, K. (2000), Creating a hybrid organizational form from parental blueprints: The emergence and evolution of knowledge firms, *Human Relations*, 53(1): 33–56.

Oliver, C. (1997), Sustainable competitive advantage: Combining institutional and resource based views. *Strategic Management Journal*, 18(9): 697–713

Ong, W.J. (1982), *Orality and literacy: The technologizing of the word*, London: Routledge.

Orlikowski, W.J. (2002), Knowing in practice. Enacting a collective capability in distributed organizing, *Organization Science*, 13(3): 249–273.

Orr, J.E. (1996), *Talking about machines: An ethnography of a modern job*, Ithaca and London: Cornell University Press.

Patriotta, G. (2003), Sensemaking on the shop floor: Narratives of knowledge in organizations, *Journal of Management Studies*, 40(2): 349–375.

Pawlowsky, P., Forslin, J. & Reinhartd, R. (2001), Practices and tools of organizational learning, in Dierkes, M., Berthon, A., Child, J. & Nonaka, I., Eds., (2001), *Handbook of organizational learning & knowledge*, Oxford: Oxford University Press.

Penrose, E.T. (1959), *The theory of the growth of the firm*, Oxford: Blackwell.

Pentland, B.T. (2000), Will auditors take over the world? Programs, techniques, and verification of everything, *Accounting, Organization & Society*, 25: 307–312.

Pentland, B.T. & Rueter, H.H. (1994), Organization routines as grammars of action, *Administrative Science Quarterly*, 39(3): 484–510.

Peteraf, M.A. (1993), The cornerstones of competitive advantage: A resource-based view. *Strategic Management Journal*, 14(3): 179–191.

Pfeffer, J. & Fong, C.T. (2002), The end of business schools: Less success than meets the eye, *Academy of Management Learning and Education*, 1(1): 78–95.

Pfeffer, J. & Sutton, R.I., (1999), *The knowing-doing gap: How smart companies turn knowledge into action*, Cambridge: Harvard University Press.

Pickering, A. (1995), *The mangle of practice: Time, agency, and science*, Chicago & London: The University of Chicago Press.

Pisano, G.P. (1997), *The development factory: Unlocking the potential of process innovation*, Boston: Harvard Business School Press.

Polanyi, M. (1958), *Personal Knowledge: Toward a Post-Critical Philosophy*, Chicago: Chicago University Press.

Porter, M.E. (1980), *Competitive strategy*. New York: Free Press.

Porter, M.E. (1985), *Competitive advantage*. New York: Free Press.

Porter, M.E. (1990), *The competitive advantage of nations.* New York: Free Press.

Porter, M.E. (1991), Towards a dynamic theory of strategy. *Strategic Management Journal,* 12(S): 95–119.

Porter, M.E. (1996), What is strategy? *Harvard Business Review,* 74(6).

Porter, M.E. (2001), Strategy and the Internet. *Harvard Business Review,* 79(5).

Postrel, S. (2002), Islands of shared knowledge: Specialization and mutual understanding in problem-solving teams, *Organization Science,* 13(3): 303–320.

Power, M. (1994), "The audit society," in Hopwood, A.G. & Miller, P., eds., (1994), *Accounting as social and institutional practice,* Cambridge: Cambridge University Press.

Prahalad, C.K. & Bettis, R.A. (1986), The dominant logic: A new linkage between diversity and performance. *Strategic Management Journal,* 7(6): 485–501.

Prahalad, C.K. & Hamel, G. (1990), The core competence of the corporation, *Harvard Business Review* 70(3): 79–91.

Priem, R.L. & Butler, J.E. (2001), Is the resource-based 'view' a useful perspective for strategic management research? *Academy of Management Review,* 26(1): 22–40.

Prigogine, I. (1997), *The end of certainty: Time, chaos, and the new laws of nature,* New York: Free Press.

Prigogine, I. & Stengers, I. (1984), *Order out of chaos: Man's new dialogue with nature,* New York: Bantam Books.

Piore, M.J. & Sabel, C.F. (1984), *The second industrial divide: Possibilities for prosperity,* New York: Basic Books.

Pruijt, H., (1998), Multiple personalities: The case of business process reengineering, *Journal of Organizational Change Management,* 11(3): 260–268.

Quinn, J.B. (1978). Strategic change: Logical incrementalism. *Sloan Management Review,* Fall: 7–21.

Ravasi, D. & Verona, G. (2001), Organising the process of knowledge integration: The benefits of structural ambiguity, *Scandinavian Journal of Management,* 17: 41–66.

Reason P. (1994). Three approaches to participative inquiry, In *Handbook of Qualitative Research,* Denzin N.K., Lincoln, Y.S., eds., (1994), London, Thousand Oaks & New Delhi: Sage.

Reason, P. (1999). Integrating action and reflection through co-operative inquiry, *Management Learning,* 30(2), 207–226.

Reason, P., & Bradbury, H. (2001), Introduction: Inquiry and participation in search of a world worthy of human aspiration. in Reason, P. & Bradbury, H. eds., (2001). *Handbook of action research: Participative inquiry & practice,* London, Thousand Oaks & New Delhi: Sage.

Reed, R. & DeFillippi, R.J. (1990), Causal ambiguity, barriers to imitations, and sustainable competitive advantage, *Academy of Management Review,* 15(1): 88–102.

Ricardo, D. (1817), Principles of political economy and taxation. London: J Murray.

Roberts, P.W. (1999), Product innovation, product-market competition and persistent profitability in the U.S. pharmaceutical industry, *Strategic Management Journal,* 20: 655–670.

Rouse, M.J. & Daellenbach, U.S. (1999), Rethinking research methods for the resource-based perspective: Isolating sources of sustainable competitive advantage. Strategic Management Journal, 20: 487–494.

Rumelt, R.P. (1974), *Strategy, structure, and economic performance.* Cambridge: Harvard Business School Press.

Rumelt, R.P., Schendel, D.E. & Teece, D.J. (1994), *Fundamental issues in strategy. A research agenda.* Cambridge: Harvard Business School Press.

Ryle, G. (1971), The thinking of thoughts: What is 'le Penseur' doing?, in *Collected papers*, Vol. 1, London: Hutchinson.

Rynes, S.L., Bartunek, J.M. & Daft, R.L. (2001), Across the great divide: Knowledge creation and transfer between practitioners and academics, *Academy of Management Journal,* 44(2), 340–355.

Sanchez, R. (1997), Managing articulated knowledge in competence-based competition. In Sanchez, R. & Heene, A. (eds), *Strategic learning and knowledge management.* Chichester: Wiley.

Sanchez, R. (2001a), Managing knowledge and competence: The five learning cycles of the competent organization, in Sanchez, Ron, Ed., (2001), *Knowledge management and organizational competence,* Oxford: Oxford University Press.

Sanchez, R. (ed) (2001b), *Knowledge management and organizational competence,* Oxford: Oxford University Press.

Sanchez, R. & Heene, R. (1997), Competence-based strategic management: Concepts and issues for theory, research, and practice. In Heene, A. & Sanchez, R., eds, (1996), *Competence-based strategic management.* Chichester: Wiley.

Sanchez, R., Heene, A. & Thomas, H. (1996), Towards the theory and practice of competence-based competition. In Sanchez, R., Heene, A. & Thomas, H., eds, (1996), *Dynamics of competence-based competition: Theory and practice in the new strategic management.* Oxford: Elsevier.

Scarbrough, H. & Swan, J. (2001), Explaining the diffusion of knowledge management: the role of fashion, *British Journal of Management*, 12: 3–12.

Schatzki, T.R., Knorr Cetina, K. & Savigny, E. von, Eds., (2001), *The practice turn in contemporary theory*, London & New York. Routledge.

Schoemaker, P.J.H. & Amit, R. (1994), Investment in strategic assets: Industry and firm level perspectives. In Shrivastava, P., Huff, A. & Dutton, J., eds, (1994), *Advances in strategic management*, 10A, 3–33. Greenwich: JAI Press.

Schofield, J. (2001), The old ways are the best? The durability and usefulness of bureaucracy in public sector management, *Organization*, 8(1): 77–96.

Scott, W.R. (1995), *Institutions and organizations*. Thousand Oaks: Sage.

Seely-Brown, J. & Duguid, P. (2000), Balancing act: How to capture knowledge without killing it, *Harvard Business Review*, 78(3): 73–80.

Selz, D. (1999), *Value webs. Emerging forms of fluid and flexible organizations*. Ph.D. Dissertation, University of St. Gallen.

Selznick, P. (1957). *Leadership in administration*. New York: Harper & Row.

Serres, M. (1995) *The natural contract*, Ann Arbor: The University of Michigan Press.

Seufert, A., von Krogh, G. & Bach, A. (1999), Towards knowledge networking, *Journal of Knowledge Management*, 3(3): 180–190.

Simon, H.A. (1945), *Administrative behavior*. New York: MacMillan.

Simon, H.A., (1957), Models of Man, Wiley: New York.

Simonin, B.L. (1999), Ambiguity and the process of knowledge transfer in strategic alliances. *Strategic Management Journal*, 20: 595–623.

Slywotsky, A. (1996), *Value migration: How to think several moves ahead of competition*. Cambridge: Harvard Business School Press.

Smircich, L. (1983), Concepts of culture and organizational analysis, *Administrative Science Quarterly*, 28: 339–358.

Sole, D. & Edmondson, A. (2002), Situated knowledge and learning in disperse teams, *British Journal of Management*, 13: S17–S34.

Soo, C., Devinney, T., Midgley, D. & Deering, A. (2002), Knowledge management: Philosophy, processes, and pitfalls, *California Management Review*, 44(4): 129–150.

Spanos, Y.E. & Lioukas, S. (2001), An examination into the causal logic of rent generation: Contrasting Porter's competitive strategy framework and the resource-based perspective, *Strategic Management Journal*, 22: 907–934.

Spencer, J.W. (2003), Firms' knowledge-sharing strategies in the global innovation system: Empirical evidence from the flat panel display industry, *Strategic Management Journal*, 24: 217–233.

Spender, J.-C. & Grant, RM., (1996), Knowledge and the firm: Overview, *Strategic Management Journal*, 17 (Winter Special Issue), 5–9.

Spender, J.C. (1996). Competitive advantage from tacit knowledge? Unpacking the concept and its strategic implications. In Moingeon, B. & Edmondson, A., eds, (1996), *Organizational learning and competitive advantage*. London: Sage.

Stabell, C.B. & Fjeldstad, Ö.D. (1995), On value chains and other value configurations. Working paper #20, Department of Strategy, Business History and Foreign Languages, Bedriftsinstitutt, Norway.

Stacey, R. (1993), Strategy as order emerging out of chaos. *Long Range Planning*, 26(1): 10–17.

Stalk, G., Evans, P. & Shulman, L.E. (1992), Competing on capabilities: The new rules of corporate strategy. *Harvard Business Review*, 70(1): 57–69.

Stein, J. & Ridderstråle, J. (2001), Managing the dissemination of competences. In Sanchez, R., ed, (2001), *Knowledge management and organizational competence*. Oxford: Oxford University Press.

Stewart, T.A. (1997), *Intellectual capital. The new wealth of organizations*, New York. Doubleday.

Styhre, A. (2003), Rethinking knowledge: A Bergsonian critique of the notion of tacit knowledge, Forthcoming in *British Journal of Management*.

Styhre, A., Roth, J. & Ingelgård, I., (2002), Care of the other: Knowledge creation through care in professional teams, *Scandinavian Journal of Management*, 18(4): 503–520.

Sutton, R.I. (1991) Maintaining norms about expressed emotions: The case of bill collectors, *Administrative Science Quarterly*, 36: 245–268.

Swindler, A. (2001), What anchors cultural practices, in Schatzki, T.R., Knorr Cetina, K. & Savigny, E. von, Eds., (2001), *The practice turn in contemporary theory*, London & New York. Routledge.

Szulanski, G. (1996), Exploring internal stickiness: Impediments to the transfer of best practice within the firm. *Strategic Management Journal*, 17 (Winter Special Issue): 27–43.

Szulanski, G. (2000). The process of knowledge transfer: A diachronic analysis of stickiness. *Organizational Behavior and Human Decision Processes*, 82(1): 9–27.

Tarde, G. (1969), *On communication and social influence: Selected papers*, Ed. by T.N. Clark, Chicago & London: The University of Chicago Press.

Taylor, F. (1911), *The principles of scientific management*, New York: Harper.

Teece, D.J., Pisano, G. & Schuen, A. (1997), Dynamic capabilities and strategic management. *Strategic Management Journal*, 18(7): 509–533.

Tranfield, D. & Starkey; K. (1998), The nature, social organization and pro-
motion of management research: Toward policy, *British Journal of Management*, 9: 341–353.

Tranter, D., (2000), Pharmaceutical science and technology today: Evolving
to reflect the modern industrial life-science environment, *Pharmaceutical
Science & Technology Today* 3(12).

Tsai, W. (2000), Social capital, strategic relatedness and the formation of intraorganizational linkages. *Strategic Management Journal*, 21: 925–939.

Tsai, W. (2001). Knowledge transfer in intraorganizational networks: Effects
of network position and absorptive capacity on business unit innovation
and performance, *Academy of Management Journal*, 44(5): 996–1004.

Touraine, A. (1971) *The post-industrial society. Tomorrow's social history:
Classes, conflicts and culture in the programmed society*, Trans. by
Leonard F.X. Mayhew, New York: Random House.

The Economist, (2000), The New Alchemy, January 20 issue.

Tsoukas, H. (1996), The firm as distributed knowledge system: A construc-
tionist approach, *Strategic Management Journal*, 17 (Winter Special Issue): 11–25.

Tsoukas, H. & Chia, R. (2002), On organizational becoming: Rethinking organization change, *Organization Science*, 13(5): 567–582.

Tsoukas, H. & Vladimirou, E. (2001), What is organizational knowledge?,
Journal of Management Studies, 38(7): 973–993.

Turner, S. (2001), Throwing out the tacit rule book, in Schatzki, T.R., Knorr
Cetina, K. & Savigny, E. von, Eds., (2001), *The practice turn in contemporary theory*, London & New York. Routledge.

Van den Bosch, F., Volberda, H.W. & de Boer, M., (1999), Coevolution of
firm absorptive capacity and knowledge environment: Organizational
forms and combinative capabilities, Organization Science, 10(5):
551–568.

Vattimo, G., (1992), *The end of modernity*, Cambridge: Polity Press.

Walgenbach, P. & Hegele, C. (2001), What can an apple learn from an or-
ange? Or: what do companies use benchmarking for?', *Organization*,
8(1): 121–144.

Weber, M. (1946), *From Max Weber: Essays in sociology*. Oxford & New
York: Oxford University Press.

Weick, K.E. (1979), *The social psychology of organizing*. 2nd edn., New
York: Addison-Wesley.

Weick, K.E. (1989), Theory construction as disciplined imagination, *Academy of Management Review*, 14 (4), 516–553.

Weick, K.E. (1995), *Sensemaking in Organizations*, London: Sage.

Weick, K.E. (2001), *Making sense of the organization*, Oxford: Blackwell.

Wenger, E. (2000), Communities of practice and social learning systems, *Organization*, 7(2), 225–246.

Wenger, E., McDermott, R. & Snyder, W.M. (2002), *Cultivating communities of practice*, Boston: Harvard Business School Press.

Wernerfelt, B. (1984), A resource-based view of the firm, *Strategic Management Journal*, 5(2): 171–180.

Wernerfelt, B. (1995), Resource-based strategy in a stochastic model. In Montgomery, C.A., ed., (1995), *Resource-based and evolutionary theories of the firm. Towards a synthesis.* Boston: Kluwer Academic Publishers.

Wilkinson, A., Godrey, G. & Marchington, M. (1997), Bouquets, Brickbats and Blinkers: Total Quality Management and Employee Involvement in Practice, *Organizational Studies*, 18(5): 799–819.

Williamson, O.E. (1999), Strategy research: governance and competence perspectives. *Strategic Management Journal*, 20(12): 1087–1108.

Winter, S.G. (1995), Four Rs of profitability: Rents, resources, routines and replication. In Montgomery, C.A., ed, (1995), *Resource-based and evolutionary theories of the firm. Towards a synthesis.* Boston: Kluwer Academic Publishers.

Winter, S.G. (2000), The satisficing principle in capability learning. *Strategic Management Journal*, 21(S): 981–996.

Womack, J., Jones, D.T., and Roos, D. (1990), *The machine that changed the world.*, New York: Macmillan.

Wood, M. (2002), Mind the gap? A processual reconsideration of organizational knowledge, *Organization*, 9(1): 151–171.

Woolgar, S., ed. (2002), *Virtual society? Technology, cyberbole, reality*, Oxford & New York: Oxford University Press.

Xu, Q., (1999), TQM as an arbitrary sign for play: Discourse and transformation, *Organization Studies*, 20(4): 659–681.

Yakhlef, A. & Salzer-Mörling, M. (2000), Intellectual capital: Managing by numbers, in Prichard, C., Hull, R., Chumer, M. & Willmott, H., eds., (2000), *Managing knowledge: Critical investigations of work and learning*, New York: St. Martin's Press.

Yelle, L.E. (1979), The learning curve: historical review and comprehensive survey. *Decision Sciences*, 10: 302–328.

Yeoh, P-L. & Roth, K. (1999), An empirical analysis of sustained advantage in the U.S. pharmaceutical industry: Impact of firm resources and capabilities. *Strategic Management Journal*, 20: 637–653.

Young, G.J. & Charns, M.P. & Shortell, S.M. (2001), Top manager and network effects on the adoption of innovative management practices: A study from TQM in a public hospital system, *Strategic Management Journal*, 22: 935–951.

Zander, U. & Kogut, B. (1995), Knowledge and the speed of transfer and imitation of organizational capabilities. An empirical test. *Organization Science*, 6(1): 76–92.

Zbaracki, M.J., (1998), The rhetoric and reality of total quality management, *Administrative Science Quarterly*, 43: 602–636.